"WHAT D'YA DO IN THE WAR DAD?"

BY BARRY PARR

' SON OF WALLY '

Note for Librarians: A cataloguing record for this book is available from Library and Archives
Canada at www.collectionscanada.ca/amicus/index-e.html
ISBN 1-4251-1073-8

Printed in Victoria, BC, Canada. Printed on paper with minimum 30% recycled fibre.
Trafford's print shop runs on "green energy" from solar, wind and other environmentally-friendly power sources.

TRAFFORD
PUBLISHING™
Offices in Canada, USA, Ireland and UK

Book sales for North America and international:
Trafford Publishing, 6E–2333 Government St.,
Victoria, BC V8T 4P4 CANADA
phone 250 383 6864 (toll-free 1 888 232 4444)
fax 250 383 6804; email to orders@trafford.com
Book sales in Europe:
Trafford Publishing (UK) Limited, 9 Park End Street, 2nd Floor
Oxford, UK OX1 1HH UNITED KINGDOM
phone +44 (0)1865 722 113 (local rate 0845 230 9601)
facsimile +44 (0)1865 722 868; info.uk@trafford.com
Order online at:
trafford.com/06-2832

10 9 8 7 6 5 4 3 2

HEALING

Sixty years ago our fathers returned,
Battle weary spirits burned.
They rebuilt our future as fine men should,
And soon they were told: 'You've never had it so good'
But they will remember as only they can,
Their fallen comrades in a foreign land.

As young kids we grew up in awe.
Often asking: 'Dad, what d'ya do in the war?'
And as years passed by and illness took its toll,
Less and less appeared at each years roll.
Yet even today old mates still meet,
Talking until the small hours, drinking whisky neat,
A shoulder to cry on, still battles to fight,
And they heal each others wounds, deep in the night.

And they will remember as only they can,
Their fallen comrades in a foreign land.

Finally fathers, hear your sons cry:
Do one more thing for us, before you die.
Put anger and hatred and bitterness aside,
And when you're gone, we will stand there.
And remember you with pride.

I DEDICATE THIS BOOK TO......
PEACE

SADLY, THE ONLY WAY TO
ACHIEVE THIS IS THROUGH...

WAR

Chapters

Preface

As the Horsa glider began its long decent through the night sky, my Dad gently touched my arm. The scene, on the cinema screen, changed to the interior of the plane. The gloom of the fuselage blended with the khaki uniforms and blackened faces - the only contrast was the fear in the whites of the soldier's eyes. As the glider hit the ground and skidded through the traps that snapped the wings on impact, my Dad suddenly squeezed my arm so tight I thought it would break.

After a brief moment of silence, doors were kicked open, screams were heard and all hell broke loose.

'Up the Ox and Bucks! Up the Ox and Bucks!' yelled the men. I could hear Dad mumbling the phrase beneath clenched teeth.

As the soldiers ran up a short incline, my Dad released his grip and sat upright in his seat. As they got to the bridge and started firing his shoulders visibly tensed.

The director cut to a long view of men swinging under the bridge expertly defusing explosives that had been set in case of such an invasion. As the picture returned to the men storming the bridge, I could see Dad flinch as each bullet was fired. My attention was divided between the action on the screen and the reaction of the man sitting beside me. As the fighting intensified I could see his arms moving as if shadow-boxing.

Thankfully after a few moments the story moved on and we were both able to relax and enjoy the rest of the film.

The place was the Granada Cinema, Sydenham in London, now long since demolished and turned into a lifeless supermarket. The year was 1962 and I was twelve years old. The film, of course, was 'The Longest Day'.

These were interesting times. The Prime Minister of the day, Harold Macmillan, had recently announced to the nation that, 'We had never had it so good'. If he had taken a stroll around my part of the world in South-East London he may not have been so sure.

Reminders of the war abounded. Our area was still littered with prefabs and bombsites. On the plus side our playground games had changed from cowboys and indians to war games. The new baddies were now the Germans. The ricochet of the Winchester rifle and the swishing of bows and arrows had been replaced with the rat-a-tat-tat of sub-machine guns and the crash of hand-grenades as we pulled out the pretend pin with our bare teeth. Inevitably some kid would shout, 'My Dad's gun is bigger than your Dad's gun', only to receive the reply, 'Oh yeh, my Dad drove a tank'.

The art of conversation, in those days, was alive and well. Television was in its infancy and when relatives visited, us kids would sit around the fire and listen to the grown-ups as they spun their yarns. As the booze flowed the stories got funnier and more exaggerated.

The highlight of an evening would often be my Dad telling the story of how he and his mates, in the war, the night before D-Day, flew over in gliders, invaded Europe and then the rest followed. I thought all dads made up pretend stories like these, to impress their kids, so that they could boast about it next morning in the playground. The difference was - in my Dad's case, the story was true!

This is not your basic war book. There are no maps with arrows pointing in all directions. Far more informed authors have already covered this ground more than adequately. Fundamentally this is a book about people, an army of ordinary people. Obviously there are the soldiers and their heroic deeds, but also you will meet their families and friends. In addition there are total strangers, with no real family connections, who somehow have been swept up with the thrill and importance of the story of D-Day.

This is also a book about a poem - a simply personal poem I wrote for my Dad just before the fiftieth anniversary of D-Day in 1994. Somehow, through forces and powers greater than my own, it has consequently been read by ten of thousands of people over the past decade. The message of the poem, and this book, is simple: By preserving, honouring and learning from the past we have a chance to produce a better future - we do this by acting in the present, the all powerful NOW.

There are some people out there who will demand to see my credentials - others will ask how many qualifications I have. To those people my answer is simple: 'I have only one - I am my father's son'.

Up the Ox & Bucks

The young twelve-year-old Wally Parr was dragged into the doctor's surgery much to his annoyance – for a while he had been complaining of chest pains and breathlessness. The medical expertise of 1930's Britain was limited – the depression that engulfed the western world catered for the mere basics. A medical for a lad that age would consist of a quick run over with a stethoscope and a 'cough and drop'. His balls were okay but the doctor did detect a slight irregularity in his heart beat. The diagnosis suggested that provided he took it easy for the rest of his life he should live to a ripe old age. As they left the surgery the doctor handed his mother a note excusing Wally from physical exercise at school for the rest of his days.

Outside an argument ensued – the young lad suggested that perhaps the doctor was talking rubbish. In the next few years he ignored his mother's nagging and threw himself into every sport imaginable. He ran cross-country for his school, as well as captaining both the cricket and football first-eleven teams.

The young Wally Parr, aged 18, looking for a war !

He learned to 'bite on the bullet' at an early age.

He came from a tough sporting family, his father has played professionally for Accrington Stanley and Tranmere Rovers in the 1920's and his brother Reg was on the books of Millwall promising to follow in his father's footsteps. Sadly it never happened, Reg died as a Prisoner of War in Japan.

The violence of 1930's Catford, South-East London was everywhere, especially amongst his four brothers Bill, John, Reg and Chris - arguments between the four boys was common-place. Work was scarce and, compounded with the hostile home life,

Dad decided on the 5th February 1939, aged sixteen years and ten months, to enlist as a boy soldier with the Gloucester Regiment. To join he had to alter his birth certificate with crude markings changing his year of birth from 1922 to 1921. He signed up for six months with a further option of seven years. He endured basic training well, yet he decided after his initial period of six months to call it a day.

Adolf Hitler had other ideas, after two weeks in Civvie Street, war was declared and as a reservist Dad was summoned back to Horfield Barracks ready for action.

He recalls Neville Chamberlain holding a piece of paper declaring 'Peace in our time'. A year later, to quote Dad, 'He may as well have wiped his arse on it for all the good it done'.

At Horfield Barracks he was greeted by his mates that had chosen to do the seven years, they thrust upon him a couple of dirty sheets and led him to the same bed he had vacated a fortnight earlier.

For the next three years he moved amongst various units in the Gloucesters, going nowhere fast. Dunkirk, the Blitz and the Battle of Britain was a war being played out somewhere else, it only touched him through the daily papers and the occasional Pathé Newsreel.

The boy soldier, Parr, in The Gloucester Regiment at the outbreak of war.
(Back row in the middle)

In June 1940 Churchill had formed a new military force of Airborne troops, their trade-mark was to become their red berets and a horse-shaped insignia. Major General 'Boy' Browning had taken command in late 1941 and it was his wife the author Daphne du Maurier who helped him choose the famous badge. It was taken from the story in Greek mythology where Bellerophon, lance in hand, is riding a winged horse called Pegasus and is in the process of destroying a dragon called Chimera. As history unfolded the names Bellerophon and Chimera were lost in antiquity but the name of Pegasus and its image of the flying horse became one of the most famous and most instantly recognisable images of the Second World War.

By 1941 Wally somehow found himself acting as a barman in the Woolacombe Bay Hotel - the place had been converted to the Southern Command Weapons Training H.Q. His job was to serve officers as they attended week long intensive training courses. About that time the Daily Mirror ran an article which urged A1-fit soldiers with cushy posts to come out of the woodwork and join in with the fighting.

Shortly afterwards a notice was pinned to the notice board asking for volunteers to join a newly formed Airborne Division based near Yeovil. Along with a dozen or so others from the hotel Dad applied for a transfer. The interview was not your run of the mill type, he recalls having a thorough examination by a high ranking doctor and an in depth grilling from what he can only assume was a psychologist.

Of the twelve who applied only four were accepted.

Dad joined the Ox and Bucks in the February of 1942 his love affair with D Company was to last over four years until his demob in Palestine, in May 1946.

It was three days after enlistment that he came face to face with Captain, later to become Major, John Howard.

The frustration of doing nothing with the 'Gloucesters', for so long, had spilled over onto his new regiment. So far, the only 'action' the young tear-away had experienced was weeding and sweeping the parade ground. Dad wanted out, he wanted to join the Paras, he wanted to be up in the sky, after all that's what 'airborne' meant, he wanted this - he wanted that.

At an interview, requested by Dad, Howard listened politely and then firmly explained that eventually he would become part of a fighting light infantry airborne unit, but first things first, before being airborne he must learn to fight. As he was being dismissed Dad thought to himself, 'I had better watch this geezer he could be trouble', no doubt Howard thought much the same!

The Ox and Bucks were stationed at Bulford Barracks, on the edge of Salisbury Plain in Wiltshire. The plain is huge, bigger than the Isle of Wight, and sparsely populated. It was the perfect location to train troops in the many aspects of warfare.

The atmosphere was different from the usual run of the mill barracks - each person present, from squaddie to officer, was a volunteer, whatever motive they had was irrelevant, the common bond was that they all felt elite and above all they wanted their platoon to be the best.

In retrospect, the average man in D Company was probably no better or worse than any other regimental member - the fact that D Company slowly emerged as the 'elite' amongst the 'elite' was the dedication and drive shown by their commander John Howard. The philosophy of he and his fellow platoon leaders was simple: 'I will not ask you to do anything that I cannot do myself'. In some instances he showed his men he could actually do it better.

At times I reflect on the ages of these young men. When Dad marched into Howard's office with all his demands he was twenty years of age, the superior officer sat opposite him was a mere twenty-seven. When Howard led his men across the bridge as a Major he had reached the ripe old age of twenty-nine!

Today's average twenty-something youth is still pre-occupied with Saturday night booze up's, football terraces and a yearly rave up in hotter climates. Respect for authority is at an all time low, older generations call for the return of National Service, 'bang some discipline into them' they cry – yet I wonder if the youth of 1940 were much different from today.

I am convinced that one of the root causes of today's unrest is boredom. Howard was well aware of this problem with his lads sixty years ago. His remedy was physical exercise. A typical day would begin with an early morning cross-country run followed by the usual morning exercises on camp, which were usually strenuous. After lunch his lads were allowed to spend any free time as they wished, provided it was with one of the sports on offer. Howard liked to combine the individual disciplines (boxing, swimming and running) with team events such as soccer or rugby - this allowed the mind to be balanced between going solo and working for your comrades. Dad enjoyed soccer and cross-country, he also discovered a new talent in boxing. A certain 'Tich' Rayner took Dad under his wing and managed to train him up to regimental standard. Dad fought forty-nine fights losing only two – the first and the last; he was left with a small scar above his lip, as a result of his last fight, which would be there for life!

Despite trying to work the boys into exhaustion some of the lads still managed to find the energy to indulge in varying degrees of yobbish behaviour, most of it was fairly harmless 'letting of steam'. Midnight raids on a rival platoon's billet and ransacking the place was considered friendly fun. It got a bit heavier on the occasional Saturday night when leave was granted so that the boys could invade the nearby town of Salisbury and hit the pubs. Inevitably they would bump into groups of American G.I.s - 'smartly dressed gits impressing the girls with nylons and fags', - was one of Dad's more polite descriptions. Many a night would turn into a mini-battlefield, before the whistles and batons of the Military Police arrived to break it up.

Occasionally people would overstep the mark. One night Dad, Billy Gray and another guy decided to raid the NAAFI (Navy, Army and Air Force Institutes – which runs canteens for the British Armed Services) just for the hell of it. They had planned the deed for midnight - but they all drifted off to sleep and didn't awake until 5 a.m. Undaunted they agreed to go ahead despite the fact that the barracks were soon about to stir. Once inside they realised there was nothing much worth pinching, so, in an act of pure vandalism, they decided to relieve the place of almost all of its soap powder – one has to ask were these guys on booze or drugs to do such a thing! The trail of soap powder outside pointed more or less in the direction of their billet and to add to the chaos it started to rain causing the powder to rise up into huge mounds of froth and foam. It didn't take a 'Maigret' or 'Gideon of the Yard' to work out who the stupid culprits were.

Howard soon had the 'Super-Foam Robbers' before him. Indiscipline at this level was not taken lightly, at this point Dad had been promoted to a Corporal in charge of snipers, but without hesitation he was demoted back to Private and given fourteen days in the glasshouse. Billy Gray and the other guy were each given twenty-eight days – maybe the longer sentence was dished out because they were already Privates and you can hardly demote them to a lower rank!

The news reached Howard's superior, Colonel Mike Roberts, who wanted Dad to be returned to unit (RTU) – Major Howard had to put up a strong case to convince Roberts to change his mind. Howard argued that, although wayward at home, men like Parr are natural leaders and would come into their own when facing the enemy. He was proved right when on a couple of occasions Dad was promoted in battle only to be busted when back on home soil.

There is a thin dividing line between a man turning into a hooligan or into a hero – the vandal who decides to channel his negative energy into good can easily become the VC winner.

Howard affectionately called this bunch of guys his 'scallywags'. In battle all these men proved to be his best fighting soldiers - sadly a high percentage of them died at the enemy's hands, as throwing caution to the wind and storming in regardless would cost them dear.

Fully trained in the Ox & Bucks

By now the men had reached the peak of their physical fitness, the task now was to train the mind as well as the body to the rigors of close knit hand to hand bloody warfare. The location and timing of these exercises was constantly varied so the men gradually accustomed themselves to expect the unexpected.

Denis Edwards in his excellent book 'The Devil's Own Luck' recalls how it was not unusual to be dragged out of bed at midnight and dumped in the middle of Salisbury Plain and instructed to get back to Bulford Barracks by sunrise. They had to use their own devices and instincts to achieve this, an added incentive was the knowledge that they had to cross firing-ranges which used live ammunition and the action usually commenced at dawn!

At other times they would find themselves in bomb damaged cities in the Midlands or on the South Coast, this environment enabled them to become experts at urban warfare - live ammunition again sharpened the senses! It is unclear how many troops were actually killed by 'friendly fire' during these exercises. Denis Edwards personally witnessed one lad peering over a sand dune and being ripped apart by his own Sergeant-Major's Sten gun burst - to the best of his knowledge there was no enquiry. Perhaps if the statistics were published the damage to moral would have been counter-productive, needless to say, for every man that died, a further ten thousand learnt how to survive.

In the summer of 1942 General Gale made the decision to send the regiment on a two month training exercise to North Devon to gain extra fitness and experience in beach and cliff fighting. D Company ended up in Ilfracombe but much of the most vigorous training was performed on the sands and cliffs of Woolacombe Bay. It was probably here that Denis Edwards experienced the fatality. Live ammunition was certainly used as the men darted amongst the sand dunes and the grenades, if not fully laden with explosives, were loud enough to do serious damage to David Wood's eardrums!

After deciding the men had fully benefited from their stay beside the seaside, General Gale announced that his men should return to Bulford Barracks – any short term jubilation expressed by the men was soon transformed into gloom when they found out that the 130 mile return journey would be taken on foot!

As always, any exercise would be treated as a contest between the companies and the march back was to prove no exception.

I have travelled the North Devon coastal road many times, thankfully always in a car – it is one of the most hilly and picturesque routes in the whole of England. After Ilfracombe you reach Combe Martin and then you begin a long slow incline up onto the heights of Exmoor and eventually after a few hours you drop down several hundred feet through Lynton and into Lynmouth at sea-level once again. I was in Lynton recently and notice that Lynton in now twinned with Bénouville in France – they made the decision in 1985, I like to feel it may have something to do with this epic march!

True to form the English weather played its usual tricks and began with two days of sweltering heat and after the men were allowed to strip out of their thick shirts, the weather changed and the final two days produced cold winds and torrential rain.

Dad has many times reminded me of Contisbury Hill, the road that leads eastward from Lynmouth back up onto Exmoor – it is a 1 in 4 gradient that the men nicknamed 'Chinstrap Hill' for the obvious reason that by the time you had marched up it, your chin was on the floor. It was probably here that D Company lost one of their men through sheer exhaustion.

Needless to say, largely due to the guidance and example of Major Howard, D Company arrived back at Bulford well ahead of the opposition – their first reward was hot showers and hot food, their second reward was that this latest 'victory' may have been the deciding factor that put them on the front line and got them selected to take part in one of the most daring raids of the Second World War.

Fitness was such an important part of D Company's life that it became second nature. When I was a young lad in the late fifties Dad would ask me to punch him in the stomach with everything I had, inevitably I would hurt my hand on his rock hard stomach muscles. Dad's fitness manifested itself in other directions, by now Mum, with my

Mum (far left) in the ATS

brother Chris, was living in Corsham, not too far from Bulford. Occasionally Dad would get the odd weekend leave and meet Mum in Salisbury. Many years later Dad was looking at a print of John Constable's famous picture of Salisbury Cathedral with my elder sister Pat. After a few minutes he turned to her: 'See that wall?', he began, 'well during the war I had a few hours leave with your Mum and against that wall you were conceived'! Dad certainly knew how to make a teenage girl blush!

I'm not sure if Major Howard would have been all that impressed if he knew that his boys on their weekend leave, instead of resting were having knee-tremblers!

As 1943 drew to an end, an air of expectancy was stirring amongst the soldiers at Bulford. The Russians under intense pressure were pushing for the Allies to open up a second front in the West. With Dunkirk a not too distant memory the timing and location had to be right, a second disaster was unthinkable. While most of the world, including Rommel, was focusing on the narrow Dover Straits and the Pas de Calais, men like Montgomery and Churchill were looking in the direction of Normandy.

I try to put myself into the shoes of my Mum and Dad during these turbulent times, by now they had two small children, brother, Chris, and my sister, Pat. Mum and Dad were married in April 1940 and Chris was born a couple of months later – what the heck, a war was on! By now, Mum in essence had two homes, one in Bristol and one in London. Apparently, according to Mum, the Luftwaffe must have had a personal vendetta against her, because whenever she left Bristol because of the bombing and went to London, the next night the very street in London where she was staying would be hit. Perhaps somebody should have pointed out that the Hun had enough bombs to bomb both cities at the same time. One particular night while staying in London with her in-laws, a raid began, but due to extreme fatigue Mum seriously thought about ignoring the warning and sitting it out. At that last moment she became frightened and headed off to the shelter with her two young children. After the all-clear she returned home, to find a house a few yards from her own had been hit but had suffered only slight damage. Almost asleep she climbed the stairs to put the children to bed, when she opened the bedroom door she was shocked to find part of the ceiling had collapsed and completely crushed the tiny cots in which the two children would have been sleeping. From then on she was one of the first to reach the shelter.

The thing that would have got to me most would be the lack of communication. For Dad and thousands of others each bombing raid must had brought fear and uncertainty, despite mass evacuation there was still the worry of stray bombs. For Mum it was different, although in relative safety for the present, at sometime in the near future she knew that Dad was about to enter a period of untold danger. Today's world of mobile phones and instant emails would have been to the 1940's man the material of science-fiction news, be it good or bad news it would take days or even weeks to reach loved ones and when it did arrive it was often hopelessly inaccurate.

But for John Howard, on May 2nd 1944, he was to receive some news that was, to say the least, probably the most accurate news he was to ever receive. He was summoned to 'Broadmoor', a codename given to Major 'Windy' Gales planning H.Q. situated near Milston on Salisbury Plain. The mansion was encompassed in the tightest possible security. Strangely 'Broadmoor' is the name of a notorious prison hospital that houses the mentally and criminally insane in England. It was at this place that Major Howard was about to meet Brigadier Nigel Poett and be given a mission, that to some, must have been dreamt up by a 'mad man'. On that day he learnt that D Company had been given a special assignment to seize intact two bridges over the river Orne and the Caen canal and to hold them until reinforcements came. Howard was then handed his orders which were marked Bigot & Top secret. The pages contained intelligence details of how many men would be protecting the bridges, what weapons they possessed and what sort of counter attack he could expect in the following hours before reinforcements arrived.

These orders were not only incredibly detailed but also up to date. Daily aerial reconnaissance flights would photograph the area and update the file in the coming weeks. Every thought and plan given to Howard had to be kept in his head, even his number two Captain, Brian Priddy, was not told of any place names. It must have seemed a lonely time for Howard, so much excitement and tension stored within - perhaps he was even terrified of talking in his sleep!

As he studied the plans Howard soon realised the key to its success relied on the element of surprise, silent gliders landing in the pitch dark was only the beginning. As well as his own D Company, amongst others, he would be given thirty sappers who had the task to diffuse explosives that had been placed along the entire length of the bridge. The more he studied the plan the crazier it became. Not only did they have to crash-land in pitch darkness, then stop somebody simply pushing a button and blowing the whole thing sky high, they also had to capture the bridge intact and hold it for God knows how long against some fairly hefty artillery and tanks and all the while they are classified as a light infantry detachment.

Dad told me many years later that unofficially the operation was classified as a 'suicide mission - that may just work!'

Regardless of the risks, Howard set about bringing Poet's plans into fruition. He began by laying out the two bridges using vast amounts of tape depicting the exact sizes of each structure. The men must have wondered what on earth he was up to. This began the game of 'enlightening' his men while at the same time, 'keeping them in the dark'. The men knew they were onto something big – it must have been important even their food had improved!

At one point Howard asked H.Q. to scan various maps to see if England could provide him with a similar canal/bridge layout as the one in Normandy. As luck would have it they came up with an almost identical location at Countess Weir, just outside Exeter. To the men it was just another exercise with its usual intensity - for Howard it was exploring every possibility of things going wrong.

Each glider had a code-name, Dad's glider was No. 1 with the code-name 'Able' - No. 2 was 'Baker' and so on. Locals looked on in amazement as these maniacs constantly stormed the bridges shouting: 'Able, Baker, Charlie' at the top of their voices as they lobbed live hand grenades at the two peaceful bridges.

The locals often complained to the authorities about the constant noise and damage being done to the environment, but if they only knew the exact nature of this mayhem perhaps their voices would have been more subdued.

The last night at the pretend bridges was spent 'invading' nearby Exeter pubs. Due to a glass shortage the enterprising guys tied jam jars around their necks to guarantee a much needed pint. Howard, although he felt a part of his men, declined the offer to join them. Instead he entrusted one of his right hand men, H. D. Brotheridge (otherwise known as 'Den' or 'Danny' to his close friends), to keep an eye on his motley crew. This proved to be a slight misjudgement as Brotheridge managed to out-drink most of his contemporaries - with the inevitable result. Howard spent most of the small hours driving around Exeter rounding up various waifs and strays while keeping residents and local police reasonably happy. Dad recalls having quite a wild night he labelled it one of our 'Last Suppers'. There would only be a couple more 'Last Suppers' before the big day.

It was around this time that Mum found herself taking a more active role in the war effort when she received official papers telling her to join up and become an operator on the anti-aircraft guns in London. She stayed with Dad's parents in South London and night after night, while her two children were safely tucked away in air raid shelters with their grandparents, Mum was risking her life operating the searchlight that tried to spot the bombers that were blitzing London.

At the end of May D Company was sent to Tarrant Rushton. Security was tight; this was the place where the boys were to leapfrog into France and history. Dad was amazed at the organisation and detail in everything that was shown to them, 'me mind boggled', he recalled, 'there was pictures of this and models of that, we were finally shown the actual place where we were to land, although we hadn't a clue where the bloody place was, but we were all pretty sure it wasn't Norway!'

As more and more details emerged so the need for the utmost secrecy was instilled into the men. Howard in no mean terms threatened his men with a RTU if they even whispered the word 'bridges' to an outsider.

As early June arrived the tension intensified. Howard covered every detail over and over again. Such was his obsession with authenticity that he even arranged outside British Tommies to dress up in genuine German uniforms speak in German tongues and stage mock battles with German weapons against D Company. These war games proved invaluable to Dad and his mates as they become familiar with the workings of the enemy's weapons. Their expertise showed them that the German Schmeisser carbine was far superior to the standard Sten gun and these were to be the first things to be looted from dead Germans and used to make even more dead Germans.

As D-Day drew nearer there was almost the danger of 'over preparing' the men, a case of 'peaking early' before a prize fight. Howard had to somehow keep the training fresh and somehow alleviate the boredom of men, razor sharp tuned for some intense action which they desperately wanted to happen sooner than later.

June the 3rd arrived and with it Howard's last intelligence report. The Germans had completed their defences around the bridge, trenches had been dug, anti-aircraft and anti-tank guns had been put in place and a heavy machine gun had been installed in a pill-box along with six light-machine guns and around fifty men were poised for any invasion threat. In essence the scene was probably no different from several thousand other defensive positions along the channel coast. The Germans must have felt like slip-fielders in a vital test match, every day being a new over - always trying to stay alert just in case the ball came their way.

Major General Richard 'Windy' Gale (above) and a
CO (below) give final briefings to the 6th Airborne

That was to be the ace in D Company's hand; if they could catch the enemy half asleep then they would smash them for six before they knew what hit 'em.

Dad knew it was all about to kick off when the big boys came through Tarrant Rushton. He heard that Montgomery had met Major Howard and had received an up-date and finally General 'Windy' Gale had gathered the men together to deliver his final battle cry. Apparently Jack Bailey reckoned that perhaps he should have been nicknamed 'Long Winded' Gale, such was the content of his inspirational talk to the troops. The only part Jack can remember is the classic quote, since used by Dad in after dinner speaking, 'Germany was like a June bride, she knew that she was going to 'get it' but she wasn't exactly sure when, or how big it was going to be'. Dad's version is much cruder.

June the 4th was kick-off time. The boys got into full kit and ate a meal, this should have been the final time they would have sat around a table and eaten normally for weeks, if not months, again it felt like the 'last supper' - for some it was. Before the food was digested the news came through that the invasion was off – you can plan something for months, even years but one thing you cannot plan against is the good old British weather and in early June 1944 it was more like November with driving rain and strong winds.

On June the 5th the dawn broke into slightly improving weather. The men of D Company went through the same routine as the day before. The only difference Dad noticed was that lunch was very low in fat, he presumed this was to prevent air-sickness, after all, he reckoned, all they were travelling in, was glorified kites! For the first time ever, most of the men lost their appetites - their stomachs over-rode their brains, their bodies knew this was it. The rest of the day dragged, I love Stephen Ambrose's quote at this point: 'Then they sat around, according to Parr, "trying to look keen, but not too keen like".' I have shown this quote to Dad to re-jog his memory, 'In actual fact,' he recalls, 'to be quite honest most of us were scared shitless!'

It is action that dispels fear and boredom and before they knew it Howard was instructing his men to get into full combat gear.

The ongoing logistic problem was always going to be weight. Overload a glider and it will drop like an out-of-control brick – for Jim Wallwork and the other pilots to have any chance they had to get the weight just right. Fairly early on they realised they had to sacrifice men in preference to equipment. Major Howard recalls thirteen-stone grown men weeping like babies when they were told they would be missing the trip in favour of weapons. Billy Gray even suggested that perhaps the married men with children should be excused – he said this in the full knowledge that his best mate Wally Parr fitted this category - Dad screamed and hollered and to keep the peace he was kept on board.

I have in my possession a list of every soldier on each glider and their battle order weights. Beside Parr is the weight two hundred and twenty-six pounds (sixteen stone and two pounds), beneath the list in his own handwriting Dad has written: 'My weight in fact was ten stone six pounds (one hundred and forty-six pounds) - I was carrying eighty pounds in equipment'. That is more than half his body weight! How the hell could he stand upright let alone run across a bloody bridge!

As they stood at the base of the glider the burnt cork was handed round so that they could blacken their faces. I have a photograph of the entire D Company – amongst them is one black guy 'Darkie Baines'. In Britain in the 1940's prejudice had not raised its ugly head 'Darkie' was a nickname as harmless as 'Dusty' Miller, or 'Chalky' White. As the burnt cork passed from soldier to soldier Dad found himself passing it to Baines - he smiled at Dad, tapped him on the arm in comradeship and

passed the cork to the next man. I have checked my list of occupants and cannot find the name Baines on any of the gliders – perhaps this story is an urban myth, anyway I include it as a tribute to all the ethnic minorities that supported the allies in the Second World War!

Fully kitted up and with blackened faces these guys must have been an awesome sight.

Before entering the glider, Dad wrote 'Lady Irene' on the fuselage of the glider, which is, of course, the name of my mother. According to Dad he was not the only graffiti artist that night – Jack Bailey scrawled something about London, probably 'Maybe it's because I'm a Londoner' and Billy Gray, a lifelong West Ham supporter wrote 'Up the 'ammers'. Its ironic that Billy rang Dad after the 1966 World Cup victory over West Germany and told him that 'West Ham' had won it with Moore, Peters and Hurst [Hammers players] yet if you think about it if D-Day had failed we, wouldn't have 'played' West Germany in 1966 we would have 'been' West Germany.

Finally after many months of preparation, a Halifax of 298 Squadron piloted by Wing Commander Duder started its engine and began to taxi down the runway pulling No. 1 Glider with Jim Wallwork at the controls and Sergeant Ainsworth as his co-pilot.

As the air speed increased, against every regulation, the lights at Tarrant Rushton came on and the hundreds of personnel on the ground waved and cheered as D Company of the 6th Ox and Bucks Regiment finally lived up to their name and became 'AIRBORNE'.

A wonderful picture of Horsa gliders awaiting their towing craft – Heathrow it ain't !

Seating plan for Horsa Glider No.1 "Lady Irene"
the first glider to touch down on D-Day, June 6, 1944, 00h16
carrying these brave men from the British 6th Airborne Division,
who subsequently captured Pegasus Bridge near Bénouville, Normandy, France

1 S/Sgt Wallwork Glider Pilot	11 Pte Chamberlain Platoon Medic	21 Spr Ramsey Engineers
2 S/Sgt Ainsworth Co-Pilot	12 Pte Bourlet Scout Section	22 Pte Edwards 2 Section
3 Sgt Ollis Platoon Sgt	13 Pte O'Donnell Scout Section	23 Pte White 2 Section
4 Lt Brotheridge Platoon Commander	14 Cpl Bailey Scout Section Commander	24 Pte Bates 2 Section
5 Pte Gray *(Bren Gun)* 1 Section	15 Spr Wheeler Engineers	25 Cpl Webb 2 Section Commander
6 L/Cpl Packwood *(i/c Bren Gun)* 1 Section	16 Spr Danson Engineers	26 L/Cpl Minns *(i/c Bren Gun)* 2 Section
7 Cpl Caine 1 Section Commander	17 Cpl Watson Engineers	27 Pte Tilbury *(Bren Gun)* 2 Section
8 Pte Baalam 1 Section	18 Pte Parr Scout Section	28 L/Cpl Tappenden Wireless Operator
9 Pte Jackson 1 Section	19 Pte Gardner *(Bren Gun)* Scout Section	29 Pte Watson *(2" Mortar)* Commanders Runner
10 Pte Windsor 1 Section	20 Spr Yates Engineers	30 Major Howard Force Commander

Normally the senior pilot
sat in the portside (left)
seat, but as they had to
make two sweeping
starboard (right) turns,
they changed seats to
have a better view of
the approach and ground.

front door

rear door

Airspeed Horsa Glider

Produced by
Paul and Bart Heux

Based on information
supplied by:
Denis Edwards
44 Penstone Park
LANCING,
West Sussex
BN15 0AJ

June 2004

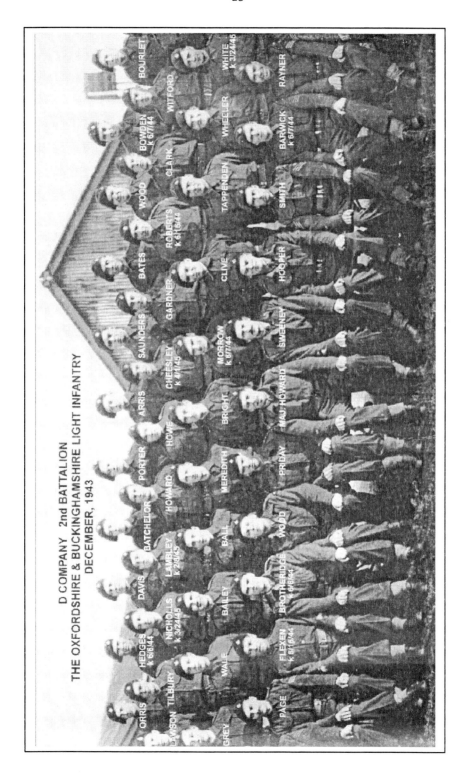

D COMPANY 2nd BATTALION
THE OXFORDSHIRE & BUCKINGHAMSHIRE LIGHT INFANTRY
DECEMBER, 1943

- 26 -

#

Coup de Main - D-Day 1944

GLIDER NO.1 - Tarrant Rushton Chalk No. 91. (Glider No. 667)

Pilot: S/Sgt. Wallwork. Co-Pilot:S/Sgt.Ainsworth,MM
Tug Pilot: W/Cdr. Duder - Halifax of 298 Sqn.

LOAD: No. 25 Platoon, "D" Company, 2 Oxf Bucks with RE attached.

Name	Weight (In Lbs)	In "Battle Order"
Lt Brotheridge	7	
Sgt Ollis	230	
Cpl Caine	233	
" Webb	237	
" Bailey	235	
L/C Packwood	222	
" Minns	242	
Pte Baalam	212	
" Bates	237	
" Bourlet	219	
" Chamberlain	252	
" Edwards	226	
" Gray	245	
" Gardner	241	
" O'Donnell	226	
" Parr	226	
" Tilbury	241	
" Watson	214	
" White	225	
" Windsor	225	
" Jackson 08	215	
Major Howard	?	
Cpl Tappenden	236	

Total 23

5092 / 231 (4859/21=231)

Royal Engineers

Cpl Watson	270
Spr Danson	242
Spr Ramsey	270
Spr Wheeler	260
Spr Yates	245

(1287/5=257.4)

The First Glider to land by the canal bridge
(Tug Pilots Note: Reached L.Z.)

My weight was in fact 11 stone Page 2
- 6 lbs

I was carrying 56 lbs equiptment

Crew and passengers of No. 1 Glider
- the handwritten note at the bottom is Dad's

Ham and Bloody Jam!

While our band of brave brothers are crossing the channel at a fair old height perhaps this is a good time to step aside and discuss the role and problems of being a 'modern-history writer'.

The basic problem is simple: We weren't there – everything we record is stolen from a third party. Ideally it should be from somebody that took part; they of course are relying on a fading memory that is digging deep over forty, fifty or sixty years. Usually us poor 'historians' are plagiarising some other writer who we hope has actually got it right. The problem further deepens when we realise that the veterans themselves were in some cases. 'There – but not actually there' – they were in the world but not of it. Fear and confusion sometimes plays strange tricks with the memory. From my own personal life I recall to my children and grandchildren my experiences of being a teenager in 'swinging London' in the 1960s – over the years the story gets more and more embellished as I seek to entertain, how long will it be before I'm claiming to have danced naked at Woodstock!

It needs to be stated that this is a personal war story – much of what I share is from intimate conversations with my father. I have made a few friends over the past couple of years who know the history of D Company backwards. No doubt they will spot the occasional error in my story-telling, I don't mind, for years most people looked at aerial photographs of the three gliders and presumed they landed 1 – 2 – 3, in actual fact they landed 1 – 3 – 2 – the reason for this will unfold shortly.

Returning to D Company flying through the dark June night, the euphoria of the cheering crowds at Tarrant Rushton was slowly subsiding – they tried to keep the mood high by singing the usual bar room songs – this was a simple act of comradeship, the theory being that if you knew the same words and the same tunes perhaps you had become as one team and you were in this 'together', in the case of D Company this was true.

I can still remember the first time I flew, comfortably numb with booze, I cruised out of Gatwick Airport reasonably confident that modern technology and a highly trained crew would ease me onto a warm Greek Island four hours later.

Dad was 22-years-old the first time he took off, stone-cold sober, he quietly doubted whether the cumbersome brute dangerously over laden with men and equipment would even leave the ground before smashing into the end of the runway.

Fortunately, the pilot, Sergeant Jim Wallwork, and his co-pilot, Staff Sergeant John Ainsworth, were quietly confident that not only would they get No 25 Platoon of D Company off the ground but also safely across the channel and down onto a spot roughly the size of a football pitch. The fact that they would be doing it in the dark, without an engine and with the aid of just a compass and a stop-watch didn't seem to perturb the duo that much - if they were scared it wasn't picked up by Major Howard and his men.

Interior of a Horsa - note that the basic construction was balsa wood – for lightness !

The six gliders were part of a convoy doing their nightly bombing raids over main-land Europe. The plan was to approach Normandy over the town of Cabourg and at that point to be cast off in a relatively quiet anti-aircraft flack area and begin their descent onto the landing zone several miles away. They hoped that if the radar operators on the ground did pick up the glider's descending they would presume the gunners had shot the planes from the sky.

The task of the glider pilots was to fly their engineless brutes the ten miles to the Landing Zone in a series of loops, upwind & downwind, the co-pilot timing each leg with a stopwatch in the hope of getting the correct approach and the correct speed.

The half-moon gave Wallwork some visual assistance but much of his judgement relied on instinct and a memory bank of endless hours of practise.

Apparently the pinpoint practise sessions went out of the window when on one of his crosswind legs he caught a glimpse of the bridges and water glistening in the moonlight and decided to veer off course and go for it early. He glided in at 95 mph although ideally he would have preferred 85 mph.

A glider pilot's view of what had to be done with only the aid of a stopwatch and a compass!

By now my father, in his position at the back of the glider was poised to force open the back door and was preparing himself for action. Ambrose quotes him in 'Pegasus Bridge': 'God Almighty, the trees were doing ninety miles an hour. I just closed my eyes and went up in my guts'. A classic example of detaching yourself from reality – it wasn't the trees doing 90 mph it was him!

At this point Wallwork decided to let out the parachute to slow the craft down – air brakes at its most basic! The chute did the trick more or less, the speed dropped to around sixty, but it achieved it by lifting the tail and setting the nose down and then lifting the craft up briefly, ripping the wheels off and eventually braking the nose off. Before this happened, Ainsworth managed to jettison the chute. As the glider slid to a grinding halt on its metal runners sparks were sent flying convincing some of the men that they were being shot at with tracer bullets.

All along Wallwork's mind was torn between two possibilities. If he was too fast and overshot he would crash into the embankment and sustain injuries with he and Ainsworth almost certain goner's, yet if he was too slow and dropped well short he had to face the fact that No. 2 glider coming in a minute later could easily have ploughed into his backside causing untold mayhem. Fortunately skill and lady luck were both on the sides of the three crews.

Exactly a minute later No. 2 glider landed, it finally slid to a halt 50 yards away from Howard's craft, the pilot Oliver Boland at first may have been a little disappointed at the gap he left, but it proved to be a blessing in disguise. As No. 3 glider approached, a minute or so later, the pilot desperate to avoid the other two, somehow managed to swerve and avoid contact, but due to its speed and angle the glider snapped in half and finally settled between No. 1 and No. 2 - this led to the simple error of most people looking at photographs and presuming they landed in the obvious order of 1,2,3. Sadly when No. 3 broke in half Fred Greenlagh was hurled into a near-by pond and was pinned down until he drowned.

Like beached whales, the gliders lay stricken in the Landing Zone

As the dust settled the men slowly began to gather their senses. On No. 1 glider Wallwork and Ainsworth had been thrown forward through their cockpit and still strapped into their seats had landed on the ground. Technically speaking they were the first Allied soldiers to touch French soil on D-Day, but they were blissfully unaware of this honour, both being unconscious.

Behind them each soldier began to recover from various degrees of concussion. It was recognised that almost everybody lost consciousness for a moment or two – thankfully no one was seriously injured although for one brief moment John Howard thought he was blinded until he realised his helmet had fallen over his eyes! When Dad came round, he quickly realised that neither he nor the trees were doing 90 mph anymore; at that precise moment he wished that No.1 platoon could now muster up half that speed and get up onto the bridge. His job was to open the back door and make easy the exit onto the ground, he recalled it as organised chaos but one way or another before he knew it, he was racing up towards the bridge looking for Germans to kill.

One of my Dad's favourite sayings was 'The only thing you have to fear – is fear itself'.

It is impossible to comprehend what must have been going through the young twenty-two-year-old's head at that time! There is a thin dividing line between heroism and cowardice – one soldier that evening had already run away from the glider at Tarrant Rushton while another on landing feigned injury and remained frozen to the spot. There is also equally another line that divides being 'brave' and being a 'nutter'! Dad was probably entering 'nutter' mode.

As his body, full of bravery, propelled him up and onto the bridge, his mind, fighting the fear, dried up his mouth, as he described: 'so I couldn't spit sixpence'.

By now the two sentries that were guarding the bridge were fully aware of the rampaging mob that was storming their position. As Den Brotheridge led his men into occupied Europe, the first sentry a mere sixteen-year-old turned and ran like stink in the opposite direction. The second, managed to fire off a flare before he was cut down by Brotheridge.

The young German was the first soldier to die at the hands of the Allied forces – in a matter of seconds the tally would tragically be equalled.

Meanwhile the flare alerted the German troops at the far side of the bridge. Complacency, boredom and the time of night had left them sluggish. This enabled Brotheridge to get close enough to pull out a grenade and lob it at the machine gun post to his right, as he did so he caught a bullet in the neck and collapsed in a heap – the grenade continued onward and wiped out its intended target. Those following behind their platoon leader continued forward and with Bren & Sten guns took out the other threatening gun post.

Dad was by now half way across the bridge desperate to get into the action. Like everybody around him he knew he had to keep yelling 'Abel, Abel', the password that enabled everybody to ascertain who was on who's side.

Meanwhile he still had the problem of spitting a sixpence from the roof of his mouth. Stephen Ambrose builds a lovely picture of Dad's frustration building up and releasing itself in anger. He relates Dad's shouting in block capitals, the only two sentences reproduced this way in the entire book – the other I will mention later, it must have touched a special place in Ambrose's thinking – I quote: 'With a great effort of will Parr finally broke his tongue loose and shouted, "COME OUT AND FIGHT YOU SQUARE-HEADED BASTARDS!".

Pleased with himself, Parr started yelling 'Ham & Jam, Ham & Jam', as he ran the rest of the way and then turned left to go after the bunkers that were his task'. Dad never did mince his words! He may have been pleased with himself but yelling 'Ham & Jam' – the code words announcing the capture of both bridges was a bit premature to say the least.

Over the past couple of decades a number of books have been published with the standard few photographs salvaged from 1944. As with the photographs there have been very few quotes used by the veterans, most of these have been recorded in Stephen Ambrose's book. I find it mildly amusing to see Dad in Normandy talking to people and going over the same old stories quoting 'Wally Parr!'

I reproduce here a well used account of how Dad, once he had cleared his throat, sprang into action: 'I stopped and looked across the bridge just for a brief second. Looked at the Very light being shot up, then I turned and one of the dug-out doors half-opened and closed again, I shot across the roadway – by this time I had a No.36 grenade; the pin out, into the dug-out opened and shut the door. The explosion went off, Charlie Gardner came in, I opened the door again and he just machine gunned inside. On to the second dug-out and the same: in with the grenade, bang the door shut, explosion; smash it wide open again Charlie finished them off. As we came back past the first dug-out suddenly there was a moan or something from inside and I pulled out a 77 phosphorous. Took the cap off, gave it a twirl, undone the tape and jumped in and that went off'.

Grenade, machine gun and phosphorus – when D Company attacked you, they meant it!

Meanwhile John Howard had set up his base holding it all together with some sort of invisible authority that permeated towards his warriors.

Behind him, Denis Fox had landed 300 yards in front of their objective – the river bridge.

Denis Fox is obviously a humble man; we know this from his observation that the real leader of his platoon was in fact Sergeant 'Wagger' Thornton.

Wagger showed his qualities early, as he and Fox headed from the glider in the direction of the bridge they immediately came under enemy fire from an enemy MG34. Wagger sensing this, had held back and as soon as he found the position of the enemy fire, let off the mortar he had set up and in no time the machine gun post was taken out, the response from the remaining sentries on the bridge was to run. I don't know the German for 'retreat' but they certainly did!

A few minutes later 'Tod' Sweeney's platoon hit the ground running and in much the same style as No.1 Platoon on Pegasus Bridge came screaming onto the Orne River bridge looking for a good old fight. All they found was Fox and his boys looking rather smug at their rather easy mission accomplished. Tod and Denis shook hands and more in relief than anything joked about 'where were the umpires' – for it turned out to be little more than a training exercise. Despite this, there must have been a period of intense pressure when they feared the unknown and the unexpected - for all they knew, the enemy could have been laying in waiting and the bridge could very easily have been blown to 'kingdom come' as they crossed it.

Both sections of D Company were in earshot of each other's action – my Dad having done his business with Charlie Gardener continued onwards looking for more Germans to take out.

As pill-boxes and trenches were silenced the sound of gunfire began to slowly decrease. Chaos receded into relative calm as No.1 Platoon gathered itself and men began to ask the question – 'where's Danny?'

Again we now enter the world of historic legend a place where in modern history every quotation is dissected. For years I thought that Den Brotheridge died in my father's arms. I was wrong. Again I quote my father's own words: 'He was lying about twenty yards from the café in the middle of the road. I thought he was a German at first and then I stopped and realised, came back..... I cradled him in my arms. Danny was not just our platoon leader but our mate. There was blood everywhere -

the first thing that went through my mind was - what a terrible waste'.

In fact Brotheridge was taken to Doc Vaughan's post and despite the doctor's gallant efforts passed away shortly afterwards.

As the son of Wally Parr I claim the right to say that Den Brotheridge's death was not a 'terrible waste' - but an unfortunate consequence as a result of crushing a tyrant that threatened our very freedom. Of course I respect my father's comments and no doubt I would have said the same if a close friend of mine had rested, dying in my arms.

As Dad cradled his comrade, nearby the first incident of 'friendly fire' occurred in the invasion of Europe on the Orne Bridge. Tod Sweeney's section had heard a patrol approaching their position. They called out the code letter 'V', expecting the response to be 'Victory'. When the response was negative they opened fire and cut down the four men approaching. On examining the bodies they discovered that one of them was a captured and gagged British Para – undoubtedly many more 'friendly fire' incidents would happen – a flying bullet has no way of recognising nationalities.

Stephen Ambrose encapsulates all these events and more in his book with a chapter entitled 'D-Day 00:16 to 00:26 hours' We need to get our heads round this – we are only talking about ten minutes!

While all this is going on Jock Neilson and his sappers had swung limb to limb beneath the bridge with the intention of defusing the detonators placed in position to blow the bridge at a moments notice – they discovered instead that the explosives had been removed and stored in a nearby shed. Years later Darryl Zanuck decided, when he was making his epic film 'The Longest Day' to have the explosives in place to create a better dramatic effect – but that's Hollywood - today we are hopefully studying reality.

By half past midnight the capture of Pegasus Bridge was all but over. Howard in his central position now ordered his wireless operator Ted Tappenden to broadcast the now famous message 'Ham and Jam' eastwards in the vague hope that Brigadier Nigel Poet and his reinforcements would pick it up. The message was in vain – in the confusion Poett had managed to team up with only one other soldier and it wasn't the wireless operator. Time and time again Ted sent out the message 'Ham and Jam', 'Ham and Jam' after a couple of 'Ham and Jams' in complete frustration he yelled down the radio 'Ham and Bloody Jam!'

To this day anybody vaguely connected with Pegasus Bridge signs off an email or letter with 'Ham and Jam', it has become an unofficial slogan.

- 36 -

When Barry Tappenden signed my hardback edition of 'Pegasus Bridge'
twenty years ago he signed 'Ham and Bloody Jam' – as the son of Ted he
has the special privilege to sign his Dad's special call sign.

In the lull before the next storm Howard assessed his position with
regards to casualties: all three platoon leaders Brotheridge, Wood and
Smith were out of action, such was the level of training amongst D
Company that the sergeants easily filled the void left behind. Without
realising it every member of each platoon moved up a notch and took on
more responsibilities.

The 'hard' bit, capturing the bridge had been relatively 'easy'. Now
the 'easy' bit, holding the bridge until reinforcements arrived would
prove to much 'harder' than expected. Howard quickly assessed the
situation: To the east, and behind him, the river bridge was intact and
secure, it proved no immediate threat. For now, as he looked across the
canal bridge, the position was stable – yet he knew as he looked past the
Café Gondrée and up towards the T junction and the village of Le Port
the enemy were getting ready to counter-attack - somewhere in the
darkness a considerable force of angry Germans wanted their bridge
back!.

For a glider-borne light infantry unit one of their biggest fears was
tanks. Their only defence was Gammon bombs and the PIAT anti-tank gun
both relatively effective if used correctly.

My Dad was one of the first to hear the drone of tanks starting up
in nearby Le Port, still on a high, adrenalin pumping, he sprinted back
towards Howard and gave him the information. Immediately Howard
instructed Dad to nip back to No.1 glider and collect the PIAT with its
ammo and also gather up the Gammon bombs. Big mistake!

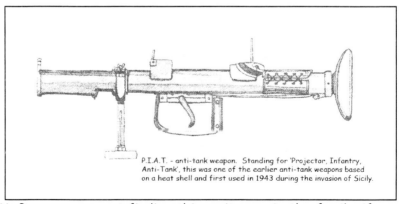

P.I.A.T. - anti-tank weapon. Standing for 'Projector, Infantry,
Anti-Tank', this was one of the earlier anti-tank weapons based
on a heat shell and first used in 1943 during the invasion of Sicily.

Us Parrs are crap at finding things, it runs in the family, if my wife,
Diane, sends me to a cupboard or a drawer to get something, I panic and

rummage through it and can never find the required article, five minutes later of course my wife comes in, goes to the same place and hey presto she find's it – it's a woman's thing!

Perhaps each glider should have taken a Wren with them whose sole duty was to tidy up the glider and give everything a dusting after the crash landing.

Needless to say, the young over-keen Parr rushed back to the glider and started rearranging the contents in a desperate attempt to find the Gammon bombs and the PIAT gun. In the darkness he never did find the Gammons and when he did eventually find the PIAT he tripped over something and dropped the bloody thing, bending the barrel and rendering it useless. In the end he returned to Howard with some ammo for the machine guns and no doubt reported that the PIAT was damaged when they landed!

The raid on Pegasus Bridge had been recorded and assessed many times – here I am trying to relate it in a personal and unique way, coming at it from a different angle so to speak. I am reminded that luck and skill need to go hand in hand, if you are to be a success and claim a victory.

Monte Cassino was a battle that by June 1944 had already been laid down in the nation's history books. When it comes to the raid on Pegasus Bridge read 'Monty's Casino' – for Montgomery and the rest of his commanders knew that if this 'night on the town' was to work, it would need an element of luck as well as a high degree of expertise and training.

The first hand dealt was the glider landings, there are two sides to every coin, on the one side the skill of the glider pilots has been described as probably the finest piece of flying in the entire second world war and indeed it was – yet on the other side, if you look at the position of gliders 1, 2, 3 you see that they have landed 1, 3, 2 and it was only 'lady luck' that sprung the last glider around No. 2 and in between 2 and 1. Two thirds of the flying force could have been wiped out before they fired a shot in anger. From the air, the landings look a shambles – either way, the undoubted skill and bravery of the three sets of pilots is not questioned. The first hand had been played at 'Monty's Casino' and the dealer had dealt 'three of a kind'.

Now we turn to 'Pontoon' or should we say 'Platoon' as the boys go headlong into the thick of it , they win another 'hand' but at a price – the 'King of Hearts' is torn away from them as Brotheridge is snatched away.

In another part of 'Monty's Casino' some of the guys join in 'crap' games as they scare the 'crap' out of retreating and hiding Germans, this night out is going okay – they were on a high yet the biggest and highest staked game was about to begin.

It was Wagger Thornton and his PIAT Gun. 'The Cincinnati Kid' was about to take on the 'Man'. A young kid against a ruddy, great tank.

Five card stud poker – winner takes all!

As the first of the two tanks came into view, Wagger was pleased that he actually had in his possession the only PIAT gun that worked and two shells to fire from it.

'Ten of Diamonds'

Slowly the tank began to trundle down towards the bridge unaware of Wagger's position.

'Jack of Diamonds'

Thornton was the man for the job, his nerve would hold – so would the nerves of men like Billy Gray on the opposite side of the road – nobody would dare shoot early and give away their positions.

'Queen of Diamonds'

Wagger had the expertise and the skill yet he knew deep down that the weapon he held in his hand was notoriously inaccurate and he had only one chance – if he missed with the first shot, by the time he tried to reload, the machine gunner on the tank would have taken him out. He needed to get the tank into a perfect position without being noticed and he needed to stop shaking.

'King of Diamonds'

The moment was approaching - the cards were nearly all on the table – his hand looked good – but so did the other guys – it could go either way – shit or bust – Wagger held his breath and for a brief moment managed to stop shaking as he took aim and fired his shell at hopefully the perfect spot.

'Ace of Diamonds' !

Bingo – all hell broke loose as the shell penetrated the armour and began setting off all the ammunition inside – the danger to Wagger and the rest of the guys was now not from the guns of the tank, but it's exploding shells and bullets.

A giant firework display came into force to celebrate the famous victory of Wagger Thornton M.M. against a tank.

The Cincinnati Kid – a 'Diamond Ace' – had saved the day!
He didn't need to reload to stop the second tank because the first one had completely blocked the road and the commander of the second crew, immediately reversed away from the T junction having no intention of ending up like his mates.

For the time being the party at 'Monty's Casino' was over – there was still a long night ahead of them, in the small hours they would wait and wonder: Would the tanks start up again? Would they attack in greater numbers? Would reinforcements gather from Caen and overwhelm them?

That night 'Lady Luck' dealt them two more good hands in the strangest of ways:
Firstly, the driving force behind the German defence, Rommel, had decided to travel back home to his wife and celebrate their wedding anniversary. His reasoning was that due to the moon, tides and atrocious weather the allies would not attempt a beach landing in the next couple of days – the truth was more than likely that his old lady was giving him an 'ear 'ole bashing' and he had better get his arse back home with a bunch of flowers or else!
Secondly, Hans Von Luck with his 21st Panzer tank division, although only a few miles away, could not launch a counter attack without clearance from higher command – in fact with Rommel's absence it would have to come from Hitler himself – and he was fast asleep with strict instructions not to be awakened until dawn!
Von Luck was out of luck because he knew that in a daylight attack he would probably be picked off by the heavy guns of the Royal Navy battleships – which incidentally had amongst the crew my future father-in-law, Bill Davies; it was very much a family affair!
In retrospect – it was probably a nagging wife and a sleep-obsessed dictator that allowed D Company valuable breathing space until reinforcements arrived.
At this point in the story we enter a 'minefield'- not your bog-standard minefield that maims and kills - to the best of my knowledge there were none around Pegasus Bridge that day – but the controversy relating to facts and figures, truth and myth.
If four young police officers were involved in a serious incident and all made notes, it would be a fair guess that quite a few of the facts

would tally and some would vary to a lesser or greater degree ....and so it was that night. The problem relates to time – some reports use British Standard Time while others may have used French. I have studied many accounts regarding the relief of Colonel Pine-Coffin and the 7th Paras and it varies from 01:30 hrs at the earliest to anything between 02:30 hrs to 03:00hrs at the latest.

The problems between the Para boys and the Airborne boys probably began that night when some of D Company men made several sarcastic comments to 7th Para when they eventually did arrive at whatever time it was. This wouldn't have gone down too well with the exhausted Paras bearing in mind that they had been scattered far and wide and it had been one hell of a job to muster in the dark and get to the bridge.

One thing in my opinion is glaringly obvious: D Company captured the Bridge but 7th Paras held it.

During the first day of the conflict D Company had two men killed and several wounded – in the same period 7th Parachute Battalion lost 68 men and had many more wounded. It is worth noting, of course, that by the time Howard's company returned to Bulford many weeks later, their casualties were on a par. It is quite natural for some of the Para boys to feel that their exploits and their dead and wounded have been pushed somewhat into the background.

I have tried to analyse the popularity of the Ox and Bucks boys compared to other units and the only analogy I can draw upon is to equate it with another historic clash between Germany and England and that is the 1966 World Cup final at Wembley. Please hear me out. I realise D-Day was far more important and of course brave men were killed. The point is that John Howard in his modesty often said that he was merely the right man in the right place.

For John Howard read Alf Ramsay, a modest man, who in my opinion was nowhere near the best manager England ever had but was in the 'right place at the right time'.

Bobby Moore the captain becomes Den Brotheridge, the consummate professional and leader of men that was cruelly taken away before his time.

At the centre of the defence Big Jack Charlton becomes Big Jack Bailey, solid, no messing and dependable.

The 'Hero' Geoff Hurst the scorer of the first ever Cup Final hat-trick is Wagger Thornton, the hero 'sharp shooter'

Gordon Banks is Ted Tappenden whose 'goal' is to send messages.

The little 'whipper-snappers' Nobby Stiles and Alan Ball are Wally Parr and Charlie Gardner, full of energy and mischief running around like 'blue-arsed flies'.

Finally Martin Peters, a West Ham player described by Alf Ramsay as a player 'ten years ahead of his time' is Bill Gray, a life long Hammers supporter who, when I met him at the 60th looked ten years younger than the rest of 'em!

As an after-thought, Jimmy Greaves, who in my opinion was the greatest England goal-scorer of all time but was cruelly dropped for the final, reminds me of the men that were withdrawn at the last minute and missed the action and may have regretted it for the rest of their lives.

There we have it – a football team that captured the nation's hearts in 1966 and another team that won us over in 1944 – there were probably better outfits before and since, but these are the boys that hold the limelight and that's life!

Soldiers march across Pegasus Bridge in relative safety – a few days earlier it was a different story

Meanwhile back to the action and for the best part of the next hour the firework display continued as allied reinforcements moved slowly nearer. It was led by Nigel Taylor of the 5th Para Brigade – as they approached they could only presume that one hell of a battle was going on somewhere in the region of the bridge - little did they know that it was only D Company sitting there and going 'ooh and aah!'. One of Taylor's Paras was the well known British actor Richard Todd.

It is the sense of humour of the British Tommie that kept him going, not only through the war, but to this day

Because of the story of the 'Demon Barber' 'Sweeney Todd' - all Todds were nicknamed 'Sweeney' and all Sweeneys including Lieutenant H. J. Sweeney of D Company were nicknamed 'Tod' The two men briefly met before the invasion and vowed, God willing, to say hello again somewhere on the battlefields of Normandy. Fortunately they managed it - I'm not sure if Todd Sweeney noticed Sweeney Todd first or if it was Sweeney Todd who spotted Todd Sweeney – confused – you should be!

Nearly two decades later Richard Todd was given the part of playing Major John Howard in the film the 'Longest Day' – not only could he give the director, Darryl Zannuck, his acting skills but also a fair amount of technical advice. At the time of the making of the film Dad, no doubt with tongue in cheek, suggested that the actor most suited to play his role would have been Charles Bronson – as a family we all agreed Groucho Marx was probably more appropriate!

Back in the real world it is now 02:30 hours – apart from the exploding tank very little action was going on. Then out of the blue a lone German motorcyclist turns a corner and obviously by mistake approached the T junction. He is immediately cut to pieces by the waiting allies – as he collapses onto the road the motorbike, still in gear on full throttle takes on a mind of its own. In the resulting crash a British soldier was hit by the machine as it spiralled out of control and eventually died of his injuries. The cards that man were dealt that night were cruel – he had suffered under the wroth of German engineering mastery, the Schmeizzer gun didn't get him – it was the peak of transportation, the BMW that took its revenge. By 03:30 hours with the arrival of Colonel Richard Geoffrey Pine-Coffin and his men the first wave of relief was complete and D Company could begin to withdraw from the west bank and gather at Howard's H.Q. on the east side of the canal and get some well earned rest.

They had much to reflect upon – their dear friend and comrade Den Brotheridge had been lost – also for the first time in their lives, after all their training they had actually fired a shot in anger. In the blink of an eye they had experienced fear and hatred - they had fuelled themselves with pride with the knowledge that they were supremely fit to undertake a job and they had done it well. Some smiled on Lady Luck and thanked her for the way she treated them - others, the pessimists amongst them – expected it to run out. They had arrived, in my father's case, as a boy of twenty-two and three and a half hours later had matured into men of war – the coming weeks and months would have a profound and deeply rooted effect on all them for the rest of their lives.

Today, history recalls that June 6th 1944 was 'The Longest Day.'

For the men of D Company this had already been 'The Longest Night'.

'Parr – keep that bloody gun quiet!'

The night on the town at 'Monty's Casino' would produce, in the cold light of dawn, the inevitable hang-over – but meanwhile in the wee small hours of darkness my Dad decided to do some exploring.

In the initial surge up from the glider very few of the men had spotted a rather large anti-tank gun positioned a few yards up the embankment from where they had landed. Curiosity led Dad to take another guy and give it a good looking over.

To his amazement, he discovered a labyrinth of tunnels and chambers underneath the gun pit. Some of them even housing sleeping quarters. All of them were empty except one – inside he found a fully dressed soldier shaking like a leaf. Throughout the night D Company had unearthed the enemy in various places – the captured men fell into two camps – the pure, highly trained German patriots and the not so keen occupied conscripts. In the initial few minutes of the attack the former held firm while the latter did a runner.

I'm not sure what category Dad's latest captive fell into – but the sight of a bayonet at the end of a rifle soon persuaded the guy to accompany him up the ladder and into a hastily erected POW compound.

As dawn rose – so did the 'Longest Day'.

Anybody who had managed to grab a few minutes sleep was soon aroused by the pounding of the huge guns of the Royal Navy as they attempted to immobilise the German defences poised on the edge of the Normandy beaches.

Soon the last great mass invasion of a country was about to commence. It has been observed that such a momentous event could never be repeated again in modern times because technology would wipe out such an attempt with two or three high-tech nuclear bombs. At dawn on June 6th 1944 the threat to Howard and his men was not nuclear fission – but good old-fashion snipers.

At night, movement across the bridges had been relatively safe and easy – in daylight it became highly dangerous. It was quickly ascertained that the general direction of the fire was up on the west bank of the canal towards Caen. Two buildings suggested the position of the snipers – the Château de Bénouville or the water tower a hundred yards or so in front of it.

In warfare, snipers are a breed apart. Their number one rule is: 'There are no rules.'

In ancient times warriors fought head to head – to shoot a man in the back was to lose honour. Not so with snipers – face, back, side or arse - all were legitimate. Anything goes – Doc Vaughan, wearing Red Cross arm bands and attending the wounded, including David Wood and Sandy Smith, found himself ducking the bullets. At one point he shook his fist and waved it in the general direction of Caen proclaiming: 'This isn't cricket!'

Quite right – it was war.

In short, snipers are cold calculating killers. They will wait hours, even days to achieve a kill; they are your basic hunter/gatherers. Their greatest weapon is not their rifle, but fear – for the enemy does not know how or when they will strike, they must be on their guard 24/7 - forever they must walk in uncertainty. The modern day equivalent would be the suicide bomber – for he/she has the same effect.

I have no problems with snipers – my Dad was one.

While British, American and Canadian troops were being cut to pieces on beaches a few miles away – Wally Parr, Charlie Gardner, Billy Gray and Jack Bailey decided to have a little fun with a certain German anti-tank gun.

In their intense training they had been taught to use almost every conceivable German weapon, but not one of these. Undaunted they proceeded to try and figure the bugger out.

In the chambers below they discovered several dozen shells that obviously fitted the gun – as they struggled up the ladder with the first one, it never occurred to them that if they stumbled and dropped it nose down it would have exploded at the bottom and set all the rest of the shells off, taking them and probably Pegasus Bridge to 'Kingdom Come!'

Throughout his book, Ambrose constantly returns to these four characters – Howard referred to them as his Scallywags, yet he knew that when these types went into battle they would provide the backbone, and how right he was.

Finding where to put the shell was relatively easy – the range marking along the side was self-evident, once you converted metres into feet and inches – the tricky bit was firing it.

After several minutes of deliberation between the men, Charlie Gardner spotted a button, and after stating the classic line: 'What's this?', pushed it and stood back in amazement as a shell screamed out of the barrel heading due south into the heart-land of Normandy. Naturally the spent case ejected itself from the back with an equal velocity, narrowly missing giving fatal injuries to Jack Bailey's ribs!

Now the boys had learnt how to fire the brute there was no stopping them. They were all convinced that the sniper fire was either coming from the top of the château or the water tower. In no time they worked out the range of the château and began their bombardment. The first shell screamed high over the top of the flat roofed building. They adjusted the range and the next one hit about six feet below the top ledge. Such was the power of the shell that it went clean through the outer wall and out the other side without exploding. Dad by now had taken unofficial control of the gun and it was he that claimed the glory. He may have changed his mind if he had realised what he was shelling – it was the local maternity hospital!

Years later he would stand by his gun – although in fact it belonged to all four – and joke about how that evening: 'Many a French maid in the later stages of labour, dropped their chicko's in double quick time and headed down stairs!'

Meanwhile Jack Bailey had grown tired of all this shelling and had decided to go down below into the gun pit and make himself a nice hot brew of tea. After the war Jack used to visit our home and I recall, unlike Dad with his beer, Jack always asked for a nice cup of 'Rosy Lee'. Due to dust filling the chamber every time a shell went off Jack had very politely, but also quite firmly, asked Dad to refrain from firing until he had made his tea. Jack was almost there when Dad thought he saw a sniper up a tree and gave him a blast with his six-pounder. The resulting blast covered Jack's head with dust and worst still turned his hot cup of tea into mud. With steam coming out of his ears he climbed the ladder ready to pull a certain Wally Parr apart, limb from limb – being twice Dad's size it would have been easy. Dad was saved from a fate worse than death because at that precise moment, John Howard intervened and informed him in no uncertain terms that: (A) He was firing at a maternity home and (B) Would he keep that bloody gun quiet because it didn't allow him time to think.

Dad, in pure Spike Milligan mode, thought to himself: 'Nobody told me it was going to be a quiet war!'

Quiet it wasn't – the initial shelling that had bombarded the beaches, now switched a few miles inland and pounded the city of Caen.

Personally, if I was positioned midway between the beaches and Caen I would have been, to say the least, a little bit apprehensive. What if some guy on the battleships several miles away had got his sums wrong and landed a ruddy great shell right amongst us? Ted Tappenden noticed the size of the shells screaming over them towards Caen and commented to Major Howard they were firing bloody jeeps!

Amongst the carnage – the British Tommy never loses his sense of humour.

Inevitably the Germans began to launch a counter-attack. Von Luck quickly realised that if he moved out from under his cover, spotters would relay his position to the war ships and that would be it. His superiors agreed with him – the decision was then made to destroy the

A rare picture of Hans von Luck, far left, discussing the situation on June 7th.
Forty years later he would be enjoying a jazz brunch with Dad in New Orleans !

canal bridge by what ever means.

Firstly they called up a fighter bomber and at around 10:00 hours it appeared from Caen flying barely above tree level. All everybody on the ground could do was dive for cover. Lady Luck had decided to get up early that morning – for although the pilot dropped his 500 pound bomb perfectly on target on the bridge tower, it failed to explode and simply bounced off harmlessly into the canal. The dent it made is still visible to this day.

Another attack was launched from the opposite direction, as a couple of gun boats headed towards the bridge having left the coastal port of Ouisterham. It must have been debatable if in fact they were actually attacking or running – bearing in mind several hundred thousand allied troops were up their arses – but one thing was certain it was coming at a full rate of knots and its 20 mm cannon was blazing away at the bridge.

Howard's men allowed the boats to come into range before Claude Godbolt let fly with a PIAT gun. Once again the notoriously unreliable PIAT proved to be okay when it mattered, catching the vessel smack in the wheel house. Although it didn't sink it was certainly rendered useless and ended up smashing into the bank. German troops emerged from within, most of them in the mood to surrender – the one exception was the young Nazi captain who showed his full arrogance to the end – shouting abuse to all and sundry and risking being torn limb from limb from the boys of D Company. Howard managed to keep them off the guy and had the Nazi marched to the POW cage in Ranville. Over the following hours a pattern emerged with regards to the capture of prisoners - they fell into two distinct categories, the highly trained native Germans who put up a fight and gave the men grief even in captivity and the conscripted soldiers who would have much rather had been somewhere else and surrendered without a murmur.

Years later Dad told me the story of how he brought one particular troublesome captured German officer to Howard's post in the thick of the battle. Major Howard, obviously wrapped up in other things, brushed Dad aside and told him to deal with it. To Howard, this obviously meant marching the bloke to the cage in Ranville – to Dad it meant something somewhat different – the pair never got as far as Ranville.

After the initial surge across the bridge and the incident with Wagger, and his Piat, most of the action involving D Company centred around the anti-tank gun. It began with Gray, Parr, Bailey and Gardner learning to fire the thing, then there was the story of Bill Bailey and his fated cup of tea, a tale that we used to laugh at when we were kids when he and Dad got together to 'spin yarns'. Years later Dad would stand over his gun and would either tell the story of him firing at the maternity hospital or how he shot at the gun-boat that came out of the glistering water coming from the direction of Caen – generations of visitors would smile as he told them how he made the bastards do a quick U turn and retreat double-time back to Caen.

My favourite gun story is when Dad, on that first morning, tried to silence the 'moaning minnies', although the tanks were rendered virtually useless, the self-propelled rocket launchers were proving to be more than effective. They were keeping the men pinned down and making movement highly dangerous. They were nicknamed 'Moaning Minnies' because of the high pitched noise they made just before exploding. Everybody, including Dad, was getting pretty pissed-off by this onslaught, so he ran over to Major Howard and expressed his opinion that he thought the accuracy of the rockets was due to spotters on the water tower relaying positions.

Keen to eliminate all possibilities, Howard gave Dad permission to have a crack at the tower with his anti-tank gun.

To quote Howard: 'You couldn't see Wally's arse for dust!'

In all probabilities Dad hadn't a clue where the spotters were – but at least he could have a bit more fun with his beloved gun.

Ambrose, in his book, then builds up a lovely scene of tension rising as Dad takes control in full military style and prepares his 'team' to fire the first shell. He describes how Dad roars his instructions in his 'loud Cockney voice' – for the second and last time in the book he uses block capitals: 'NUMBER ONE GUN – PREPARE TO FIRE – FIRE'.

His voice had briefly silenced the battle around Bénouville and Le Port – both sides stood and watched as the first shell was fired – loud cheers went up as it hit the water tower – being armour piercing it went clean through and out the other side without exploding. Half a dozen shots later the structure was littered with holes – the ground beneath got a thorough soaking, and the 'moaning minnies' continued their carnage.

Howard, not a great lover of my Dad's gun, ordered him to stop.

Fifty years later, the great bellowing Cockney voice was just as strong. If he ever babysat my daughters, Jennie and Sandra and they misbehaved, he would scream at them: 'Get up to bed or you will get six lace holes up your arses!' My daughters had two granddads: My wife's father 'quiet grey-haired granddad' and 'shouty six-lace holes granddad'!

Back in Bénouville the Gondrée family had slowly emerged from their café and made themselves known to the allies. In the coming decades the building would become a shrine as the first building to be liberated in the invasion of Europe. Once the owner George Gondrée realised what had happened he immediately went to his garden and dug up bottles of vintage Champagne that he had hidden from the hated Germans.

The Gondrée family have been serving drinks to the British ever since.

I am writing this book from the perspective of a working-class son of your bog-standard squaddie. While doing so I am trying to embrace all ranks and all class structures that made up the British army.

I note with interest the attitude of the upper-class higher ranks.

For instance, at around 09:00 hours on the morning of D-Day while men of D Company were hurrying and scurrying at full speed and crouching down Major Howard spotted three men, all immaculately dressed and over six feet tall strolling in unison at full height towards

Pegasus Bridge. The men were General 'Windy' Gale and Brigadiers Hugh Kindersley and Nigel Poett.

The three men had just left Gale's headquarters in Ranville and had decided to 'stroll over' to Pine-Coffins H.Q. in Le Port. The fact that there was a raging battle going on seemed not to perturb them in the least. Howard recalls that seeing these three magnificent figures marching towards his men was awe-inspiring – Richard Todd described it as: 'for sheer bravado and bravery it was one of the most memorable sights I've ever seen'. As they marched across the bridge they were shot at and never flinched – Lady Luck decided to deal them three kings.

I've no problem with these guys – if they decide to put their own heads on the block and it remains intact fine – either way they put their own fate in their own hands.

By 13:00 hours the men were beginning to feel the strain – for them the 'Longest Night' had merged into the 'Longest Day'. They continued to 'hold until relieved' but relief seemed a long way off.

By 15:30 hours relief materialised in the form of Lord Lovat and his company. They heard them, before they saw them – Bill Millin dressed in kilt and sporran announced their arrival with a full blast from his bagpipes. Although first impressions may have been that this was an act of nationalism, in fact it was a coded message which was awaiting a response from a D Company bugler – one tune would announce all was clear and another would warn that a battle was still raging.

The bugler played a tune of caution to the advancing reinforcements.

They approached along the canal path travelling south out of Ouisterham. It was the obvious and safe way to travel - the higher road to the west would have taken them through the hamlet of Le Port where there was heavy fighting going on. Anyway it is the 'pretty route', the way many of us 'foot passengers and pilgrims' still take to this day.

Back in 1944 as Lovat and his men marched along the path the welcome they received was ecstatic – Lovat in his white jumper and full battle smock oozed authority his green beret contrasted proudly against the occasional red of the airborne troops – I use the word 'occasional' because most men wore the camouflaged steel helmet as a protection from the constant onslaught from the enemy.

As Lovat drew level with the café, George Gondrée appeared with a tray of Champagne and offered a glass to Lord Lovat, who being the consummate professional thanked him and brushed the offer aside.

At this point the accounts of events begin to blur somewhat. The controversy lies in what manner Lovat then crossed the two bridges.

History recalls that Lovat then met with John Howard – they exchanged a few words of greeting and then as Lovat began to continue eastwards across the bridges in the direction of Ranville, Howard warned

Pegasus Bridge – a few days after D-Day

him to cross the bridges with extreme caution as they would be under attack from heavy sniper fire.

Some accounts say that, undaunted, Lovat decided not to heed the advice but instead ordered piper Bill Millin to strike up a tune on his pipes and he then proceeded to march his men across the bridge.

I have read several versions of Bill Millin sharing the next few minutes and the gist of each account was that basically it was pretty hairy. If the bagpipes were played, along with the sight of soldiers marching across the bridge, they were certainly sitting targets for the snipers.

There is a unique Britishness about keeping a 'stiff upper lip' the problem is that in the wrong circumstances your 'stiff upper lip' can turn you into a 'stiff'.

Several men were killed – most died due to bullet wounds to the head. Historians note – almost with embarrassment – that future troops crossing wore helmets and used the crouching position.

If this is true, surely I can't be the only person that is slightly disturbed by the action and decision of Lord Lovat at this moment.

For a person to receive news that a loved one had perished while fighting to defeat an enemy is one thing – but for that same person to be shot in the head while, to all intents and purposes, they were taking part in some kind of a 'Victory Parade' or at best 'a show of strength', disturbs me, to say the least.

When Gale, Poet and Kindersley displayed themselves a few hours earlier the only lives they were putting at risk were their own – who has the right to march men across a bridge as an act of defiance knowing their lives may be needlessly taken?

In true Parr tradition I can feel a demotion coming on – by now I may have risen to the dizzy heights of Corporal, but I have a funny feeling that after writing the previous paragraph I may be consigned, if not to the glass house – at least back to being a Private and perhaps the dog house!

Shortly before Lovat's arrival a gun boat had appeared, chugging up from the direction of Caen. This again was part of the enemy's counter-attack, albeit a single boat with no particularly high expectations. The eagle eyes of the four musketeers soon spotted the threat and rushed over to their trusty gun and then entered into a heated discussion as to its range before firing off a shell from their favourite toy. The confusion was probably due to the range markings on the gun being shown in metres and the boys thinking in feet and yards. The first shot was well short, by the time they reloaded for the second shot, the boat had done a quick U turn, yet they managed to catch it on it's stern, although not seriously enough to stop it limping back to Caen.

On many occasions in the future Dad would lean against the railings surrounding his beloved gun and charm tourist with this story and the one about him shelling the maternity hospital – I have numerous photographs of him pointing his arm upstream.

The afternoon drifted into evening – the noise and smells of war intensified for D Company as they held their ground. Thankfully Von Luck and his Panzers had been kept at bay by the heavy artillery of the

How time flies – just one year later John Howard and David Wood join George Gondrée in a toast to freedom

battleships – when they did attempt a breakout spotters would relay their position and pin them down.

By midnight Howard's 'mission' had been accomplished – they had captured and held the bridge until full relief had arrived. Their 'finest hour' had lasted almost exactly 24.

When the Warwickshire Regiment arrived Howard handed over to their commander – meanwhile Dad grabbed a Sergeant and gave him a crash-course on how to fire a German anti-tank gun. I'm sure if Dad had it his own way he would have taken the bloody thing with him, but it was on the heavy side to say the least!

The role of D Company was to change radically – instead of being a highly trained singularly motivated unit that had only one mission in mind they now had to merge into the rest of the Ox and Bucks regiment and become a 'bog standard' fighting unit. Howard, for some time had been answerable to Pine-Coffin and Poet, but now his orders were to be given by Mike Roberts the Battalion Colonel. The men themselves would quickly realise that storming bridges was one thing – but fighting trench warfare up to their necks in muck is an entirely different ball game. In short in the next few hours they would revert from sophisticated Second World War combating to the horrors of the First, so called 'Great War'.

So it was this brave band of brothers found themselves marching away from their beloved bridge in the wee small hours, not so much in a blaze of glory but rather unceremoniously pushing and pulling a ruddy great ox cart! On it was all their heavy equipment and supplies.

Their immediate destination was Ranville and beyond that, the villages of Herouvillette and Escoville. The progress, without a

Escoville – where Dad received his first serious injury

convenient ox or horse was slow - the men were physically and emotionally drained, they had had little or no sleep in the previous forty-eight hours. On the rough narrow roads, despite the efforts of all concerned the cart would veer off the track as if it had a mind of its own – I know the feeling as every supermarket trolley I have ever

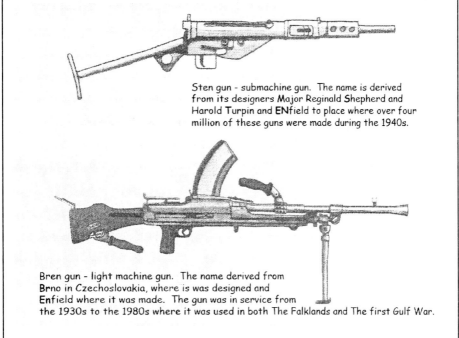

Sten gun - submachine gun. The name is derived from its designers Major Reginald Shepherd and Harold Turpin and ENfield to place where over four million of these guns were made during the 1940s.

Bren gun - light machine gun. The name derived from Brno in Czechoslovakia, where is was designed and Enfield where it was made. The gun was in service from the 1930s to the 1980s where it was used in both The Falklands and The first Gulf War.

Instruments of war – above the British Armour and below the German

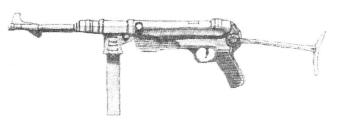

Karabiner 98k or 'Mauser' - bolt-action rifle. Adopted by the Wehrmacht in 1935 as the standard rifle for use within the German Army.

Schmeisser MP40 - submachine gun. Developed specifically for use in the Second World War. Over one million were manufactured during the conflict.

pushed, acts the same.

According to Dad, the language used by the boys as they struggled with this cart was bad, by even their standards – it was not so much the 'Ox and Bucks' as the 'Ox and F***s'!

After a few hundred yards the project was abandoned and the men continued carrying what they could. They were now literally in the dark, lost in the countryside they couldn't find the rest of the regiment – which when you think about it must have been pretty big! It should have been somewhere near Escoville, but Howard had been given the wrong map bearings and had marched nearby to it on at least two occasions before finally making contact at around 03:00 hours. Shortly afterwards they managed to grab a couple of hours sleep – their first on French soil. This was to be one of many such nights spent in Normandy – most believed the Allies would swiftly advance inland to the town of Caen, they talked of hours, at worse days – in fact it would be many weeks of bitter hand to hand fighting before Caen fell – the casualty rate would be high.

After a brief rest the boys found themselves in the thick of it – the enemy at the bridge had been mainly lightly trained conscripts eager to retreat as soon as possible - now in the fields and woods their foe was elite fighting warriors whose allegiance to their Fuehrer was unquestioned, their training, second to non. Von Luck and his 21st Panzers would meet them head on with an arsenal of weapons ranging from tank, mortar and self-propelled rocket launchers to sniper and artillery fire. For a light infantry unit to compete against these boys they would have to dig deep.

For the next couple of days the progress varied between advance and retreat. At one point Dad found himself, along with Jack Bailey organising an evacuation of wounded men, bringing them back from Escoville to Herouvillette. Acts of heroism and deep compassion for your fellow soldier stood beside utter contempt for your enemy – emotions over-rode the logic that tried to tell them that they were all human beings – the law simply stated: 'kill or be killed'

It was during these weeks that Dad came into his own - as a sniper.

Denis Edwards in his highly detailed book 'The Devil's Own Luck' gives numerous accounts of going out on sniping sorties with Wally Parr and Paddy O'Donnell. In pure 'hunter/gatherer' mode he describes days in relation to the number of 'kills'. In true upper-class Britishness I almost expected him to record getting a 'brace of Germans' much as you would shooting pheasants.

It is ironic that most infantrymen, whenever possible, would swap their home produced weapons for the much prized Schmeisser and the P38 pistol - a German being shot by a gun built by one of their own countrymen really was adding salt into the wound.

The mayhem of full frontal face to face warfare is one thing – by and large each side knows what they are up against. In contrast the sniper offers a totally different concept of fighting. With tanks, artillery and planes, you usually get some sort of warning if only a few seconds – a sniper gives you none, yet in some circumstances you may be aware of his presence 24/7.

There are two qualities a good sniper needs – patience and accuracy - if they possess these, they literally have 'time to kill'.

I recall a story my Dad told me when he was on a patrol near Escoville with Edwards and O'Donnell. For three consecutive days they went to the same slit trench and observed the enemy. The opposition had dug-in a few hundred yards away – there had been a temporary lull in the fighting, everybody was waiting and watching, trying to anticipate the next move.

On the first day Dad had noticed a gap in the hedge where a young German, probably no older than sixteen, had walked past at precisely 09:30 hours dishing out drinks to his comrades. On the second day he checked to see if the routine was the same – he appeared like clockwork. By now, when he told us the story years later he had given the young lad the name Fritz – according to Dad all Germans were either called Fritz or Hans, leaders were called Adolf.

On the third day at precisely 9:30 hours Dad looked through his telescopic lens, pulled the trigger and took Fritz out. He showed little emotion when he told us the story – he had a job to do and he did it – his face did break into a smile when he finished the story by commenting that the next day the new tea boy did the job on his hands and knees!

As kids, the stories our dads and uncles told us never really touched the true horrors of war. One of our favourites was the one about a monkey standing on a wall and peeing all over Jack Bailey in India. Dad never mentioned grown men crouching in trenches trembling with shell shock – even shooting themselves in the foot – anything to get them back to Blighty.

For many, morals and standards went by the wayside – apparently one French farmer tried to show his appreciation to the liberating allies by offering his all too willing daughter to pleasure the eager sex-starved men.

After Mum died Dad did mention a certain young French girl. Be it French Champagne or a French maiden 'take it when you can' was Dad's philosophy –'there was a war on, today may be the last cup of tea, shave or shag you ever have!'

Years later, during a quiet intimate moment with Dad, I asked him to describe the real horrors of war, to forget the glamour and the glory and get down to the nitty-gritty.

For a while he just stared at me - then he lit up a cigarette and poured himself a large one.

'There are no atheists in a slit trench,' he began, 'when the bullets fly and the mortars start dropping you cry out to God. You tell Him if He gets you out of this mess when you get home you will be a good boy, go to church and even run for Pope. Yet amid the carnage and madness sometimes you detach from it all and start cursing - you find somebody or something to blame. Where's the supplies?...Why doesn't the bloody radio work?...Why can't I have a decent cup of tea and where's all the bog paper gone? Stupid thoughts that have nothing to do with survival. Then the mortars land nearer and although you are already laying flat on your face in the mud, you dig down even deeper - somehow you manage to embed all your fingers a couple of inches further into the ground and you kid yourself that along with your metal helmet you have somehow made yourself a bit safer. After half an hour eternity the barrage stops - you turn to your mate on the right. "Okay Harry?" He nods with weary eyes. Then you turn to the guy on your left. "Joe are you alright?" There's no answer, you look at the back of his neck, a piece of shrapnel has entered turning the mud blood red - you turn him over, his eyes stare heaven-ward and you thank God that for him, it is all over, the pain has gone. Then you realise, that you aint really scared of death - what did the Good Book say: "Greater love hath no man than to lay down his life for his brother."

He aint going to Hell, this is Hell right here, this moment on Earth. No, what you really fear is getting wounded - going blind or losing an arm or a leg or suffering for days or weeks before you finally cave in.'

Dad stopped talking, he drew one last drag from his cigarette and finished off his whisky.

Weeks later as I reflected on these words it occurred to me that, 60 years on, in essence nothing much has changed. True, the technology of killing people has improved - nowadays we eat our dinner watching the six o'clock news and look at footage of bombs homing in on their targets with pin-point accuracy. Yet when we see buildings destroyed it somehow reminds us of arcade computer games - our minds detach from reality, we don't comprehend real bombs killing real men, women and children. Yet away from the sophistication of modern warfare for Tommy Atkins in the trenches nothing much has changed. In the 21st Century, boots melt in the Gulf War heat, desert dust clogs up modern radios and men die because there is a shortage of body armour and they have just lent theirs to a mate. And when the rocket-propelled grenades start screaming some grown men still huddle on the ground and cry out to God in confusion not really knowing whose God is on whose side - and some still crap themselves, and would you believe it they are still running out of bloody toilet paper!

For Dad D-Day plus 44 was the day that his worst fears turned into reality. It was the 20th July, the British army was still bogged down in the fields of Normandy – Berlin seemed a long way off – Caen, a few miles inland still hadn't been taken, deadlock was the order of the day. Between the odd skirmish and the occasional sniper outing, life was about surviving and nothing else.

I now quote from Denis Edwards: '*The day ended on a good note around teatime, fresh supplies arrived and included real tea, sugar and tinned milk, which makes a wonderful change from the foul 'mixed monkey' tea cubes. This new stuff tasted like tea.*

There was a severe stonk a short while later, and whether the fresh tea went to his Cockney head I don't know, but Wally Parr was hit by two chunks of shrapnel. I was not around when it happened, but I was told that his wounds were not too severe, but enough to put him out of action for some time. Wally was a collector of interesting items! Apparently as he was being placed upon a stretcher he said to one of the orderlies: "ang on a minute mates,' then he called out to one of the lads, 'hey mate do me a favour, nip over to me trench and get the little pack for me, it will make a nice pack for me as they cart me back to Blighty'.

As he went he called out: 'Don't worry mates – I'll be back'.

Wally was one of those brave characters who seemed to be in his element during warfare'.

'I'll be back!' - very Arnold Schwarzenegger!

Dad recalled vaguely about the incident – 'all I can remember is that I wanted to refill my water bottle, my helmet was at the bottom of the slit trench, I couldn't be bothered to retrieve it yet I felt instinctively that I had to protect my head so I reached into my smock and put on my red beret - Paddy O'Donnell said "where are you going?" "to fill my bottle" I replied – as I approached company H.Q., scream of shell – all I remember is appearing to turn three somersaults and shutting one eye and blokes were all around me – I stammered and they dragged me out of the trench. An eye witness told me that I actually received the entire force of the shell that exploded after hitting a tree about twenty yards in front of me, under which four D Company blokes were being instructed by a Sergeant. None were injured yet I caught the full shock-wave and a couple of pieces of shrapnel in me head.'

Within a few minutes two stretcher bearers appeared and carted him off to the first-aid post.

For Wally Parr aged 22, his war effort had come to a brief interlude – if Messrs. Churchill, Montgomery and Howard wanted to advance onwards, roughly in the direction of Berlin and take out Mr. Hitler they would simply have to carry on without him!

Down in the Ardennes

'They dragged me out, put me on a stretcher, then an ambulance – I passed out – I came too – I passed out – I couldn't open my right eye, I thought I had lost it but in fact it was clogged up with congealed blood – eventually opened up, everything was white – thought I was in heaven – opened again and there was a Queen Alexandra Nurse, grey uniform edged with red, white pad on shoulders, she said: "You're alright – you're going home". I closed my eyes, she squeezed my arm – I woke and they were putting me on a landing craft – came to a couple of times – eventually wound up in Portsmouth – then I was taken to Cosham – looked up and thought "bloody hell, that's good of them taking me to see my wife in Corsham"!'

These are the rambling thoughts Dad shared with me concerning the immediate aftermath of his wounding – I have not added punctuation for I feel they perfectly sum up his mental and physical condition. It is worth noting that Cosham is just outside Portsmouth while Corsham is many miles away in Wiltshire where Mum and her two children were staying.

In actual fact, on arrival in Portsmouth Dad was taken four hundred miles north to a hospital in Scotland, which is about as far away from Corsham as you can get!

It is amazing the difference a letter or a number can make – John Howard a few weeks after Dad's injury was wounded by a mortar attack. The message his wife Joy received was not that he was in hospital with a 'mortar wound' but with a 'mortal wound' – a significant difference!

Even more dramatic is the story of Arthur 'Robbo' Roberts aged 21.

In the height of action another A. Roberts was killed in action. Somehow company H.Q. cocked-up the paper-work and sent a message of condolence to the parents of the wrong A. Roberts – eventually the mistake was rectified when the living Arthur Roberts sent a letter home telling his mum and dad how he was getting on!

In the years that followed Arthur carried the notification certificate, announcing his own death, around in his wallet – proud to show it to anyone interested. Sadly he passed away not long after the 60th anniversary of D-Day.

Meanwhile, the young Wally Parr had arrived in the hospital in Scotland. The concussion soon subsided – the shrapnel was removed from his head – it was presumed there will be no long lasting brain damage – although those amongst us, who know him the best, may question that!

For several weeks he was allowed to rest and recuperate in the serenity of the Scottish Lowlands – Normandy and his mates were a million miles away.

Yet the horror's of war continued. I have in my possession a letter that John Howard sent to the parents of Pete Barwick one of his men who was killed at Escoville. It is particularly poignant to me as I have met Pete's brother, Ted, many times over the years, not only on the bridge, but also travelling down to Honiton in Devon and staying with his family with my Mum, Dad and wife.

The letter was written on the 11th July 1944 - as a battle raged all around him John Howard still managed to find time to write a letter of condolence – it sums up the man's compassion and also highlights the intimate horrors of war. I have reproduced it in full:

Dear Mr. Barwick,

I have managed to get your address from Sgt. Webster because I want to pen you a few lines of sympathy over the loss of your son, Sgt. Barwick.

I was his company commander and have felt his loss more than I can ever say. He was without a doubt the best NCO one in whom I had complete faith. He'll do any job I gave him to do, well. His popularity was terrific both as a soldier and a man. That he was a born leader goes without saying, his men would follow him anywhere. I am sure you would like to know how he, was faced up until he was killed. His platoon was part of my special force that took off from England at 23:00 hrs (11pm) Monday 5th June with the important task of capturing two vital bridges, before the seaborne assault next morning. Your son's glider unfortunately, landed in the wrong place, some ten miles away from the proper objective. There were two officers with him Capt. B. D. Priday and Lieut. C. Hooper, both of whom are now wounded. They managed to fight their way back to us through swamps meeting odd German patrols all the way.

It took them a good twenty-four hours. Sgt. Barwick reached us in very good spirits. The life really suited him. The rest of my force landed in the right place, and as you have read in the papers we captured and held the bridges.

On Wednesday we attacked and moved into Escoville. The Huns counter attacked and our company and all but surrounded. During this attack Sgt. Barwick was killed together with other men of this platoon. He was lying in a ditch when an enemy armoured car strafed them. Your son went down fighting hard and calling them all the names he could lay his tongue to. He died immediately.

We were driven out of the place but I personally later took a fighting patrol back for his and other bodies. He is buried at Herouvillette along with many other comrades. I had a great personal liking to your son, his London wit and cheerfulness under all conditions impressed me. I am a Londoner myself and felt that we had much in common. The thoughts of his young wife and baby daughter he only saw once sadden me terribly.

May God Bless Them Both.

If this letter comforts you and your family I am glad. I write it as a tribute to a very fine soldier. He lived a fine life and died a fine death.

Yours very sincerely,
Major Howard.

But Dad was cocooned from all this in the peace and quiet of Scotland. By mid-August Dad felt he was on the mend. The hospital ward was led by a matron who, in true tradition ran the place with a rod of iron. One of the rules was that nobody was allowed to leave the premises without her specific permission and then they must wear a special blue uniform. Dad had tried his luck on several occasions but for some unknown reason she was having none of it. Unperturbed he managed to convince another patient to lend him their uniform and on a bright sunny Monday morning he ventured out into the nearby village.

He had several things to do. Firstly, there was the small matter of his postal orders. In Normandy he had managed to work a right old fiddle with the company clerk. Apparently there were loads of American issue French francs scattered everywhere.

'Everybody thought they were worthless, people were lighting their fags or wiping their arses on them,' says Dad.

But he had other ideas – he would collect them from dead German bodies or from wherever else he could find them and worked a deal with the clerk. Somehow they were converted into £2 postal orders – some for the clerk and some for Dad. On the day he was wounded the young entrepreneur, in his top pocket had 39 £2 postal orders – 78 quid in real money, a small fortune in those days. When he asked for his rucksack as he was being carted off - it wasn't because he wanted to use it as a pillow, it was because inside he had a couple of dozen good quality watches taken from the bodies of dead Germans!

French francs - printed in America to be used by the allies when they invaded France - it was these notes that enabled Dad to make a few quid !

The first task was to cash the postal orders.

He joined a small queue at the post office. Eventually he made it to the front; he placed the postal orders on the counter and asked the old lady behind the desk to cash them. She looked at them suspiciously and then informed him they had to be signed. By the time he finished signing them the queue was out the door and to make matters worse the poor old dear doubted if she had enough cash left in the till to last the rest of the day!

Feeling like a millionaire, young Wally headed to the nearest pub - his face soon dropped when the landlord informed him he wasn't allowed to serve men in hospital blue uniforms. Seeing the look of disappointment on Dad's face he told him to go round the back and in no time he had knocked back three pints of bitter.

On a high he wandered into the local picture palace and sat through the afternoon matinee, watching the main feature twice. Afterwards he strolled back to the pub, had a quick pint and a wee dram of single malt whisky - the second drink was Dutch courage, needed to survive the onslaught of the dreaded matron!

As he entered the ward the matron was standing there waiting for him instead of giving him a rollicking she had a slight smirk on her face. 'I don't know what you have been up to young man but I hope it was worth it, you've got visitors!'

Dad looked across to his bed and on two chairs beside it sat my Mum and her sister, my Aunt Lilly.

They had faces like thunder - if looks could kill - Dad was dead, twice! He gave them a quick peck in the cheek and immediately retreated to the other side of the bed, hopefully out of arms and harms way.

For the next couple of minutes the gruesome-twosome gave him a right old ear 'ole bashing – in no uncertain terms they told him how they endured the over-night train from London and then had to wait two hours for a further connection to get to this God-forsaken town in the middle of nowhere, They then rambled on about how that had been sitting and staring at his empty bed since lunchtime, wondering if he had deserted or even run off to the Highlands with some wee Scottish nurse!

As their nagging approached its crescendo Dad gave up listening, reached into his top pocket and threw seventy-odd quid in old fivers onto the bed.

Immediately Mum and Lilly stopped nagging and, with eyes nearly popping out of their heads, the mood changed dramatically.

'Not to worry, my darling,' cried Mum, 'How's your wounds? You were so brave, we are all so proud of you'.

All of a sudden Wally Parr was flavour of the month.

Within the hour Dad had convinced matron that his wife and sister-in-law were in fact trained nurses and were capable of escorting him back home. She probably didn't believe a word of it but there was a bed shortage and she would have been glad to see the back of him. By the next morning the papers were issued and the three-some were on their way back to Corsham in Wiltshire.

As they waited for the train, the cash began to burn a hole in the girl's pockets. 'We need sheets!' cried the girls 'we can't get any in Corsham because of the rationing'.

Dad took them to the nearest shop that looked like it may sell some.

'You can nah hav' any unless ya hav' the coupons', was the Scottish shopkeeper's response.

'Sod the coupons,' was Dad's reply, 'will these do?'

Then in classic Spiv style he rolled-up his left sleeve and displayed a dozen or so quality watches.

'Nah problem', replied the shrewd Scot.

The going rate was two watches for a pair of sheets – Dad brought the girls an armful!

After a train journey that lasted several hours they eventually arrived back in Corsham – Dad double-checked the sign at the station, just to make sure it didn't say Cosham.

He had been given ten days compassionate leave – he used the time to get to know his young children and also to have as much compassion as his tired body would allow.

In his quieter moments his thoughts turned to his mates, still slogging it out in Normandy. The daily news was vague and often confusing – he figured that if the Government told all, the enemy would be aware of the facts as well.

All too quickly his leave was over and he was told to report back to the Ox and Bucks H.Q. in Colchester, Essex. His journey was uneventful until he reached Liverpool Street station in London – there he was informed that the line to Colchester had been bombed and it would not be open until the following morning.

With several hours to kill, he decided to get his hair cut. After a long wait he finally found himself in the barber's chair and took his red beret off.

One side of his head looked relatively normal but underneath his beret side his scalp was almost hairless due to his operation to remove bits of shrapnel.

'What do you want me to do with this lot?' asked the barber.

'Anything you like', was the reply.

The barber had no choice other than to shave the lot off – a 'short back and hard luck' of the first order. As he cut his hair the barber asked Dad how he got wounded. For the first time Dad shared his experiences at Pegasus Bridge – the barber and the waiting customers listen intensely – the poster outside that warned the public that 'careless talk costs lives' was ignored as they hung on to his every word.

When the haircut was finished the young soldier stood up and asked the barber how much he owed him. There was a short pause.

'How much you owe me?' cried the barber, 'no, my friend, it is how much do I owe you?'

With that, a couple of the waiting customers gave a polite clap and Dad slightly embarrassed, and truly humbled, left the shop without paying a penny.

'Cheapest haircut I ever had'. He would remark years later – yet in many ways it was also the most expensive.

He spent the rest of the evening and night at the station, sleeping on a hard bench. By the following morning the track had been cleared and he got the first available train to Colchester,

His orders were to report to the barracks by 21:00 hours the previous day but through no faults of his own he finally made it to the Military Sergeant over twelve hours late. He handed in his papers and was told to go to the mess hut – he almost made it to the door before a loud yell from the officer told him to about turn and get back to his desk double quick. Within seconds the Colonel was called and in no time Dad quickly realised this guy was completely mad.

For a good five minutes he screamed and ranted at Dad informing him that he was on a charge and he would be busted for reporting back late – before he knew it he was in the guard-house minus his stripes. He learnt at a later date that the 'Mad Colonel' was later discharged on medical/mental grounds, but this didn't help Dad in his present situation.

For the next couple of days he was locked up with various other misfits and deserters until the matter was sorted and he was eventually driven back to Bulford Barracks.

He arrived there around mid–August it was a strange eerie feeling, the rest of D Company were still in Normandy, some of the beds previously occupied by his buddies were being slept in by total strangers – these were raw recruits, called up by age to replace the dead and dying.

To these guys, Dad was a war veteran – the exploits of D Company were already legendry in the mess hall of Bulford and soon Dad's skill as a story teller was being put to full use.

On the 3rd September 1944 a small convoy of trucks rumbled in to barracks – aboard was what remained of D Company.

They had left, on the night of June 5th, 180 men strong – they returned three long months later with only forty personnel , plus of course Wally Parr who had had a brief holiday in Scotland and now formed the backbone of the welcome home committee.

The true realisation of the loss and carnage that manifested itself during those days in Normandy struck home to the men when they saw their beds. Many were empty, some were occupied by 'trespassers', young upstarts who had no right to sleep in their dead mates beds without asking – the empty beds were like unmarked graves in which a fellow comrade could lay down his grief like a wreath of flowers.

Dad can remember John Howard coming into the room and giving the men their first inspection since the return only a few hours earlier. Although obviously weary his true professionalism still shone through as he welcomed his new men and encouraged his old comrades before they left on a well deserved two week leave. As he was about to dismiss them he spotted Dad in the corner.

'Parr, it's good to see you, welcome back, I'm glad to see that you've made a full recovery'.

He was just about finished when he noticed Dad's lack of stripes. 'What happened this time?' he asked wearily.

Dad briefly gave him the story of bombed railway lines and mad

Colonels. 'It wasn't my fault Major Howard – honest sir!'

Howard gave him the benefit of the doubt.

'Put those stripes back up Parr,' he bellowed, 'and this time BLOODY WELL KEEP THEM!'

Throughout his army career Wally Parr was a Private, a Corporal, a Private, a Corporal, a Sergeant and was on the verge of being busted back to Corporal just as his de-mob papers came through. Somehow army authority and Wally Parr just couldn't get it quite right.

Meanwhile there was a war on. The onward march into Europe continued. At Bulford a second wave of gliders was being prepared to fly back into occupied enemy territory – this time targeting the Bridges at Arnhem and Nymegen.

Compared to Arnhem the raid on Pegasus Bridge had been a stroll in the park. After four days fighting Wagger, along with many others, was captured. Although I have a special soft spot for my own father, without doubt, in my opinion Thornton was the consummate professional infantrymen whose bravery and skill was second to none.

There has been much speculation amongst war historians as to whether D Company should have been brought back to Bulford earlier and prepared for Arnhem – but considering their losses, particularly amongst the platoon leaders, I think it was a too tall an order to ask.

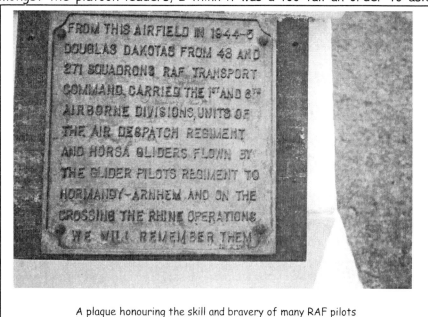

A plaque honouring the skill and bravery of many RAF pilots

Psychologically and physically they were shattered – it would have been like asking a football team to play two cup-finals back to back.

Yet after a couple of weeks break, Howard set about rebuilding his team. Things were going well – this time the training had a different emphasis no bridges this time – hand to hand fighting was the order of the day. In true Churchill style, they would fight them in the hills, they would fight them in the woods and fight them amongst the streets and houses of Europe – pushing them back all the way to Berlin.

Howard had somehow managed to rebuild a second D Company – would he carve his name into a second piece of history?

The simple answer was 'no' – while travelling to Oxford to visit his wife he decided to relieve his jeep driver of his duties and drive the vehicle himself on the grounds that he could drive the damn thing much faster. While passing an American convoy of trucks coming in the opposite direction one of the trucks decided to pull out and move up the convoy - the truck hit Howard's jeep head on.

Howard, always a man that lived on the edge had eventually fallen off – he sustained serious leg and hip injuries and was on the critical list for over a fortnight. He remained in hospital until the spring and despite frantic efforts to return to fitness his army career was over.

For the rest of his life he walked with a limp that steadily deteriorated, causing him to firstly use a stick, then crutches and eventually a wheel chair.

Perhaps it was destiny that the raid on Pegasus Bridge was to be his one and only 'Finest Hour' – anything after that may have been an anti-climax.

With Howard gone the regiment had the almost impossible task of filling his well-worn shoes – this was achieved by promoting Captain John Tillet, the Battalion Adjutant during the Normandy campaign, to Major. Tillet was to eventually reach the rank of Colonel before retiring from the army.

In many ways I feel sorry for John Tillet – we all know that Alf Ramsay was manager of England when they won the World Cup, but how many of us can remember, or indeed care, who followed him. Needless to say, the same training, initiated by Howard continued. As Christmas 1944 approached the men were promised a bonus of Christmas at home with their families - this was cruelly dashed two days before leave was due when they were informed that they were heading back into Europe. Their destination was the Ardennes, in Belgium – for D Company the Battle of the Bulge was about to begin.

Although technically airborne troops, due to the atrocious weather conditions, they found themselves travelling into Europe by boat, leaving from Dover and being one of the first convoys to enter Calais after it had been cleared of mines.

It was Christmas morning when they transferred into canvas covered trucks and were driven towards Belgium in freezing conditions. En route they were given small tins of bully beef and told to share it with two others. As I write I can almost feel Dad recalling it, with violins in the background – I am reminded of some Dickensian saga when times were tough, very tough - yet somehow Dad would put lightness to the story, trying to make it not as bad as it was.

They spent Christmas night in a small town outside Brussels. Thankfully they were billeted into local houses – the townsfolk showed their appreciation by giving them slap up meals and warm beds to sleep in. Dad spent the night in a room with Charlie Gardner. After a huge meal and loads of wine they slept peacefully. Next morning they continued their journey in the drafty trucks heading deeper into snowbound Europe. After a few miles Charlie confessed to Dad that he had so much wine the previous night that he managed to wet the kind people's bed – so much for a British soldier's appreciation!

Eventually they arrived at the river Meuse – it was cold – bloody cold – everywhere was a white-out.

Every family has its pet-phrases, if it is the parents and they are trying to stop their kids moaning or complaining it usually begins along the lines of: 'You think you have got it tough – when I was your age, etc. etc.'

Well, my Dad had a special saying that covered every complaint from the weather to being hard done by... 'You call this cold - when I was down in the Ardennes it was so cold, etc.'

No matter how cold it got in England the Ardennes was colder – once he told us it was so cold that when the chickens laid their eggs you didn't have to hard boil them 'cos it was so cold they laid them rock solid to begin with!

In fact he didn't always use it to describe the weather, often if something was going pear-shaped he would simply tell us; 'You think this is tough, down in the Ardennes......'

I'm sure all families survive this way, the philosophy is simple: If you think you have hit rock-bottom relax – it may improve but believe me it could get a whole lot worse!

Apart from the weather and the fact that Dinant was a beautiful village on the river Meuse, Dad told us very little about his Battle of the

Bulge.

According to Denis Edwards most of the time was spent sitting around and trying to keep warm. The Americans did most of the donkey-work as the fog and snow began to clear and they began to drive the Hun further and further back into their homeland. By the end of February 1945 D Company was heading back to England and the relative safety and warmth of Bulford Barracks.

Of course the Germans were not so much 'retreating' as 'regrouping' – gaining a mile in Belgium was one thing, gaining ground in Germany was a completely different ball-game.

Dad and his mates were soon to find this out on their next sortie into Europe – the Rhine Crossing.

As young kids the first funny rude song we learnt was; 'Three German officers crossed the Rhine, parlez vous!' God knows why – this certainly wasn't a barrel of laughs.

This time the boys came in by glider, unlike Pegasus Bridge there was no element of surprise – gliders were being destroyed before they hit the ground. Forever etched in Dad's mind is the sight of blazing planes spiralling to the ground men falling out of the flimsy fuselage and plummeting hundreds of feet to their deaths. Dad's plane was lucky, it landed without any casualties yet once on the ground, between the 24th and 25th March 1945 the regiment suffered 183 killed and many more wounded.

Amongst the wounded was a certain Wally Parr. He remembers it happening at night and again it was his old mate, shrapnel. This time he managed to get back on his feet – his platoon leader took one look at him and gave instructions to get himself over to a nearby château that was being used as a first aid post. He had been hit in the leg so he used his rifle as a crutch and staggered there as a walking wounded. A medical orderly gave him a quick examination, dressed his wound, told him to stop moaning and instructed him to brew up some tea for the overstretched medical staff.

'No holiday back in Scotland this time', he thought to himself.

Although not as serious as the first episode, shrapnel did enter his leg. The medical orderly did a good enough job on the field to take him out of any danger but presumably somebody, somewhere expected him to have a small operation at a later date to remove the remaining shrapnel, but it never happened.

Years later one of Dad's favourite party tricks was to roll up his trouser leg and let us feel the shrapnel buried half an inch inside his thigh – another one was for him to clench the muscles in his stomach and tell us to punch him as hard as we could - the stomach was rock solid and inevitably we would hurt our hands – I noticed he stopped that trick when I became a teenager, I'm not sure if this was because I was getting stronger or he was getting soft in his old age, probably 'six of one and half a dozen of the other' as Dad would say.

In the passage of time the wound did give him some discomfort, but to counteract it he would take large swigs of Scotch out of Mum's bottle – if he got caught nicking it while Mum was out of the room he would simply reply; 'Shrapnel medicine my love – it's for the shrapnel'!

About the time of Dad getting wounded his old mate Harry 'Nobby' Clark also copped it, although the injuries Nobby received were much more serious.

It happened on the 5th April – while chatting to Nobby recently I pointed out to him that this date was Wally's birthday.

'It certainly wasn't mine!' was the response.

He and a few others were on patrol just as the light was fading – from nowhere machine gun fire burst into action, the guy beside Nobby was killed instantly while he caught two bullets in the hand and one in the wrist. As a result he had to have his right hand amputated – although his army days were over it would be a further thirteen months before he was discharged. The reason for the delay was because the policy of the British Army was that they desired, as near as possible, to discharge their men in roughly the same shape as when they enlisted and in Nobby's case it took all that time to fit an effective false hand that half worked. He has long since given it up and manages to get by with just his left hand.

There is a sad irony to this story – the burst of gunfire that did all the damage was from a British Bren as no Germans were reported to be in the area at the time. Nobby always maintains that he had a rough idea who the culprit was, but refuses, quite rightly to name names.

I am still intrigued as to why these incidents are recorded under the heading 'Friendly Fire' – 'Cock-ups' seems more appropriate to me.

The action on the Rhine was as intense and fierce for D Company as it was around Escoville and the Château Saint-Côme in Normandy. Somehow the four 'usual suspects' found themselves time and again in the thick of it together. Billy Gray shared with me recently how they once found themselves in a railway signal box of all places. It was near a river and beside a partly built section of a revolutionary new road called an 'Autobahn' – German expertise was years ahead of Britain, it would be another decade before we began our motorway system. A few hundred yards away was the advancing Gerry, 'Loads of the buggers!' according to

Billy. Charlie Gardner was using one Bren gun out of one window and Bill Gray was shooting out of another. Wally Parr, Jack Bailey and Paddy O'Donnell were supporting them with rifle fire. The action went on for a good few hours – nobody was prepared to predict the outcome – would the enemy retreat or would reinforcements arrive. They all took turns on the Bren – Billy recalls while bullets were flying left, right and centre he looked across into the corner and there fast asleep was Charlie Gardner. Charlie always did have a reputation for being an easy going, laid-back sort of guy and if he fancied forty winks he was going to bloody well have it!

Needless to say they all got out alive.

They arrived in late March and slugged it out until the first week in May. On May the 8th 1945 Germany surrendered – Hitler was 'bunkered' – and Wally Parr and Billy Gray found themselves doing a bit of relaxing by pilfering a small yacht from an exclusive sailing club on some lake or other and trying their hand at sailing.

They found sailing down-wind a piece of cake – when they hit land at the far end and then attempted to tack up-wind they were buggered. After several goes they gave up and decided to have a swim. It was a beautiful day – the war in Europe was over it was time to chill out. After a while Billy emerged from a deep dive looking rather stressed – he drew a deep breath and dived again. Dad was on the boat, having a fag, oblivious to everything. Eventually Billy appeared on the surface again and yelled to Dad he needed help. It turned out that Billy had lost his front three false-teeth and they were somewhere on the bottom of the lake. Dad couldn't jump in for laughing, after half an hour Bill gave up. For the next 60 years, when they met at reunions, Dad still asked him if he has found his false teeth yet. It puts a whole new meaning to the poignant saying 'somewhere in a far corner of Europe, there is a part of me'. In Billy Gray's case – it's his false choppers.

Before they knew it they were flying out of Germany in Dakotas and heading back to Blighty.

For many years I thought soldiers were demobbed a few weeks after victory over Japan in August 1945 but, of course, I was wrong.

When Dad and his mates returned from Europe they found themselves being scattered here there and everywhere. Dad was issued with full jungle kit and before he knew it Billy Gray was hanging on the end of a parachute as he was transferred to the 9th Para's.

1945 drifted into 1946 and at the ripe old age of 24 Dad was a seasoned soldier and Colonel Tillet had promoted him to the dizzy heights of acting Sergeant. It was around this time that Wally Parr found himself taking, not a slow boat to China, but a slow one to India. From there he boarded a very slow steam train that rumbled its way

Bailey, Dad and a mate in Palestine

through the sub-continent in the general direction of Palestine. Apparently the train was so long and so slow that he was on it for seven days! Men used to sunbathe on the roof and occasionally, if they fell asleep and slid off, they would dust themselves down, get up, run after the train, and jump back on. I think this should be filed away in the 'chickens laying hard boiled eggs down in the Ardennes' department, but with Dad you could never quite tell – he loved to spin a yarn.

What was becoming apparent was that the world and its politicians were stepping into a new arena - they had begun to take on the role of 'Policing the World' and their first objective was sorting out the Arab / Jew conflict.

Dad shared with me his thoughts on this: He could see the point of standing firm and defending his country when some bugger was about to overthrow it – but what the hell was he doing a couple of thousand miles away sorting out two nations who had been at each others throats for centuries?

I'm sure it is a sentiment shared by many soldiers to this day.

By the time the slow train reached Karachi Dad was feeling distinctively unwell, his condition worsened and a couple of days later he was stretched off to the local hospital , 'it wasn't malaria but some other tropical lurgy' Dad recalls.

In no time they had given him medicine, washed away his sweat and tucked him up in a nice clean white gown. As he slowly drifted off to sleep a violent slap in the face brought him back to his senses and then he looked down and saw blood and guts oozing onto his chest. He yelled for a nurse at the top of his voice and when she rushed in, she took one look and called for assistance.

You may have heard of the expression: 'The shit hitting the fan,' well this is a slight variation: Apparently, a stray bat had entered the ward and flown straight into the fan above Dad's bed and the poor animals fate was to be shredded all over Dad.

Before he knew it, four hefty orderlies appeared, stripped Dad naked, washed him down, grabbed an arm and a leg each and spread him face down over the bed. The next moment a doctor appeared with a hypodermic needle, 'the size of a javelin', and after muttering the immortal words: 'This may hurt a little', gave him an injection that made him yell so loud that he woke up the natives in the next village. When asked what he had done to deserve that, they explained that the bat in question would most probably have had rabies - the injection was merely a precaution.

'Most obliged!' was Dad's abrupt response.

Jack Bailey and Charlie Gardner visited the hospital a few days later and brought him the customary bunch of grapes and in true British tradition ate them in front of him, spitting the pips all over the floor. Needless to say Dad recovered fully and eventually found himself in Cairo.

Although up to this point he hadn't heard a shot fired in anger – his wounds were just as troublesome as they had been in Europe. Again he found himself in another hospital, this time with a severe case of piles – or 'roof tiles' as we Cockneys affectionately call them!

History repeated itself once again as he was placed face down across a table minus his trousers and underpants. A doctor then place a contraption up his rear-end that 'spread my arse hole to the size of a dinner plate!' according to Dad.

Beside the doctor were four giggling young nurses who peered up as the doctor began to snip each pile off with a pair of scissors – after the first snip Dad gave a loud shriek and the girls giggles turned to hysterics. At this point Dad decided to pull rank: 'Listen ladies, you are looking up a Sergeant's arse at a Sergeant's piles and I am bloody well ordering you to stop laughing!'

They somehow managed to muffle their giggles.

After the fourth snip Dad pulled up his pants and trousers and walked out of the room, looking like a cross between John Wayne and a gorilla. As the door closed the laughter explode again.

Dad wasn't amused – it was about this time that Dad came to the conclusion that India and the Middle East were distinctively anal!

Dad eventually found himself in Jerusalem, a place where major religions clash side by side.

On one of his daily exercises he would find himself against the Wailing Wall – he and his mates used to do a regular ritual against it - and it wasn't praying!

True to form, good old Dad eventually blew it. One day against army regulations he was caught drinking with the privates – as an acting sergeant he was in danger of being court marshalled. I personally find this incomprehensible, but rules are rules and Dad always a bit of a 'barrack room lawyer' knew them well. He was dragged before Tillet and the book was about to be thrown at him – fortunately alongside the book was his de-mob papers. Colonel Tillet actually had a soft spot for him and told him to lie low and instead of demotion he would soon have him on his way back to Blighty.

Meanwhile Billy Gray had decided against jumping from airplanes and fancied a bit of sunbathing – being a couple of years younger than Dad he knew he still had a bit of time to do and fancied meeting up with his old mates in the Middle East.

By an incredible coincidence while Dad was several hundred miles south of Jerusalem being driven home in a truck, he passed another one coming in the opposite direction. Through the dust he made out the figure of Billy Gray –they briefly waved to each other; it would be many years later before the next reunion.

It was touch and go as to whether Dad left the army or if he was thrown out. In actual fact it's irrelevant – the love/hate relationship they had for each did them both a power of good – it turned my father into a man and for his efforts he helped turn my country into a victorious nation.

If I was to have asked him if he could have turned the clock back and spent his war years serving drinks in a quiet bar or go through it all again I'm sure his response would have been along the lines of: 'COME OUT AND FIGHT YOU SQUARE HEADED BASTARDS!'

Roll of Honour

2nd Battalion Oxfordshire & Buckinghamshire Light Infantry
6th Air Landing Brigade, 6th Airborne Division

List of men killed in action in Normandy - June-July-August 1944

NAME	RANK	DATE	KILLED	BURIED
AYRES,K.S	Pte	3/8	Breville/St.Come	Herouvillette (from 1st Bucks Bn).
BANNATYNE,G	Pte	25/8	Advance to Seine	Beuzeville
BARWICK,C.C	Sgt	7/6	Escoville	Herouvillette
BLAIR,R.G.	Pte	16/6	St. Come	Ranville
BOWDEN,P.W	Pte	7/6	Escoville	Ranville
BRARNER,M.J	Capt	19/6	? Died in UK from wounds	Ruislip
BROOKS,B	Pte	10/6	? Died from wounds	Hermanville
BROTHERIDGE,H.	Lt	6/6	Benouville (Canal)	Ranville churchyard
BULFORD,P.	Lt	25/8	Maneville le Raudt	Beuzeville .
CANTWELL,H.E.	L/C	14/6	St. Come	Ranville
CHICKEN,G.C	Lt	8/6	Escoville	Ranville
CLAPTON,M.C	Pte	27/8	Advance to Seine	Fatouville Grestain
CLARIDGE,R.A	Pte	10/8	St Come	Ranville
CLIFFE,W	Pte	22/8	Advance to Seine	Vauville churchyard
COTTLE,D.T	Pte	10/6	Escoville/Herouvillette	Ranville
CREW,J.W	WOII	19/6	St.Come	Ranville
DANIELLS,R.C	Pte	19/6	St Come (No known grave)	Bayeux Memorial
DEACON, T	Lt	5/6	Explosion in UK	Plymouth ?
DEACE,C.E	Pte	7/8	? Died of wounds in UK	Wellingborough
DREW,A.C	Pte	14/6	St.Come	Ranville
DREW,J.R.A	Cpl	17/8	Advance to Seine	Ranville
EARLE,C.E	L/Sgt	2/7	Breville ? Died of wounds	Ranville
FOXLE, F.J	Pte	7/6	12? Died of wounds	Bayeux
EVERETT,E.J	Pte	7/6	On journey from Dives	Ranville
FAVELL,E.V.M	Major	19/6	St Come	Ranville
FITZGERALD,P.E	Lt	19/8	Dozule -Advance to Seine	Ranville (Intelligence Corps -
FLEXEN,R	WOII	16/6	St. Come	Ranville
FROST,S	L/C	9/6	Escoville/Herouvillette	Herouvillette
FULLER,C.H	L/C	20/6	St. Come	Ranville
GEORGE,E.T	Pte	24/6	St Come	Herouvillette
GILMORE,T.A	Pte	5/7	St Come (No known grave)	Bayeux Memorial
GREENHALGH, F	L/C	6/6	Benouville	Douvre la Deliverande
HEDGES,W.P	Pte	6/6	Varaville/Dives	St.Pieriers-En-Augh
HIBBARD,J.A	Pte	19/6	St Come (No known grave)	Bayeux Memorial
HIGGINS,C.H	Pte	9/6	Escoville/Herouvillette	Ranville
HIGGINS,L.G	Pte	7/6	12? Died of wounds	Bayeux
JAMES,J	Lt(QM)	19/6	St. Come	Ranville
JOHNSON,K.F	Cpl	15/6	St. Come	Ranville
KELLY,E.D	Pte	7/6	Escoville	Ranville
KNOX,H	Cpl	6/6	Benouville	Benouville churchyard
LANGHER,J	Sgt	11/6	Escoville/Herouvillette	Ranville
LANGBRIDGE,E.H	Pte	27/6	Le Mesnil?	Ranville

Page No.1

ROLL OF HONOUR

Appendix B - Page 2

Name	Rank	Date	Place	Burial
MARRIOTT,J(GM)	Capt	10/6	Escoville/Herouvillette	Herouvillette
MILLS,D.	Pte	10/6	Escoville/Herouvillette	Herouvillette
MILTON,C	Pte	6/6	Landing Zone	Ranville
MINNS,F.L	L/C	9/6	Escoville/Herouvillette	Herouvillette
MORLEY,G	Pte	16/6	St. Come	Ranville
MORROW,T	Pte	7/6	Escoville	Ranville
NEWELL,E.C	Pte	7/6	Escoville	Herouvillette
NICHOLLS,J.D	Pte	25/6	Le Mesnil?	Herouvillette
PANKHURST,J.A	Lt	14/6	St. Come	Ranville
PARK,J	Pte	7/6	Escoville	Ranville
PARSONS,W.C	Pte	20/6	St. Come? Died of wounds	Ranville
PEDLER,C.E	Pte	27/7	?	Ranville - 5th Bn att.9 Para
PEER,T.G	Pte	30/6	Died of wounds in UK	East Ham.
PEPPERALL,D	Pte	15/7	St. Come	Ranville
PHILLIPS,C	Pte	25/6	Le Mesnil?	Herouvillette
PONTIN,D.A	Cpl	19/6	St Come ? (No known grave)	Bayeux Memorial
POWELL,R.F	Pte	17/7	St Come ?	St Manview.Miles W of Caen !!
READER,C.A	Pte	13/8	?	Banneville Le Campagne
REEVE,G.E.	L/C	7/6	Escoville	Ranville
REEVES,J.W.C	Pte	7/12	Presume in UK?	High Wycombe
REVELL,F.J	Pte	27/7	?	Ranville - 5th Bn att 9th Para
REVNELL,G.L	Lt	23/7	St Come ? (No known grave)	Bayeux Memorial
REYNOLDS,W	Cpl	25/6	Le Mesnil?	Herouvillette
ROBERTS,C.L. (23)	Pte	7/6	Escoville? Died of wounds	Ranville
ROBERTS,L.H (94)	Pte	15/6	St. Come? Died of wounds	Ranville
RUSSELL,P.J.N	Pte	4/7	St Come?	Ranville
SEFTON,F.J.D	Pte	7/6	Escoville	Ranville
SILVESTER,W.J	Pte	9/6	Escoville/Herouvillette	Herouvillette
SMYTH,P.B	Pte	19/7	St Come ? Died of wounds	Ranville
STACEY,J	Pte	23/7	Advance to Seine	Tourgeville Nr.Deauville
STARR,J.F	Pte	9/6	Escoville/Herouvillette	Herouvillette
STEWART,A.H.	Pte	19/8	Escoville	Ranville - 5th Bn att 9th Para
SUMMERSEY,A.A	Pte	7/6	Escoville	Ranville
SYMONDS,W.R.C	Pte	9/6	Escoville ? Died of wounds	Hermanville.
TRESIDDER,W.E.P.	Pte	13/6	St.Come	Ranville
VAN KLAVERAN,G	Lt	13/6	St. Come	Ranville
WALKER,F.W	Pte	13/6	St. Come	Ranville
WHITE,A.D	L/Sgt	7/6	LZ?	Bayeux
WHITE,H.W	Pte	29/7	? (Detached to RAMC)	Lewisham, London
WILKINS,W.S	Pte	7/6	Escoville	Escoville
WILKS,V	Pte	7/6	Escoville	Herouvillette
WILLCOCKS,C.F	Pte	7/6	Escoville	Ranville
WILLIAMS,E.E	WOII	9/6	LZ. Died of wounds In UK	Forest Row
WILRYCK,D.A	Pte	15/6	St. Come ? Died of wounds.	Ranville
WREN,L.M	Cpl	13/6	St. Come	Ranville
YOUNG,H.G.	Pte	13/6	St. Come	Ranville
YOUNG,K.E	Pte	25/7	In U K?	Oxford

From: Denis Edwards,
Who will always be pleased to add information received, and provide further copies. 26/7/1994

Rebuilding the Future

It is 1946 and at the ripe old age of 24 and after giving six years of his life to King and Country, Dad walked into the local Labour Exchange, de-mob suited and booted, and asked His Majesty's Government for something in return.

He waited in the long queue for over an hour and eventually found himself seated opposite a weary clerk who would much rather had been somewhere else.

The clerk glanced at Dad's papers showing little interest.

'What qualifications have you got young man, what are you good at?' he began.

Dad thought for a while. 'I'm an expert at killing people!' he replied enthusiastically.

The clerk looked up for the first time, peering over horn-rimmed glasses. 'Very funny my son,' was the response, 'if you did that last year, they gave you a medal - do it now and they'll hang yer!' He then handed him a piece of paper with an introduction to a dead-end job and told him to leave.

As he walked out Wally Parr realised, like thousands of others, that the reward for serving King and Country was freedom, a de-mob suit and a piece of paper - it would have to do, because that's all there was.

Billy Gray - Paddy O'Donnell - Bill Bailey - Wally Parr - Charlie Gardner
Outside Dad's house in Lee Green in 1947

Post-war Britain was about survival. The Blitz spirit still prevailed. Clothes to wear, food to eat, and a roof over your head was the order of the day. In some ways the family that Wally and Irene Parr produced was divided into two, the 'War' children and the 'Peace' children. My brother, Chris, was born in Bristol in 1940 resulting in Mum and Dad getting married. Sister, Pat, was born in 1943 conceived in the grounds of Salisbury Cathedral. Apparently if you look at the famous picture painted by Constable it was against the wall on the left! By a remarkable coincidence Pat entered the world in a make shift maternity home in Corsham that was eventually bought by a certain Colonel Wood.

Throughout the forties Mum followed Dad on his travels, from Bristol, to Devon, to Wiltshire. Eventually, after the war, they ended up in London and in March 1950 I was born in Byron Close, a block of council flats in South East London. Eight years later my younger brother, Bob, arrived, completing the full house.

Memories of growing up in the fifties consisted of tastes and smells. Everybody had a box Brownie camera but rarely used it. Old black and white photographs of holidays to Bournemouth never captured real life. I will never forget the taste of fruit salad and black-jack sweets - both purchased at the price of four for an old penny in the corner shop at the top of the park, in those days 'luvly jubly' was a refreshing ice triangle and not a clever catch phrase used by TV sit-com writers. Taste memories touch one level but smell memories go deeper, clinging to the very soul.

The smell of Sunday roast lamb or beef cooking to the sound of Two Way Family Favourites on the radio still stir something within me. Trivial thoughts remain; all eight-year-olds knew that BFPO meant British Forces Posted Overseas when requests were read out over the airways. Conscription was still in force, the enemy was defeated, but the British Empire still felt the need to police the world.

As a young child I suffered from regular bouts of bronchitis, the standard cure was to look out for the men Tarmacing the road and drag the kids down to the site and get them to inhale the nearby Tarmac as it bubbled and boiled in the containers. Our part of South East London had been heavily bombed, as the pre-fabs were demolished and the roads rebuilt it was easy for me to get my regular fix of Tarmac sniffing, I'm not sure if it worked, but to this day if I see any road resurfacing I stop my car, wind down the window and breath in my childhood.

Occasionally, a huge man used to knock on our door and Dad would embrace him. This man smelt of leather boots, itchy khaki and Woodbine cigarettes. I remember he had a Red Beret pinned to one of his

London, 1952. "D" Company Reunion: *Front row*: Evans; Ron Stock; 'Bill' Bailey; Major John Howard, DSO; Col."Tod' Sweeney, MC; 'Gus' Gardner. *Back row*; Arthur Roberts (?), 'Eddie' Edwards; Wally Parr; Glider Pilot Budds; Bob Hill; Harry Goodsir; 'Smokey' Howard.

With thanks to Denis Edwards – author of 'The Devil's own luck'

Another reunion a few years later with Billy Gray seated between Dad and Jack

shoulders, the urge to go round the back of the settee and un-pin it when he sat down was almost too much for a ten-year-old. Mum told us the man was called 'Uncle Jack'. In those days there were two different kinds of uncles, real uncles that were related and pretend uncles. Pretend uncles were also divided into two categories; they were either people that your Mum was having it off with or they were your Dad's war buddies. Thankfully this Uncle was the latter. Uncle Jack was none other than Jack Bailey.

Dad and Jack's war stories were remarkably similar: they both joined pre-1939 as boy soldiers. Dad left before the war started due to family financial pressures. Jack left about the same time due to ill health; he was invalided out as a result of a heart condition. At the outbreak of the war both young men decided to rejoin. Dad was accepted while Jack was refused due to his heart condition. Unperturbed Jack tore up his medical papers and went to another recruitment centre on the other side of town. This time conveniently not mentioning his medical condition, he managed to be passed A1 fit after a brief examination.

During the early part of the war their paths never crossed, it was when John Howard took charge of D Company that their lives were drawn together. They remained close friends throughout all the training and fighting and both more or less stayed in one piece until the bitter end. It was pure coincidence that peace-time placed them in London living less than a mile apart - we in Byron Close, shining modern council flats and Jack in a rundown block called Kent House Buildings on the opposite side of the park.

Throughout my childhood, Uncle Jack would appear, once or twice a year, unannounced at our front door, always in uniform, always smelling the same. Basically Jack was the eternal bachelor, a man that could never quite divorce himself from his first love, the army.

He tried to leave once or twice but 'Civvie Street' was not for him.

Throughout the fifties and the sixties it was a small band of ex-comrades that kept the memory of that momentous night on the eve of D-Day alive. John Howard, Jack Bailey and a handful of others would perform a small ceremony at midnight on June 5th/6th with Monsieur and Madame Gondrée on the site of the glider landings. Locals would look on with mild interest; the rest of the world looked away showing little interest.

In 1962 when the film 'The Longest Day' was being filmed, Jack was in Normandy as a technical advisor to the director Darryl Zanuck. The part of John Howard was being played by the actor Richard Todd; ironically Todd could also have been an advisor as he was involved with Howard on the actual raid in 1944.

Jack not only loved the army but also France. He tried to settle there a couple of times, living in Normandy, learning French and painting in the Pointist style of the Impressionists, but his wandering mind eventually brought him back to London.

On the set of the film 'The Longest Day'. The actor Peter Lawford played Lord Lovat, 2nd left, while Richard Todd played John Howard, far right

After Dad's unsuccessful visit to the Labour Exchange in 1946 he tried his hand at various jobs including helping his brother at bricklaying. Finally, in sheer desperation he brought himself a second-hand ladder and decided to become a window cleaner.

'Just for now luv,' he told Mum, 'until something better turns up'.

Forty-four years later, he eventually gave up his ladder and scrim when something better, did turn up - it was retirement!

It was the winter of 1947 when he embarked on this new career. It was the longest and coldest winter of the century. The temperature between the middle of February and the end of April never rose above freezing. Long queues formed at coal merchants, people desperate to scrounge even a small bag of fuel. Dad was philosophical about the weather, he reckoned no other idiot would try and start a window cleaning round in these conditions. Dad just about scraped a living. The injuries sustained in the war nagged at him in the cold; in fact they got steadily worse as the years passed by. Occasionally he would swig Scotch from Mum's bottle, 'Shrapnel medicine', he called it. He had no car so in the early days he got the bus and picked up his ladder from the last customer of the previous day, eventually he bought a push-bike and balanced his ladder on his left shoulder. From day one, his war-time motto; 'Bite on the bullet, shoulder your pack, and soldier on' and his fitness, from the years of training, stood him well.

In present day conflicts, we hear of soldiers returning home from battle with conditions such as post traumatic stress, or 'Gulf War Syndrome'. In 1947 men and women never had the privilege of such names, in those days it was called; 'Getting over the war.' There were no professional advisors on hand, you just got on with life the best way you could.

Pat, me, Dad and Chris in front of Byron Close Sydenham in 1952, Jack Bailey lived $\frac{1}{4}$ mile away

The way Dad coped was through discipline. He was strict, but not hard. In the 1950's all youngsters respected authority. It was the norm for a beat policeman to give you a clip round the ear if you stepped out of line. At home Dad, along with Mum, ran a tight ship.

For my elder sister, Pat, and older brother, Chris, he must have seemed like a Sergeant-Major. He would inspect their rooms, running his finger over every surface, looking for dust. To rebellious teenagers entering the new freedom of the early sixties this was hard to take - eventually Chris joined the Merchant Navy and a few years later Pat joined the regular army and was stationed at Catterick Garrison in Yorkshire.

Family life was different in those days. Forget 24 hour television and endless video games. The BBC in its infancy was staid and limited. During the afternoon it used to close down for a couple of hours – probably to allow the ancient sets to cool down!

We made our own entertainment, I've mentioned earlier about the famous war stories but some of my early childhood memories weren't all so favourable. For instance when Aunty Mary or Aunty Babs used to visit, Mum would at some point in the evening drag me into the kitchen and prepare me to do my 'party piece' – this consisted in covering my face with black Cherry Blossom boot polish and making me rush into the front room, go down on one knee, stick both arms out wide and cry 'Mammy!' This was, apparently, a hilarious impersonation of Al Jolson.

It probably worked the first time but not after – I've forgiven Mum now, but the hour it took to get the bloody polish off my face remains embedded in my psyche!

By the early sixties Dad had

Smoking his pipe with attitude !

mellowed considerably as he concentrated on his 'peacetime' children. Discipline had become much more relaxed – no doubt my elder brother and sister felt that we 'got away with murder'.

The Prime Minister of the time, Harold Macmillan informed the nation that 'we had never had it so good'. Compared to being bombed out of your home day and night I suppose it was good - at that moment in time nobody told me that by my mid-teens I would be loosing sleep with worry because our old mates, the Russians were seriously thinking of dropping a nuclear bomb on my head.

Looking back though, I had a good childhood – on our council estate everybody was more or less equal, Mr. Davies on the second floor was the first person to own a car, yet Mr. Parr on the third balcony was one of the first to get one of those new telly's that had 625 lines so that you could get BBC2.

TV in those days made you feel secure – you knew where you were, you knew what day it was. As a child every afternoon I would 'Watch with Mother'. Monday was 'Picture Book' - Tuesday 'Andy Pandy' - Wednesday 'The Flowerpot Men' – Thursday 'Rag, Tag and Bobtail' – Friday 'The Woodentops'. On Saturdays we all sat quietly during 'Sports Report' while Dad checked his pools coupon to see if he had eight draws in a row – we knew he hadn't when he said 'oh well, work Monday.' Sunday was, you've guessed it: 'Sunday Night at the London Palladium' – that was bath night and the time Mum did the ironing. Throughout the year there was special events we all watched as a family, there was the Cup Final, The Grand National, The Last Night of the Proms with Sir Malcolm Sergeant waving his baton to Land of Hope and Glory and on a cold grey morning in November we would all listen in silence as Richard Dimbleby talked us through the Remembrance Day Parade in Whitehall.

The most memorable Christmas of my young life was in 1958. I was eight years old and we were all desperate with worry – Dad had been diagnosed with TB, he had developed a huge lump on his neck and the doctors feared the worst. The standard treatment was to send him to an open-air hospital overlooking the sea just outside Margate. I have a mental picture of him tucked up in a bed outside in December staring at the crashing waves. It occurred to us if the TB never killed him pneumonia would! Times were desperate; being self-employed there was no money coming in. I remember my granddad coming over and giving Mum a few quid to get us something for Christmas. Then a week before December 25th Mum got a letter from the hospital saying it was a mis-diagnosis it was only an abscess and he would be home on Christmas Eve - we spent that day doing a huge poster that said; 'Welcome Home Dad' in glitter.

Dad, holding his legs, in a TB sanatorium in Margate, 1958.
Note the baskets in the background – patients made these as
a form of occupational therapy

I only got two presents that year the first was an Osmiroid fountain pen so that I could learn italic joined-up writing at school and the second was the best of all – I got my Dad back!

Another thing I remember is not only did I get gifts at Christmas and my birthday but also when my big brother returned from his trips to Australia and the Far East. Chris was a laid-back easy-going type of guy with little or no ambition. He joined the Merchant Navy as a cabin boy and left six years later as a cabin man – promotion and getting ahead weren't in his thinking. While away, sometimes for six months at a time, he found little to spend his money on, he didn't drink much or gamble, the traditional way sailors wasted their money – so he spent most of his money on presents for the family and his girlfriend Val.

Unknown to all of us, a medical time-bomb was ticking away in the body of my elder brother, Chris. By the time he returned from his last trip abroad he shared with Mum and Dad that for the last few weeks his body had been racked with aches and pains.

Our local doctor gave Chris an examination and then referred him to Lewisham Hospital. After a long series of tests we were given the devastating news that he had contracted Multiple Sclerosis. As a ten-

Brother Chris with the classic 50's look

year-old I didn't understand what this meant but soon learnt that it was a condition that affected the central nervous system.

By now Chris had married his girlfriend Val and despite the steady decline in his physical condition they had two children, Gary and Joanne.

Throughout my teenage years and my early twenties I watched my brother deteriorate – firstly he used one walking stick, then two, eventually he was confined to a wheelchair.

When first told of his son's condition and then informed that there was no known cure Dad's immediate response was to tell them to; 'Bloody well find one!'

When the medical profession was of no help he tried the church and the power of prayer – when this failed he turned to a Spiritualist Church and watched their faith healers fail to turn the tide.

It was at this time that he began his own spiritual journey in a quest to find a cure for his own son. He developed a faith and understanding that went beyond religion he almost became a 'Hippy' before they emerged at the height of the 'Swinging Sixties.'

From my bedroom window I would occasionally see him walk bare-footed across the morning dew in the park opposite – when he reached the old oak tree in the middle he would hug it and receive strength and energy – he was a tree hugging New-Ager ten years before his time.

Alongside pursuing a spiritual quest to find a cure for his son, Dad still found time to serve the rest of his family. By now my sister, Pat, had left the army and had moved back to London and married Jim, a Scottish soldier she had met at Catterick – in the wedding photographs brother Chris, the best-man, was leaning on a walking stick – by the time my wedding came round a few years later he was sat in a wheelchair.

As I approached my teens I was getting into playing and watching football big time. A typical day for Dad would consist of eight hours window cleaning, then cycling home, grabbing his dinner, a quick visit to Chris to see if he and the family were okay – then over to the park to manage the five-a-side football team I was in. Football played a big part in the Parr household – my Dad's dad was a professional playing for Tranmere Rovers and Accrington Stanley before the First World War and Dad's brother Reg was on Millwall's books just before the outbreak of the war but sadly was killed as a POW in Japan. Like Dad, I could play a bit and managed to play for the Thames Water Board without actually working for them – not so much a 'ringer' more like a 'washer'! To add to the fun, brother-in-law, Jim, given the right breaks, could have made the grade – and looking to the future Jim and Pat's grandson, Josh Payne has recently signed up to Portsmouth FC and looks certain to go all the way.

Once Jim arrived on the scene, England vs. Scotland games at the end of the season took on a whole new passion.

Although my local club was Crystal Palace with Johnny Byrne my hero, I soon switched my allegiance to North London when the mighty Tottenham Hotspur won the cup and league double in the 1961/62 season. The first big game Dad ever took me to see was Spurs vs. Glasgow Rangers in 1962 – it was for the Cup Winner's Cup and was billed as 'The game of the century'. At 13 I saw my all-time hero Jimmy 'Twinkle-toes' Greaves for the first time. We thrashed them 5-2, the previous week we had beaten Manchester United 6-2!

'Wait until we get ye to Ibrox!' was the Scottish cry as they left the ground – a few weeks later Spurs travelled across the border and stuffed them 3-2.

In 1964, while on an outward-bound holiday in Scotland with my school I received news that John White one of Spurs' most gifted players had been struck by lightening and killed. I was 400 hundred miles from my Dad's comforting arms – I went into the toilets and cried like a baby.

In 1966 we watched England win the World Cup – much to my Scottish brother-in-law's annoyance. While managing the eleven-a-side club, I played for in 1965, Dad came up with the tactical idea of playing in a 4-3-3 formation instead of the usual 5-3-2. It worked well and we won the cup that year – Alf Ramsay used the same formation in 1966,

Dad swears Alf copied it from watching Sydenham Rovers, but I have my doubts!

In 1969 I married my childhood-sweetheart, Diane. She grew up in the same block of flats as me – she was not quite the 'girl next door' more the 'girl one down and five across.'

It was another 'Summer of Love', the sixties were swinging, we were pretty skint, yet we fancied a honeymoon somewhere exotic like Ibiza but we decided to settle for an English seaside resort.

I asked Dad for a suggestion – he came up with a place I had never heard of: Combe Martin in North Devon. It was then that he reminded us of his epic walk from Ilfracombe to Bulford. While staying at Combe Martin, Diane and I walked along the coast into Ilfracombe, although it was only five miles it knackered us – but then again we were on our honeymoon and energies had been used on other activities!

By the mid-seventies I had two young daughters, Jennie and Sandra – sadly my youngest daughter Sandra never got to really know my brother Chris because he died when she was a couple of years old.

The death of his son devastated Dad.

It took him back to the war and the passing of deep, personal mates– the difference was that in Normandy their deaths were often instant or at worse it was over in a few hours – with Chris the agony had lasted over a decade.

Mum & Dad with Chris towards the end

Before his eyes a slow-motion drama had unfolded - from a strapping six-footer, his son descended to a hunched-up cripple in a wheel-chair – he lost his speech, movement of his limbs and near the end he was virtually blind – in the end pneumonia filled his lungs.

The day before his son's death, Dad cried out to him and asked for his forgiveness for not finding him a cure – all Chris could do was look into his father's eyes and half-smile, my brother never complained once, in all his years.

Dad took it badly – he had questions to ask and when he met Him, God better have the answers!

After the funeral Dad bit on the bullet and carried on – in his early fifties he was still cleaning windows – tough as old nails he hadn't bothered to learn to drive, instead he carried his ladder and bucket on his left shoulder while he cycled and steered his bike with the other hand.

This worked reasonably well until one day in 1977 he found himself coming down a steep hill when the brake on his right side snapped - travelling at a fair rate of knots - a main road was looming up ahead and he realised the only way to stop was to crash-land into a nearby tree – Jim Wallwork would have been proud of him!

The result was a shattered knee cartilage and eventually an operation. Afterwards the doctor informed him that he may still be able to climb a ladder but he would never be able to ride a bike.

It was then that I decided to give up my office job, buy a ladder roof-rack for my car and join him as a 'glazing hygiene contractor.'

I was half his age but it took me many months to reach the fitness level that he was at.

The seventies drifted into the eighties. Dad approached 60 – as he stared retirement in the face he prepared himself for a time of quiet reflection – but a certain person had other ideas in mind.

I have in my possession a newspaper cutting sent to Dad by Stephen Ambrose. The date on the paper was Sunday October 9th 1983 although Ambrose probably sent the piece two years after this date. The article was mainly about his epic work on the life of Eisenhower.

Towards the end Ambrose circled a paragraph and wrote in the margin: 'Dear Wally, thought this might amuse you!'

The paragraph read: 'It's not likely that Ambrose will suffer work withdrawal pangs for long for he and his wife leave for London. His sabbatical from teaching duties at the University of New Orleans extends until January. "I'm going to do a book about a bridge called Pegasus that had to be held to keep the German armour from the French beach head in the Second World War," he says, "so we're going to go up to Oxford to interview the man who led the action. It's a fabulous story. They put six gliders in the air with 30 men in each and at 14 minutes past midnight on June 6th those forces came down and held that bridge. Then I'm going to do a book on one day in the lives of 180 men," he says, "but what a day – it was D-Day".'

For my Dad who, along with the rest of his band of ageing brothers, had thought that the world had forgotten them were soon to be awakened from nearly 40 years of slumber – for history was about to come alive!

Talking 'til the Small Hours

There are certain people that enter a room and fill it with their presence. The energy they emit is either negative or positive, it could be the persona of a friendly television entertainer or the menace of an East-End gangster - one thing is certain, everybody in the room becomes happy, either happy when they arrive or happy when they leave.

Wally Parr had this X-factor and different people met him with mixed emotions depending often on past encounters be it good or bad.

In the summer of 1983 Stephen Ambrose travelled to England to begin interviewing various veterans. He had already spoken to Jim Wallwork in America and the obvious first interviewee was John Howard in Oxfordshire. Interestingly the next person was Wally Parr, whether or not this was on the recommendation of John Howard I'm not sure, all I know is, when you read Pegasus Bridge, Dad appears with almost embarrassing regularity.

The list of interviewees is quite impressive and covers a wide spectrum of people. It is interesting to see that there is a joint interview held with Bill Gray and Henry Hickman. Henry was in fact an ex-German prisoner of war who spent some of the war in prison camps in England and after the war settled here and married a local girl. By an incredible coincidence Billy and Henry had fought against each other in Normandy and somehow met years later at a reunion and struck up a strong friendship. This enabled Ambrose to get stories from both sides of the fence.

As well as England he also travelled to the continent and spoke to Thérèsa Gondrée and Hans Von Luck.

If you read Pegasus Bridge it soon becomes obvious that it is not your basic historical war book, but an in-depth and personal account of a group of men training and preparing for a specific purpose. This theme was to be continued of course in Ambrose's most well-known work 'A Band of Brothers' which thanks to the Spielberg TV series turned him into a household name.

The amount of material collected by Professor Ambrose for 'Pegasus Bridge' must have been extensive. He recalls that some of the events shared by the veterans varied quite a bit, but by careful analysis he managed to develop a very accurate picture of events nearly 40 years ago. It couldn't have been easy for men to remember what happened four decades previous, my Dad at times couldn't remember what happened a week ago or the names of his grandkids!

One thing was obvious: Ambrose was looking for the human interest in this book and above all for characters. Throughout the book, whenever there was trouble, there were the usual four suspects - Billy Gray, Charlie Gardner, Jack Bailey and Wally Parr. Whether it was raiding the cookhouse or trying to fire a German anti-tank gun the same characters seemed to be in the thick of it.

I know this caused some ill feeling amongst other veterans in later years and to be honest I can sympathise with them, I'm sure many worthy deeds went un-noticed and un-heralded but in fairness to Ambrose he could only cover so much ground and above all he was trying to write a book that was not overly long yet still sellable.

The book was eventually finished in time for the 40th anniversary celebrations in June of 1984.

The magazine 'Readers Digest' wrote to Dad in early April of that year and asked him to read through a condensed version of the book which was to be published worldwide a month later.

The jig-saw puzzle that had been the writing of the book finally fell into place and revealed the full picture when Stephen Ambrose and John Howard, in June 1984, re-united the boys of D Company when they all returned to Bénouville.

Reunited in Bénouville - Jack Bailey, Hans von Luck, Tod Sweeney, John Howard and Dad

For many of the lads this was their first trip to the bridge since D-

Day – most had kept contact with the odd reunion and yearly Christmas card – but for some it was like meeting up with old school buddies who had matured into men nearing retirement.

I know from Dad's experience of the time, that he still looked up to John Howard as his Major and although he didn't exactly salute him when they first met, it was many weeks if not months before he stopped calling him 'Major' or 'Sir' and felt confident enough to call him John. For the rest of his life whenever Dad was talking to a third party he would always talk about 'Major Howard.' I guess I would feel the same, if after 40 years I met up with an old school teacher that I had once respected.

In June 1994 Georges Gondrée had been dead for many years – his wife Thérèsa although very old and frail just about managed to host the midnight ceremony before passing away a few weeks later. Her deep felt patriotism for her country and her hatred for the Germans continued until her dying days – when John Howard arrived at the café one day with Hans Von Luck, she eyed him with suspicion and it took all of Howard's

Mum with John Howard and Frankie Bourlet on the right

persuasive skills to convince her he was in fact Polish, which of course he wasn't. By this time Arlette and Georgette, the daughters, were taking a much more leading role in the running of the café and after their mother's death continued the tradition of the midnight ceremony.

It was about this time that Dad gave me, my brother and my sister copies of 'Pegasus Bridge'. At that time there was only two signatures in the front; John Howard's with his famous 'Ham and Jam' signature and a personal message from Dad. Two decades later, I now have my Dad's copy as well .The inside two pages of the two books are covered with the names of many fine men, sadly many of them have passed away, but they remain embedded in one of my most prized possessions.

Dad's book in particular reads like a Who's Who of D-Day. Some are unique, Hans Von Luck signed: 'For Wally from the man of the other side of the hill'. Another said: 'For Wally Parr – without whom there would be

Dad with Mum, Lady Irene, at the
40th Celebrations

no book' – Stephen Ambrose. The actor Richard Todd simply said; 'GO TO IT! WALLY' while his best mate Billy Gray signed: 'To Wally My father figure' – I'm not sure whether this one was tongue in cheek - with these guys you never can tell. There are four full pages of names – on the contents page dated 1992 are the signatures of Viscount Montgomery and his wife.

Without a doubt the publishers Allen and Unwin made a huge error in estimating the popularity of the book. The first edition sold out in no time and a second edition was very quickly needed. I shudder to think what a first edition signed hard back copy like would sell for on eBay. It is irrelevant because it ain't for sale!

Dad travelled over with Mum, this was certainly the first time that any of the wives had met each other – I'm sure they had some interesting natters while there, probably working out which husband over the years had exaggerated the most!

Lord Lovat boycotted the 40th anniversary some say in protest that he felt the whole proceedings had degenerated into a bit of a circus. I certainly hope he didn't think that Wally Parr & Co. had jumped on the bandwagon and become hangers on – while in fact the truth was that for many of D Company they had spent the previous 40 years building their lives and struggling to bring up their families and get a decent roof over their heads.

If they had come from a more privileged background they may have made the trip sooner. They had gone their separate ways for forty years – now irrespective of financial status or social standing they were reunited in one cause.

Needless to say whatever the motives were of people – 1994 was the year when life at Pegasus Bridge changed forever and I guess the man we have to thank for making it all possible was Stephen Ambrose.

The media interest was at last beginning to happen with regards to D-Day and Pegasus Bridge. This was reflected when Thames Television contacted some of the veterans and asked them to appear on a pilot television programme called: 'Surprise, Surprise'.

The basic formula for the programme was to arrange a meeting between long lost friends, colleagues, or family members. The producer decided that the first event should comprise of members of D Company meeting up with a long forgotten comrade. The only problem was, Stephen Ambrose had rounded up the usual crowd for his book and the producer would be hard pressed to find anybody else that would qualify as a surprise.

On the evening of the recording Dad, Mum, my wife Diane, my brother Bob, his wife Beryl and I were all piled into a huge limo and driven to the South Bank studios beside the Thames. When we arrived a dozen or so of the boys, with their families were waiting. After a short while, D Company were escorted to the bar and the rest of us were plonked in the audience.

The star presenter of the show was Cilla Black, who at the time was the queen of British light entertainment; her co-presenter was Christopher Biggins.

The show was being pre-recorded, so from an audience point of view, it looked pretty chaotic. Eventually the boys were ushered on stage and placed in various armchairs - they looked quite relaxed, I guess the half-hour in the bar had been well spent.

Cilla Black appeared from the back and some guy with a clipboard raised his hands above his head and started clapping madly, this apparently was a cue for us to join in, which we did. Cilla began to sing the theme song and after much applause she started to introduce the show. She pointed to the boys and briefly outlined their Pegasus exploits to the audience and then explained to them that she had a wonderful surprise for them. At this point there was a huge drum roll and from behind a cloud of smoke this bloke appeared wearing the Regimental Jacket and a Red Beret. They all stood up and looked utterly surprised - this was because most of them hadn't a clue who the guy was! Everybody then sat down and pretended to be excited. When Cilla finally

Surprise, Surprise studio – family and Ginger Bleach enjoy a drink afterwards

mentioned the guy's name a few of them nodded and could actually recall who he was, it was Denis Edwards, but the passage of time had altered his appearance and the boy's memories.

Cilla was genuinely interested and decided to find out more, she then made the fatal mistake of asking Dad! 'Now tell me Wally, chuck, what happened that fantastic night after you and yer mates landed in those gliders?' She began, in her broad Scouse accent.

'Well Cilla, we run round like bloody maniacs killing people!'

I burst out laughing, my brother sniggered, my Mum put both hands to her face and the rest of the audience were stunned into silence.

'That's marvellous,' replied Cilla, nervously, 'what happened next?'

Dad gave a safer, if more boring answer, and by the time the programme went out the following week, the first answer had been cut and you couldn't notice the join.

The rest of the programme continued without mishap as we sat through other people being 'Surprise, Surprised'.

Afterwards we were all invited upstairs to the bar to meet Cilla. As I expected she was a wonderfully natural person and it was good to talk to her and her, now sadly departed, husband Bobby. At one point she came over to my wife, Diane, and observed that they had similar protruding front teeth. I nearly replied that I wished they had similar protruding bank balances put I decided one Parr committing a 'faux pas' in an evening was more than enough.

At this time, the spring of 1985, the media were giving D Company maximum coverage. After 'Surprise, Surprise', Thames Television decided to give Tod Sweeney a 'This is Your Life' programme. Originated by the BBC back in the 1960's this programme is part of the British institution. Anybody who is anybody has been featured, although when they cover a pop idol in his early 30's it hardly been 'a life'!

The usual suspects, including Dad were dragged out to meet Colonel Sweeney, but this time they kept Dad in the background, instead they asked Jack Bailey to give a tribute - once bitten twice shy!

The icing on the cake came when Dad received a letter from Stephen Ambrose asking him to speak at the University of New Orleans, all expenses paid! It was to be an ambitious project spread over three days.

The speakers were to include Hans Von Luck, commander of the 125 Regiment of the 21st Panzer Division, John Howard, Jim Wallwork and Wally Parr of D Company. Finally, in order to give a talk on his father's contribution to the victory, The Viscount Montgomery of Alamein.

Dad had no problem rubbing shoulders with this mob, his only worry was that he didn't have a decent suit to wear, so he borrowed mine.

This conference was a natural progression of Stephen Ambrose's work as a military historian and would eventually culminate with the opening of the D-Day Museum in New Orleans in the year 2000. Dads red beret with the hole caused by flying shrapnel is on display there.

Dad's original beret in the
D-Day Museum, New Orleans

– it still bares the shrapnel hole

The choice of speakers was inspired; Ambrose had managed to gather a unique cross section of people that covered every aspect of warfare. Howard was the class, the well-spoken English major, Wallwork was the craftsman, the epitome of intensive training, Von Luck was the enemy made good, Montgomery of course was the ace - here was the aristocracy of war. Last but not least was Parr, the infantryman with the common touch, the salt of the earth.

Jazz Brunch in The Preservation Hall, New Orleans.

The conference began on Sunday morning in an unusual way - all the speakers and sponsors were taken to the Preservation Hall to have a Jazz Brunch breakfast. This place is the world centre of New Orleans jazz. As far as Dad was concerned he could have died and gone to heaven, as this was, and still is his musical roots. The building was nothing more than a glorified shed, the seating was hard wooden benches; the floor was covered in saw dust, its purpose, no doubt to absorb the spit. Dad found himself on the front bench sitting beside Hans Von Luck. At this point they had merely nodded when introduced but within a few minutes they were tapping and swaying in unison at the sweet sounds of the band. It was there, feet in sawdust, that the two men forged a friendship that surpassed nationality, politics, or race. Their joint love of the 'music of the soul' produced almost a 'two sides meeting on Christmas Day to play in no-man's land' moment and it was to last until Hans' passing a decade or so later.

The rest of the day consisted of a tour of the city and the site of the Battle of New Orleans and an evening banquet where the speakers were invited to share their memories of the last months of the war.

Monday morning was to consist of Parr, Howard, Wallwork and Von Luck doing their business.

Here the diversity of the speakers came into its own. John Howard, forever the gentleman and the utmost professional would describe a certain event happening at 01:30 hours - as far as Dad was concerned it happened at 'arf-one in the morning' both were technically correct it just depended on which manual you read.

'Same meat, different gravy' as Dad would say.

Each style was balanced against the other, according to an earlier letter sent to Dad by Ambrose, the conference would be attended by both 'Hawks and Doves', hopefully all persuasions were satisfied.

Dad began his presentation by using a famous quote from June 1944: 'With regards to the second front, the nation of Germany was like a 'virgin spring bride' - she knew she was going to get it, the only problem was, she wasn't exactly sure when, or how big it would be!'

Dad giving a lecture at The University of New Orleans

From there on in he had them eating out of his hand. No doubt Dad's powerful ego spurned him on and I'm sure the audience rode a roller coaster of emotions as he switched from frivolous Cockney humour to deep personal insights.

The conference was three days of non-stop talks and events, in no time it was over and everybody was packing up and heading for home. The problem was that Dad in his infinite wisdom had booked a cheap flight that returned him back to London in seven days and although Ambrose had paid for his flight and hotel they presumed he was clearing off home at the close of the conference. They quickly re-booked Dad into another hotel, albeit a cheaper downtown version

At the conference reception

and left him more or less to his own devices. Fortunately he had met a young local guy, Kirt Garcia who kept an eye on him over the next few days.

Over the years Kirt has become a family friend who has travelled to Europe on a number of occasions and stayed in our homes. Kirt had become involved with Stephen Ambrose and the University of New Orleans on a voluntary basis doing whatever was asked

The silk map in the D-Day Museum, New Orleans

of him, usually in the field of administration. The picture on page 106 was taken by Kirt and I include his account of how he met Dad and the rest of the guys - it is a good insight into the enthusiasm held by many young Americans.

'You wanted me to give you some stories about Wally. Well, let me start at the beginning. I met Wally in April 1988 at the University of New Orleans. I was a senior in College studying history. That semester I was taking Stephen Ambrose's class on modern US Presidents. One night, without prior notice, Dr. Ambrose came to class with John Howard, Hans Von Luck, Jim Wallwork and Wally Parr. He had brought them to New Orleans along with some other veterans. I've never found out the reason why they were here, but it was probably to benefit the Eisenhower Centre, they were gathering the oral histories of D-Day veterans at the time. Dr. Ambrose just cancelled his planned lecture for the night and gave us the chance to hear from the veterans who many of us had read about in his previous class

National D-Day Museum, New Orleans
- the home of Dad's beret

entitled Modern Military history. (Pegasus Bridge was one of the required books for the class, which by the way, I also took).

John Howard and company told the stories that you and I have heard a thousand times by now, but on that occasion it was special because we were hearing it (apart from Ambrose's book) for the first time. It was a great treat for us to be in the same room with them and to hear the stories directly from the participants themselves. Afterwards we were able to approach them personally and to get to know them in a friendlier manner. I had my copy of Pegasus Bridge which most of them signed. I was talking to a class mate when I felt a jab in my rib cage. I turned back toward the front of the class and there was John Howard holding his cane upward, mischievous grin across his face and asked; "do you want me to sign that?" Every time I saw him after that he always managed to jab me in the rib cage with that damn cane!

The class ended and I was walking outside towards the parking lot when I felt a tap on my shoulder. I turned around and standing there was Dr. Ambrose with Wally and Jim. He then asked me if I could take them back to their hotel while he drove John and Hans to theirs. I didn't know how the night could've gotten any better until that moment. I replied "yes sir" and gladly drove the battle of the Little Big Horn and the painter Picasso. How they went together I don't recall but I remember laughing heartily. I never knew you could be this close to history.'

Kirt's enthusiasm and imagination are inspiring to say the least!

Towards the end of Dad's stay in America he got bored and decided to leave the safety of his seedy hotel and experience the 'real New Orleans'. At the reception he asked the guy to point him in the right direction for some action. The man suggested Canal Street, a few blocks to the east, but forgot to mention that the only safe way to get there was by taxi.

Dad set out on foot, dressed in my ill fitting cheap suit.

He may had well been wearing a sign on his back saying; 'Naive English Tourist Please Mug Me'.

Within a few yards he noticed three local punks following him. Dad increased his pace. So did they.

He broke into a gentle trot. So did they.

He sprinted - the tight trousers of my beloved suit gripping at his thigh muscles, restricting his natural rhythm. So did they.

In desperation he glanced at the traffic roaring past him to his left. In an instant he saw a gap and shot across the road jay running amongst screeching brakes and blazing horns.

He glanced across the road and saw that the three men had missed their moment - in frustration they shook their fists and spat on the pavement.

He entered the first bar he came across, and had several drinks before getting a taxi back to the sanctity of his hotel.

Dad was philosophical about his experience.

He saw the irony of the fact that many years previously he had survived the wroth of a Nazi Germany Youth only to nearly come unstuck through the hatred of the young of his Allies.

Dad made many friends in America as in the end he made more than one trip. Over the following years he would be kept busy with photographs and letters crossing the Atlantic – one particular favourite of his was Jim Osborne the Chairman of Board at the Indiana Military Museum, they met with each other a number of times over the years in New Orleans, London and Normandy.

Jim Wallwork, John Howard, Hans von Luck, Dad & Stephen Ambrose

New Orleans taught Dad many things.

Perhaps the greatest lesson was on the last day of the conference.

It was at a book signing and all the main speakers, including Dad were sat at the top table. Guests were moving along the front of the table presenting their copies of 'Pegasus Bridge' to be signed by the speakers.

Dad was at the end of the table. He glanced to his left and noticed the people who were signing each copy.

Then he was reminded that in war 'No man is an island.'

It occurred to him that Churchill was only as good as his Field Marshals. Brigadiers were only as good as their Majors. Majors were only as good as their platoon leaders and platoon leaders were useless without the infantry men that were in the thick of things, with cold steel, bullets, blood and shit up to their necks. With this in mind he watched the first book making its steady way up the table towards him.

Eventually it arrived. He glanced briefly upwards toward the man that was presenting the book and then read the signatures that he had already collected: Professor Stephen Ambrose, Major John Howard, Colonel Hans Von Luck, Jim Wallwork and The Viscount Montgomery of Alamein.

Dad was seated beside the son of perhaps the greatest soldier of the Second World War. Without hesitation Dad picked up his Biro, licked the tip with his tongue and proudly wrote: 'Wally Parr of Catford'.

Contents

- 108 -

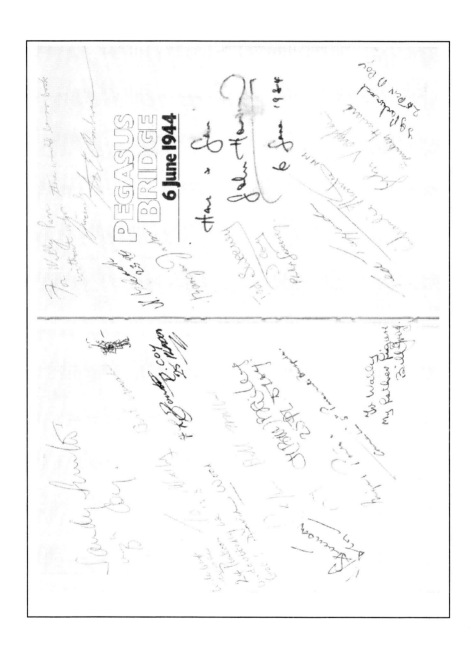

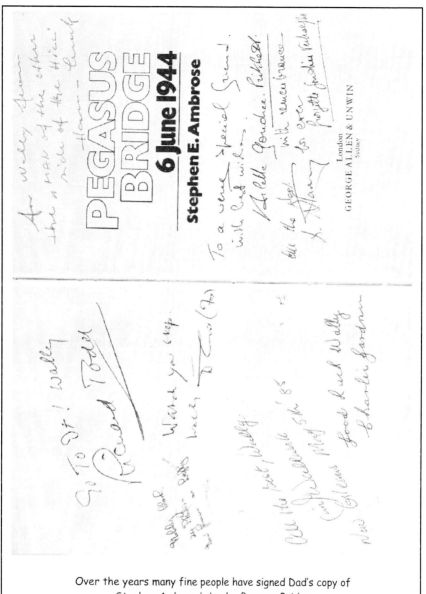

Over the years many fine people have signed Dad's copy of
Stephen Ambrose's book - Pegasus Bridge.

Riding with the wind

At 6 a.m. on the morning of May 4th 1986 I received a frantic phone call from Dad. Mum was desperately ill and I was to get to him immediately. My wife, Diane, and I arrived within 15 minutes and it was obvious that Mum had suffered a massive stroke. We called an ambulance and she was rushed to Lewisham Hospital. As the day progressed she began to deteriorate steadily so we decided to call my sister, Pat, from Basingstoke, brother, Bob, had been with us throughout the day.

Pat arrived at Mum's bedside at 3:15 p.m. and at 3:17 Mum passed away.

At the funeral I read the prayer of Saint Francis of Assisi (Make me an instrument) and we sang her favourite hymn, 'How great thou art'.

Dad took his 'Lady Irene's' passing badly. On the plus side the newly resurrected interest in all things Pegasus kept him more than occupied.

A year later on the first anniversary of Mum's passing Diane and I decided to take Dad away for the weekend to ease the pain of the previous year. I thought it would be symbolic to travel to the West Country. For it was here that Dad had so many good memories. Mum was born in Bristol, she gave birth to their first son, Chris, in the same town, and Pat was born in Corsham a few miles away in a maternity house that was eventually converted back into a private residence and owned by a certain Colonel.

I still hadn't been to Normandy to visit Pegasus Bridge but I decided to visit the land of Dad's training first, and re-live his war story in the order it happened.

For the first hour of our journey we were immersed in the traffic chaos of suburban South London. The second hour took us down the M3 through the satellite towns of Surrey and Hampshire, eventually we hit the A303 and we are in the true countryside. This is the gateway to the West, we were entering a mystical land - before us lay the ancient stone rings of Stonehenge and Avebury. Beyond them Glastonbury and Tintagel, myth and legend combine in the land of Avalon. New-agers consider this part of England to be the spiritual centre of the Western World.

In no time we were on the edge of Salisbury Plain. Dad informed us that it is the same size as the Isle of Wight, if you are not sure how big the Isle of Wight is, well it's roughly the same size as Salisbury Plain. We passed a roundabout and suddenly to our right, Stonehenge appeared. The mysticism of our oldest national monument has been crushed by modern day commercialism; a huge circular barrier keeps people 50 yards away from the stones. A visitor centre nearby educates the tourists, but rarely enlightens.

Bulford Barracks is in the middle of Salisbury Plain.

Dad began to reminisce: He told us the story of one day when D Company was doing a regular exercise on Salisbury Plain in 1943, the men were exhausted and John Howard decided to rest them within sight of Stonehenge.

In those days there were no buildings nearby yet the MOD had decided to encircle the stones with a six foot ring of barbed wire due to the fact that bored soldiers had taken up the habit of carving their initials on the granite of one of our national treasures.

Howard believed in not only training the body, but also the mind and

Bulford Camp Church – the end of the epic march from Ilfracombe

began to give the men a rather intense lecture on the origins of Stonehenge as they sat around gathering their strength. He went to great pains to explain how ancient men dragged the massive stones from Wales, a hundred or so miles away. He gave his own theory how this was done, concluding that they probably used logs, taking months if not years to get them to the site and then erecting them perfectly in a position that aligned with the rising summer solstice sun.

The men listened in awe, mouths opened taking in every word. After

A visit from Granddad was always different.
My daughter Jennie in hospital (above) and Sandra (below)

a brief silence, a voice at the back broke in: 'Cor' blimey Major Howard, imagine those poor bastards 'aving to drag those stones all that way and then finding they've got to lift 'em over that bleeding barbed wire!'

Dad was still smiling at his story as we descended a hill and I saw a sign for Bulford Barracks. Without asking I instinctively turned into the B road that led to the entrance. In those days, pre Gulf-Wars, security was relaxed, we got in easily. We approached the guard house, I let Dad wander around, while I spoke to somebody that looked like he was in charge. He was politely interested and pointed me to a few faded photographs on the wall.

Dad looked lost, he tried to get his bearings but nothing registered. Perhaps the odd building had been demolished, certainly they had given it a lick of paint - this was Bulford Barracks in modern Technicolor, Dads memories were in black and white, even sepia.

This place had no soul, it was lifeless, and he had the distinct impression that the cook-house hadn't been raided in years!

As I mentioned earlier, in the summer of 1942 the battalion had completed a round trip of over 250 miles to Ilfracombe from Bulford, the return trip being made on foot. As we left the barracks we were driving in the opposite direction that the men had walked. Since I was a young lad Dad often referred to 'Chin Strap Hill'. He used this when we encountered something strenuous, and when 'Down in the Ardennes' was

The two towns twinned in 1985

having a day off! We were now entering a landscape that brought this all home.

As the flatlands of Minehead gave way to Porlock Weir I began to realise what he meant - for before us was a sign-post that read: 'Porlock Hill, caution 1 in 4'.

We were heading westwards, so in effect the boys would have marched down this brute - but from my experience of fell-walking in the Lake District, the strain of walking down-hill is just as strenuous, it just affects different sets of muscles on the legs and back. My car managed to climb up the 1 in 4 in first gear - it's the first time I've ever driven up a brick wall! On the top of the hill we were on Exmoor, the road soon left Somerset and entered Devon; the Bristol Channel was on our right with Wales in the distance. Contisbury Hill cancelled the rise of Porlock Hill as we descended into Lynmouth. Contisbury is as steep as Porlock but twice its length - Dad dug deep into his memory banks and informed us that that was the famous 'Chin Strap Hill'. His thoughts turned to his comrade that died from exhaustion during the trip - the sign announcing Lynton's twinning with Bénouville reinforces his nostalgia.

Dad looks back at Chinstrap Hill, Lynton and
remembers his march back in 1943

Dad continued his history lesson by sharing with us the story of the Lynmouth flood disaster of 1952, when dozens of locals were killed when torrential rain caused the East and West Lyn rivers to burst their banks and swamp the village. Such is the terrain of this area, that Lynmouth is called 'Little Switzerland.' We found ourselves climbing yet another 1 in 4 as we rose up again and drove further along Exmoor to our hotel in Combe Martin.

We spent a pleasant evening in a local pub and next day continued the last ten miles to Ilfracombe and the start of Dad's epic march.

He recalled staying in Ilfracombe for a while and doing rock climbing exercises on the cliffs. Denis Edwards in his book 'The Devil's Own Luck' mentions this time. Dad also remembered live ammunition exercises on the sand dunes nearby.

From Ilfracombe we travelled even further west to Woolacombe Bay. This was the land and life that Dad lived in before he had heard of the Ox and Bucks. It is 1941, Dad, still in the Gloucesters, had been transferred to the Southern Command Weapons Training School, based at the Woolacombe Bay Hotel.

On arrival the lads were asked if they had any trades to assist in the running of the place. Dad said the first thing that came into his head and told them he was a waiter. In no time he was serving drinks to the officers in the mess and before he knew it, he was promoted to head waiter.

Although only 19 he was married and my eldest brother, Chris, was on the scene, a case of cart before the horse, but what the hell - there was a war on. Mum had managed to get digs nearby, Dunkirk and the Battle of Britain seemed a million miles away.

Life was safe if a little boring.

Somehow, Dad, in his spare time befriended a local farmer who had a white stallion that needed exercising. Whenever he could he would take this horse and gallop him, bareback, across the vast expanse of Woolacombe Sands. Occasionally the brute would throw him off on to the soft sand. Dad would remount and off they would go, it was a battle of wills.

Dad never broke the horse - and the horse never broke Dad.

Then one day a notice appeared in the officer's mess, it asked for A1 fit soldiers to enlist in a new airborne regiment preparing for a special mission.

Dad approached his CO and told him that as an A1 soldier he should be doing more. The officer liked Dad and told him not to worry, he could downgrade him to B7 and he could sit out the rest of the war serving drinks to ageing officers.

So it was that Diane, Dad and I found ourselves standing on the same spot where he, back in the war, as a young man, had had to make the most important decision of his life.

Woolacombe Bay Hotel – the place where the young Wally Parr made one
of the most important decisions of his life

Behind him was a hotel that would give him safety. He could sit out the war, with his wife and child nearby, serving drinks and perhaps die of boredom. In front of him was a sweeping bay where he could mount a white stallion, ride with the wind, and take his chances.

For the young 19-year-old, the decision was easy.

He chose 'Pegasus' and never regretted it for the rest of his life.

Touching the Bullet Holes

I had never been to Normandy and Pegasus Bridge but now was the time to go. I had done the ground work, the foundations had been laid.

The June circus had been to town and left, I wanted to live the experience quietly and personally, far from the madding crowd, I chose a quite weekend in September.

Diane, Dad and I drove to Portsmouth to get the midnight ferry to Caen. We were inexperienced at this cross channel lark and forgot to book a sleeping cabin. We spent a couple of hours in the bar and then tried to sleep in any horizontal position we could find. It was hell.

Dawn light brought welcome relief and the port of Ouisterham. We had left our car in England. Dad's new-found friend Claude was picking us up and giving us accommodation for the 60 hour short stay.

Claude Potier is central to this story. He had met Dad a year or so earlier in Bénouville. At that point Claude, a French Norman from Vernon, a couple of hours drive south from Pegasus Bridge, knew very little English, yet in the space of a few months had gone to night-school and learned almost perfect English so as to get alongside Dad.

Eventually Dad would fall in love with Claude's mother-in-law Louise, but if she was an item at the moment he was playing his cards close to his chest!

Claude had a holiday apartment overlooking the beach at Cabourg, a few miles to the east of Ouisterham, but spent no time in taking us straight to Pegasus Bridge

It was early morning

My wife, Diane, outside a deserted Café Grondrée

when we arrived at Bénouville; few people were around, certainly no tourists.

The short drive from the port brought us to the top of the village. We turned left and drove towards the bridge; we passed the Café Gondrée on our right. I half expected us to park in the space between the café and the museum but Claude continued over the bridge and parked his car beside a gun on the east bank of the canal.

I contemplate the original Pegasus Bridge for the first time

The four of us got out of the car; I tried to gather first impressions in my mind. To me the bridge was somewhere between ugly and boring. A cantilever structure, in rusting grey, which had certainly seen better days. My fears were confirmed when it was decided by the French Government to replace it with a new bridge a couple of years after my first viewing. In their wisdom they replaced it with an exact replica, although it was slightly wider and stronger.

I looked across the canal and saw the Café Gondrée from a distance for the first time. A square detached building, again unremarkable in appearance, yet vibrant as it displayed four huge flags, English, American, Canadian and French on its front windows.

A distinguished looking lady was beginning to lay cloths on the dozen or so tables placed out the front. People started to arrive.

The anticipation began to rise in my body as I prepared to hear Dad unfold his story. We walked away from the bridge along the canal and a little to the left and stopped at a small obelisk.

'This is where No. 1 glider landed,' he began, 'the other two landed there and there'

He pointed a few yards further back and we noticed two more obelisks standing innocently amongst tall grasses and a small pond.

'When we hit the ground we must have been doing nigh on eighty miles an hour. The impact was so great that most of us were knocked out for a moment. When we came round, I got about doing my job, which was to open the back door. The bugger was jammed and I needed me mate Paddy to give me a hand to fling it open'.

He was now in full flow. He began to walk steadily away from the plinth up the short incline to the beginning of the bridge. We followed him like obedient tourists behind an expert guide.

'It was about here that I started firing. The fear was so great the whole of my mouth dried up. I couldn't spit sixpence'.

He was now entering well documented folklore. Steven Ambrose had recorded this incident in 'Pegasus Bridge,' but we waited for him to continue in much the same way as a crowd calls out for a pop idol's greatest hit.

'Eventually I got some saliva and yelled at the top of my voice: "Come out and fight you square headed bastards".'

By now a small group of people had congregated, Dad had shouted his war cry at full volume. I hoped none of those within earshot were German or daughters of vicars! Dad continued for a few more minutes sharing graphic details of machine gun bursts and unwinding phosphorous bombs. We were in full flow half way across the bridge when his dramatic and sombre mood changed and after a short pause a smile beamed across his face.

'There was one thing that always bugged me,' he began, 'for months and months we trained, we practised and we trained again. We went through every possibility 'til we were blue in the face. But they forgot one thing: What if we got here, landed, and went running up the incline machine guns blazing and the bloody bridge was raised!'

For a second we paused, imagined the scenario and then collapsed in fits of laughter.

This was often the style used by Dad, one moment he would be describing horrific scenes and incidents and the next moment he would cut in with a humorous or irreverent observation. It was his way of coping, too much pain drained him, and his Cockney sense of humour was his safety valve.

Bob with his life-long friend, Pete Quick, make their first visit

We continued to walk across the bridge and stopped at a point just past the Café Gondrée. 'By now the firing was at its height,' he continued, 'somebody yelled "Where's Danny (Brotheridge)?" because nobody had seen him for a few minutes and we looked upon him for leadership. I remember running past a body about here, (he pointed to a spot on the ground) and then turning in my tracks and bending down to see who it was'.

At this point I make no apology in reproducing transcript that has been reproduced in a number of publications: 'Where's Danny?' Parr repeated. The soldier did not know and said that he had not seen Brotheridge since crossing the bridge. 'Well', Parr thought, 'he's here, Danny must be here somewhere'. Parr started to run around the café when he ran past a man lying opposite the café in the road. Parr glanced at him as he ran on. 'Hang on', he said to himself, and went back and knelt down.'

'I looked at him and it was Danny Brotheridge. His eyes were open and his lips moving. I put me hand under his head and lifted him up. He just looked. His eyes sort of rolled back. He just choked and lay back. My hand was covered in blood.

I just looked at him and thought, "My God, what a waste!" All the years of training we put in to do this job - it lasted only seconds.' Jack Bailey came running up. "What the hell's going on?" he asked Parr. "It's Danny" Parr replied. "He's had it". "Christ Almighty", Bailey muttered.'

Happy days outside the Café Gondrée

I knew this passage almost word for word but it took on a new dimension as I relived it on my knees with Dad in the Normandy dust. For a while Dad stared across the road resting in silence, then he took one last drag of his cigarette and flicked the butt into the gutter - still smouldering it took on the form of a tiny cremation - I thought of saying something clever like 'Ashes to Ashes' but declined, instead Diane, Claude and I joined him in respectful contemplation.

A minute or so later a motorbike roared across the bridge and disturbed the peace - I put my hand around his shoulder and together we walked towards the café.

As we approached we spotted Arlette Gondrée laying tablecloths on the tables in the forecourt. Dad introduced us and Arlette instantly forgot our names as she began the French custom of hugs and double kisses on each cheek - by the time she had worked through the four of us she must have been quite giddy!

Those were happy days in the Café Gondrée, the tyrant that is jealousy and misunderstanding had yet to raise its ugly head.

We stepped inside the café and were bombarded by dozens of photographs, drawings and memorabilia celebrating the exploits of the British liberators. Behind the bar was a photograph of John Howard shaking hands with royalty, beside it was a large drawing of Dad in his red beret, the likeness was remarkable.

The smell of the café was typically French - a musty aroma of real coffee and Gauloise cigarettes battled with the fragrance of expensive perfume.

Dad and Charlie Gardener continue to educate Marc Jacquinot!

As I wandered around the place I was amazed at the price of the tacky souvenirs. One look at the menu confirmed my suspicion that this was not a 'labour of love', but a lucrative business. Despite this, there was no mistaking the genuine affection Arlette showed us.

We stayed awhile, had a quick beer, signed the visitor's book and then departed to the museum next door.

Opened in June 1974, its purpose was not only to preserve the memory and educate the public of the events surrounding the immediate area in June 1944, but also to give a personal account to the veterans and their families.

The emphasis was more towards memorabilia than simply showing weapons of war. The building was fairly un-inspiring, the best way to describe it would be two Portakabins placed on top of each other.

The lack of architectural grandeur was out-weighed by the obvious enthusiasm for the curators.

It was mid-morning when we arrived, a dozen or so visitors were congregating in the main area on the first floor surrounding a huge relief map of the two canals and bridges. Out of the window I could see the Café Gondrée and Pegasus Bridge in the background; it made the perfect background for the speaker, a certain Marc Jacquinot, to begin his lecture on the exploits of D Company on D-Day

He gave Dad a quick wink, they obviously knew each other well, and then began to ask the group their nationalities. It emerged we comprised of English, French and German speaking people. He then reached for a long stick and started to unfold the events of June the 5th and 6th pointing to each position on the huge relief map before him, at times he had to lean full stretch, such was the size of the map. He spoke initially in French for a couple of minutes and then repeated the same segment in German and finally in English. Each language was fluent, such was his confidence I got the impression that if there were Dutch, Italians or Russians present he would have given it a go!

As he concluded in each language he mentioned the name Wally Parr No. 1 glider and the relevant group glanced in our direction and Dad acknowledged their attention feeling slightly embarrassed at his lack of foreign languages. Mark finished his talk, the visitors clapped politely and he came over to chat to us.

'Ow is my friend Wally, ze D-Day 'ero?' he began.

Over the years I have got to know Marc well. He is a free spirit, always with a smile on his face and a twinkle in his eyes. A bachelor, his dress sense is 'laid back' to say the least.

I remember watching him one time in a line waiting to meet Prince Charles - he had his usual jacket on with non-matching trousers. As the Prince approached, Marc wet his fingers and attempted to flatten his flyaway hair, he then twiddled his huge moustache and cleaned his shoes on the back of his trousers - this was Marc's idea of a spruce-up!

We chatted for a while getting away with handshakes instead of all that kissing and hugging lark. We spent a good hour in the museum absorbing a vast amount of information - it was obvious my grasp of the events only touched the surface. After a while we bode Marc farewell, as we left, he invited us to a barbecue at his 'mobile 'ome beside the canal' for the following day, it was to prove an unforgettable experience!

We left the museum and began to walk back across the bridge to our car parked near the landing zone. By now the sun was high in the sky and as I glanced upstream towards Caen in the south a heat haze gave the distant building an air of mystery. On the west bank about half a mile away was the Château de Bénouville - this was to play a prominent role in the next part of Dad's story.

When we arrived at the end of the bridge we dropped down towards the canal bank and joined a small group that was leaning on railings peering into a fairly large gun pit. The ten foot barrel protruded from a German anti tank gun. A French guide was giving a lecture to a group of students.

This was of course the famous No. 1 gun featured by Stephen Ambrose, I knew the story well, having read the book, but Dad proceeded to tell Diane and anybody else that was prepared to listen, the tale of how he and his mates learnt to fire a certain German artillery gun.

In no time the French guide stopped talking and instructed his

The gun with the châteaux, lost in the mist behind

students to listen to the man speaking and get the facts from the horse's mouth! He told them how Charlie Gardner, Jack Bailey, Billy Gray and he set about the task. It occurred to me they must have been like four vandals trying to start a stolen car they had just nicked. Their ages wouldn't have been much older than the students. There was a roar of laughter when he explained what happened when the first shell went off nearly decapitating one of his mates with the recoil of the spent shell! He told the story of the German gun boat approaching from the direction of Caen and how with his first shot he fired across its bows sending it into a rapid U turn and a hasty retreat back in the direction whence it came. Germans retreating raised a small cheer amongst the partisan French but the story of dust and soot filling Jack Bailey's beloved brew as he sat beneath the gun as Dad fired yet another shell, was somehow lost on the French sense of humour - anyway Diane found it funny.

He reminded us that one of the biggest threats to D Company on that first day was constant sniper fire. Major Howard had deduced that one of the snipers was probably firing from the top of the château half a mile or so up stream and could Private Parr possibly shut the bugger up with his new toy.

Like a kid on Christmas Day he was away. The first shot went a little to the right and hit a water-tower next to the building. He then realised the shell he was using was armour piercing and instead of exploding, it went clean through and out the other side, producing two torrents of gushing water. The second and third shells went whizzing over the roof

Château de Bénouville

and exploded a couple of miles further on.

The fourth was spot on and hit the château about six feet below the top gutter but thankfully went clean through the building and out the other side without exploding. I say thankfully, due to the fact that un-known to Dad the top floor of the building was being used as the local maternity hospital!

Dad felt proud that he helped a few French ladies finish the last part of their labour in double quick time! As soon as Howard realised that Dad was firing at the local maternity home, his instructions were snipers or no snipers, stop firing the bloody gun, especially at pregnant ladies.

It's ironic that years later war historians recorded that when the German army retreated from Caen, as an act of revenge they shelled the local maternity hospital - perhaps we shouldn't blame the Germans for everything!

Dad finished giving the people his party piece and the crowd began to disperse. Then a couple of youngsters came over and asked Dad to sign photographs, he looked embarrassed, I felt embarrassed. Perhaps we both didn't realise at that time the respect the French held for their liberators.

Before getting into the car we strolled over to the main turret of the bridge and Dad pointed out a huge dent near the top of the structure. He then shared the story of how at one point of the day on June 6th they suddenly heard a German plane come out of the sun from the direction of Caen. They barely had time to dive for cover when they heard the pilot jettison his 500 pound bomb and they listened to the whiz and waited for the explosion. It was a perfect hit - but instead of death and destruction all they heard was a loud clang as the brute hit the bridge and failed to detonate. Thankfully all it did was bounce off the steel and plop into the canal.

I stared up at dent and contemplated what might have happened.

By now it was mid-afternoon on the Saturday and we hadn't had any decent sleep since Thursday. On top of that we still had to meet Renée, Claude's wife, who was probably expecting us for breakfast!

It was a short drive to Cabourg from Bénouville. This part of the coast, east of Ouisterham, has a different feel from the 'Landing Beaches'. The war almost passed it by, the towns of Deauville and Trouville have a sophisticated atmosphere with their casinos and racecourses, and you could almost be on the Riviera. Further along the coast you have the gem that is Honfleur, Van Gogh or Cézanne could have lived and painted here. Tucked amongst all these is Cabourg, where Claude and Renée had bought a very nice apartment, overlooking the sprawling sandy beach. It was back to double kisses and hugs as we were introduced to Claude's wife - but it was quite enjoyable as I wallowed in the aromas of good perfume and exquisite French cuisine wafting from the kitchen.

As I mentioned before, Claude and Renée are central to the success of many reunions of D Company veterans over the past two decades. Such was their dedication that, within a year or two of first meeting Dad, they decided to sell their apartment in Cabourg and buy a large detached house in Bénouville and make a base for veterans as and when the need arose. Such was the success; they needed to build a large extension to accommodate a table that seated at least twelve. Many a drunken night have we spent around that table - more of this later!

For the first time in my life I tasted real French cooking, not to mention the non-plonk red wine. We instantly felt part of the family and they even gave me and Diane a little time to walk along the beach and watch the sun set over the sea in the direction of Bénouville - very Dubonnet!

Next morning, slightly worse for wear, we continued our explorations. This day was to be our own personal 'Remembrance Sunday'. Within fifteen minutes of leaving Cabourg we drove into the car park of Ranville Cemetery. I could see in the background a huge sprawling Cemetery but Dad chose to initially ignore this and took us to the Chapel and the handful of graves that surrounded it. We walked around the back and stopped in front of a particular tombstone. We could have been in an English churchyard, the burial could have civilian. The only difference was the headstone it was the first of thousands that I would see bearing a regimental emblem. Before me was the price paid for the cost of war.

It was the grave of H. D. Brotheridge – 'Den' or better known to Dad as his friend and comrade 'Danny'.

At that point in my life I had lost relatives but never friends, I tried to get into my Dad's mind and emotions but failed. To understand some things in life you have to experience them. My time, my tragedies, will come. All I could do was to allow him to share his grief and his regrets any way he chose.

After a while we left and a short walk across the road led us into Ranville Cemetery in all its glory.

Compared to the World War 1 sites in Belgium and the American D-Day cemeteries further along the coast this is modest - but it took my breath away. Row after row of matching headstones stood in perfect symmetry - on parade, awaiting inspection. We wandered around randomly. Dad, Claude and Renée went one way while Diane and I went the other.

The names never registered, it was the ages: seventeen, eighteen, nineteen, a 'veteran' was twenty-five. I was acutely aware that not every coffin housed complete bodies. I also had no doubt that the arm of one soldier could easily have been buried with the head and torso of another. My fears were confirmed when I stumbled upon a headstone that bore the names of four men from the same regiment. The inscription read: 'Killed by mortar attack'. Obviously a direct hit, all they could do was collect the remains and place them in a pile. This was death and carnage at the deep end - yet on the surface the pristine white headstones and the immaculate gardens, tended by the War Graves Commission, gave an impression of peace and serenity. The lush green grass between the graves had not only been watered by the gardeners - but also by the tears of countless relatives and surviving veterans. Every person should visit these places at least once in their lives - world leaders should visit them once a week.

We gathered in the car park and eventually drove further inland. At the time I hadn't a clue where we were but found out later that we ended up at a place called Escoville. For a while we walked through a field until on the edge Dad pointed out a long dip in one of the corners - this turned out to be the remains of a slit trench Dad help dig on D-Day plus four. He described how a Panzer tank came within a few feet of them one night and all he could do was crouch in the trench and shit himself.

We got back into the car and drove a little further. We stopped at a small farm and Claude knocked on the door and started a long conversation with the occupants. The woman was roughly the same age as Dad and kept looking over towards us. After a while Claude called over to us and said it was okay to wander around. Dad took us to a small out-house and pointed to a window on the ground floor. The building was probably two hundred years old, it was made of thick grey stones and the wood in places had completely rotted away.

While we stared at the building Dad entered through the gap that used to be the door and peered at us through the broken window. He explained that he and Denis Edwards sometimes used this position to snipe Germans. The enemy obviously knew where they were because the building was covered in bullet holes! Some were literally six inches from the window opening. I put my finger in some of them, they were at least an inch deep, if it did that to solid stone what would it do to a man's face.

I returned to my 'What if' mode. 'What if' that 500 pound had exploded on the bridge? 'What if' one of these bullets had been six inches to the right?

Then it occurred to me that I would have been born to a different father - perhaps a millionaire or film star. But then again my different Dad might have been a right git so perhaps I'll stick with the devil I do know!

In many ways this place was sacred. It was away from the tourist trail and all the razzmatazz - this was personal. The stories my Dad told me today were unique, these are stories you only share in front rooms after a few beers.

By now it was lunch-time and we had a barbecue date with Marc in his country residence over-looking the canal. To get to this haven you have to drive to the east side of Pegasus Bridge and then follow the canal past several industrial warehouses until, neatly nestled between a refinery and a scrap-yard, you find Monsieur Jacquinot's mobile 'ome.

About to embark on a Marc Jacquinot 'Barbie Special'

When we arrived he was waiting for us fully prepared - the drinks, varying from vintage Calvados to single-malt whisky were laid out on the bar (the bonnet of his car) and the 'barbecue' (half a dustbin, Caribbean style) was in full flow.

We all embraced and then Diane and I were introduced to Marc's partner, his dog Ranville, so named because that's where he found him!

In no time the alcohol kicked in and the good times rolled.

After a while the food appeared. I tucked into the excellent salad and eagerly await my second experience of French cuisine à-la-outdoors. I was eventually presented with a kebab of meat that was interesting to say the least.

It was so interesting I felt compelled to ask exactly what it was.

'Well, this piece is ze 'eart,' Marc began, 'this piece is ze kidney and this is how you say? The gizzard and this is the liver.'

All the meat was oozing blood, I dare not ask the identity of the animal - I put the meat back on the barbie and tried to get it to enter the category of 'cooked'. Eventually I took a bite, Renée's this was not!

I noticed his dog Ranville sitting under a nearby table and chairs, Diane was sitting there discreetly passing pieces of meat to him, I joined her and followed suit – you will not be surprised to hear that Ranville is the fattest dog in Normandy!

Needless to say the rest of the day was spent in warm sunshine drinking beer and Calvados and staring back up the river to the café and bridge.

It had been an amazing weekend, almost too much to take in. As the sun set Claude drove us to the ferry, we were tired, hopefully we will to grab some sleep on a couch or something.

Claude and Renée waited at the quayside and waved us off.

As the ferry slipped into the channel I looked back up the canal to Caen in the distance, we would return many times. This had been my first time, not necessarily the best, but it had been unique.

All the films, all the books and a lifetime of hearing stories about the war had finally been set in stone.

An Englishman dans Vernon

By the spring of 1991 Dad had long retired. He made the trip to Pegasus Bridge as often as he could – without fail for the June 5/6th celebrations and whenever the family or his growing circle of friends felt inclined to take him over.

Unknown to us Dad had been developing a rather intimate relationship with Renée's mother, Louise. The crafty old sod had been getting his wicked way with a woman of his own age – not bad at sixty nine!

In London he kept himself occupied by answering the many letters that arrived from around the world and from his fellow D Company mates. Every lunch-time he would make the 15 minute walk to his local pub, The Copperfield, at Catford Bridge.

One day as he approached the pub a group of four black teenagers ran up the stairs from Catford Bridge station and bumped straight into him – Dad immediately put his arm up to protect himself and told them to be more careful. The next second the three boys started to punch Dad while the girl stood back laughing. The blows came thick and fast – Dad instinctively resorted back to his army boxing days, crouching his body, head down, arms protecting his stomach and chest. Occasionally he managed to throw a punch back, a straight left, a right upper-cut, he even managed to elbow in the face the lad that was hitting him from behind.

The onslaught lasted 45 seconds, a minute at the most, then the foursome ran off down Catford Road laughing and screaming as they went. Fifteen feet away a group of people stood at the bus stop – mostly elderly, they looked on helplessly, choosing not to get involved. The busy traffic on the South Circular Road carried on at its slow crawling pace, nobody had been willing to stop on the double yellow line.

Dad briefly leant on the brick wall and spent a short while getting his breath back before continuing the last couple of yards to The Copperfield. Inside he ordered a pint and a large Scotch and then found a quiet corner to gather himself.

It was nearly a fortnight before Dad shared this experience with me. I noticed that he had been quieter than usual but didn't know why. When he opened up he began to sob violently.

'The bastards never put me down!' he kept repeating.

'I never went on the floor so they could give me a good kicking,' he continued, 'I stayed on me feet son!'

His emotions were a mixture of pride and shame.

He was proud that at nearly seventy he could still stand firm and fight off whatever the enemy threw at him – yet he felt shame that the very country that he was prepared to die for, had turned away and not helped him in his hour of need.

One month later he had packed a few bags and we moved him out to Vernon to live with his beloved Louise.

He had left the country for good.

Dad's farewell party with Bob, Pat and me

Dad moving to Vernon not only gave him a new lease of life but also opened up a whole new area for us.

Two hours drive south of Pegasus Bridge; Vernon is in the heart of Normandy, Calvados country. Nestling on the banks of the Seine, ancient Norman buildings abound, it reminds me of Canterbury or Stratford upon Avon. The jewel in its crown is the nearby village of Giverney with Monet's house and garden. Visitors from all over the world visit this treasure – it is only a 50 minute train journey from Paris.

Dad soon settled into Louise's tiny apartment – it was basically a bed-sit with a small kitchen and bathroom. Set in a small block situated in the grounds of the Château de Bizy, it was warden-controlled with meals provided daily from the kitchen in the château. Twice a year the Mayor of Vernon visited and put on a banquet for the residents, they were then provide with a huge hamper and a case of fine wine – the French certainly know how to look after their elderly.

Louise was soon showing off her prize catch to all the other eagle-eyed ladies in her block. 'This is Wally Parr, my 'ansome D-Day Cockney 'ero!' she would proclaim proudly. Some would smile, others would grunt.

Dad reckons every one of them scared the bloody daylights out of him!

As you probably know Dad enjoys a drink or two and by moving to Vernon he was in boozer's heaven. Apart from cheap wine and beer there was the famous local brew, Calvados. Made from apples it is fermented into a brandy-type spirit that could strip paint – cider it ain't! Dad's favourite soon became Pastis, an aniseed based spirit which has a big brother called Absenthe, drink that and you go mad or blind or both.

As soon as Dad had unpacked, Louise poured him a rather large Pastis and lemonade – several more followed before Dad was allowed to drift off into his usual afternoon nap.

Next day Louise went to the shops, leaving Dad alone for the first time. He soon found his way around – the Pastis was in one cupboard and the lemonade in another. Hands trembling he poured himself a large one – it didn't taste quite the same a yesterday's, but he put it down to the hangover. After the third it was going down like nectar. Eventually he drifted into a contented sleep clutching his empty glass, the two bottles beside him. A while later he was woken by Louise's violent shaking.

'Wally my darlin' what have you been drinking?' she cried.

'I only had one', he lied.

'I don't care how many you had my precious, but you have been mixing it with cooking oil!'

For the next 24 hours he was rarely less than ten feet from the nearest toilet – he quickly learnt to read French bottle labels.

Within a few weeks he became well-known in the cafes and bars of Vernon. 'Crazy Englishman' was his nickname – I wonder why?

He remembers the first time he went into a bar and ordered a beer and the bartender presented him a tiny glass with a three inch frothy head. 'What's that?', asked Dad.

'A beer monsieur.'

'No mate,' Dad said, pointing to the pint glasses at the back, 'I want a proper beer that big'.

'Ah, une grande bière, monsieur.'

'Oui, mate!'

Dad would then take his grande beer and sit in the sunshine outside, he ignored the custom of waiter service at tables – the French looked on and smiled.

In all the time he was in France, Dad only managed to learn a few words in French – yes, no, beer and bread. 'I learn something one day and forget it the next,' was his excuse. 'I'm making the buggers learn English, after all God was English!'

Soon Louise's tiny apartment turned into a mini D-Day museum as she built a shrine to her 'D-Day 'ero'.

In the spring of the following year they got officially engaged. In France engagement is as important as the marriage ceremony – they decided not to go the whole way as that would have devalued Louise's widow's pension – love may be blind but it still counts the pennies.

They got engaged at the June celebrations – the Mayor was there and their picture appeared in the local press.

As Dad and Louise emerged from the hall like young innocent lovers the rest of the D Company boys returned to their barrack-room humour and gave Dad a right ribbing. At one point, while the photographs were being taken, Ted Tappenden spotted a ' no entry' sign laying in the road and thought it would be funny to place it in front of Louise's midriff - I'm sure the old man ignored that sign, but there was definitely one sign he did stick to and that was 'no U turns'!

Life in Vernon during those days was good. Claude and Renée lived in a lovely old house five minutes drive away. Once a week they would all eat together – three hours of French extravaganza culminating with Dad and Claude polishing of a bottle of single malt whisky or vintage Calvados.

At least once a month the four of them would make the two hour journey up to Bénouville and stay at Claude's house for a few days. Every day Dad and Claude would take the short stroll along the canal to the café and have a few beers. Dad always took his beret or regimental jacket, thus allowing any tourist to recognise him as one of the veterans

Dad, newly engaged to Louise – 'Wagger' gives his blessing

... and a lighter moment as Ted Tappenden gives his advice

– café owners didn't mind, it was good for business.

Dad was never a 'professional veteran' ripping people off, yet he would gladly talk to anybody as long as they were interested – if they offered him a beer during the conversation, so be it, most people would agree they got their beer's worth.

While Dad struggled with his French, Louise's English was coming on in leaps and bounds. In those days, before their health began to take its toll, they would occasionally travel over to London. When they stayed with us, the secret was not to talk to Louise in school-boy French, if you did, she would revert back to babbling on 'nineteen to the dozen', then my wife, Dad and I would stare at her not having a clue what she was on about – if she laughed at the end we would all laugh together pretending

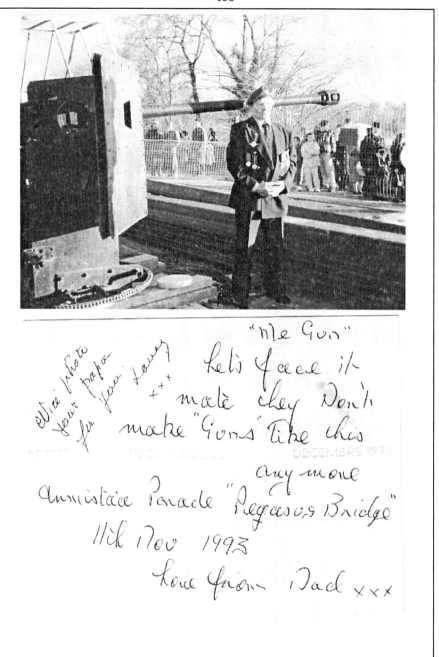

"Me Gun"

Nice photo for your papa for your Louis xxx

let's face it mate they Don't make "Guns" like this any more

Armistice Parade "Pegasus Bridge"
11th Nov 1993

love from Dad xxx

to get the joke.

It also had its good points – if they had a row, both Dad and Louise would curse and swear in their own language and that way no lasting damage was done!

At the time of the engagement Louise had a wonderful opportunity to show off her newly acquired grasp of the English language. It was June 6th, the wreaths had been laid at the memorial and everybody was getting ready to cross back over the bridge and get down to some serious drinking. Dad was amongst all the various dignitaries and officials not to mention several members of the press. One of the visitors had a classic E Type Jag - to me a car that sums up my misspent youth in the 'Swinging Sixties' - as Dad was admiring it, the owner offered him a lift across the bridge to the café. Dad as you would expect accepted - as he sat himself down in the passenger seat Louise pushed herself through the surrounding crowd and without hesitation plonked herself down firmly on Dad's lap. He immediately crossed his eyes and gave out a loud yelp. The Mayor and his entourage found this mildly amusing, but the smiles soon turned into hysterics when Louise cried out: 'What is the matter Wally my darling, am I sitting on your bollocks?'! All of a sudden

Dad being 'E-Typed' !

everybody was bi-lingual. The three years leading up to the 50th anniversary of D-Day were halcyon days - not only for Dad but for the rest of our family. One memorable trip was when my wife, Diane, and I went over with my sister, Pat, and her husband, Jim. We stayed in Vernon for the first time and obviously we couldn't stay in Dad's place so we asked them to book a nearby hotel - Dad left the arrangement to Louise - BIG MISTAKE!

Louise booked us into an old friend's hotel that overlooked the Seine. On the outside it was a perfect example of 19th Century Norman architecture - the problem was that during the war the place had been used as the local brothel and the madams that run the place were still there and they hadn't quite got round to doing the dusting! After a couple of minutes of arrival we began to walk out of the place backwards pretending not to understand a word they were saying - half an hour later we checked into the more luxurious Hôtel d'Evreux by the town square and only a two minute walk to Dad's place.

Dad & Louise's home in Vernon. – first floor on right
Hardly big enough to swing a 'chat' !

In the four day visit we did Vernon, Monet's Garden, Paris and a round day trip up to Pegasus Bridge with Dad. This was my sister's first trip to Bénouville - it was good to see a father and his daughter share special moments – I did my best to give them space.

While in Bénouville we went back to the tiny farmhouse where a few years previously I had put my finger in the holes created by bullets aimed at my Dad. The original owners had either died or moved on – the new owners had made a half-hearted attempt at renovating the place. In their supposed wisdom they had decided to fill in all the holes on the outside of the building – I was tempted to knock on the door and scream: 'How dare you cement over history!' But the better of me told me to not be so stupid. The irony is that there was a fair chance that the new owners were probably Brits and if it wasn't for the bullet holes they would have still been slaves to the Hun!

Another time we went over with my eldest daughter Jennie and her husband Gary.

On this trip Dad didn't come from Vernon to the bridge because we were getting the afternoon ferry home from Ouisterham and had decided to take in the Bénouville experience after travelling up from Vernon, 'the pretty way round' and stopping off in Honfleur and Cabourg.

It was up to me to give Jennie and Gary the historical tour, starting with the landing, then the story of granddad's gun, followed by the charge across the bridge and finally a look at the café and the museum next door.

Dad & Louise with actor Richard Todd who played
John Howard in the film 'The Longest Day' - 1993

As I stood by the gun giving them the facts, nearby people would glance over and hang on to every word. I felt proud sharing with Jennie and Gary as others looked on, the next generation were becoming aware of living history – I enjoyed my brief career as a guide.

My first few trips to Pegasus, including this one, had been taken during relatively quiet periods – along with John Howard I was not a great lover of the circus coming to town - it is intimate times like these when you have time to reflect and time to take in the enormity of it all.

The tension between Arlette Gondrée and the veterans was beginning to raise its ugly head. Jennie was aware of this and when I took them into the Café Gondrée to show her the photographs that still adorned the walls she left by signing the visitors book: 'Jennie Phillips, grand-daughter of Wally Parr and proud of it!'

I hoped in my naive way that these words may have said something to Arlette but of course they didn't.

The other memorable event of that visit was that after 18 months of trying, my daughter conceived her first child in Vernon.

It's ironic that in the land that her grandfather lost so many good friends and comrades should finally give back to him yet another great-grandchild - thank God they never followed the Beckham's tradition and called him 'Vernon'!

The circle of Dad's friends and ultimately mine was growing steadily, one of my favourites was Robbie Jones, and we have spent many a happy hour with him at Claude and Renée's dinning table over the years. I recently asked Robbie to share his story, it was revealing to say the least!

John Howard begins to question Wally Parr's sexuality !

'Wally Parr - well what a man. My name is Robbie Jones retired Special Branch officer now resident in France somewhere near Pegasus Bridge for 18 years and affectionately known to Monsieur Parr as THE BRISTOL FEELTH (Filth, Old Bill, Rozzer, Copper, Blue Bottle or any other term of sentiment he could throw at me).

I first met Wally on the 6th of the 6th 1987 when my good friend, Noel O' Driscoll, former Wiltshire Regiment and 22nd S.A.S. and I completed a walk from Bristol to Pegasus Bridge, Normandy. This was to raise funds for B.L.E.S.M.A. (British Limbless Ex-Service Man's Association.) I had decided to carry out this walk in memory of my Father Jack (44th R.T.R.) who was severely wounded in Libya in 1941 and had died in 1985. Dad had introduced us to Pegasus Bridge whilst holidaying in Normandy many years before.

After a long hot last leg of our march from Ryes, not far from Sword Beach, we arrived at Pegasus Bridge at the Café Gondrée. To greet us was Major John Howard and some of his coup-de-main party who were all sat at tables in the sun outside the café. They were a grand bunch of ex-soldiers and I was to become firm friends with all of them over the ensuing years. They were all resplendent in red berets with Ox and Bucks cap badges - blazers adorned with polished medals from many campaigns and of course the obligatory beer in one hand and a pen for signing autographs in the other. There was big Ted 'Ham and Jam' Tappenden whistling a tune. There was Arthur 'Red Jacket' Roberts, Big Bill Bailey. Martin Charles Thornton M.M. (known only as Wagger - I never did find out why!) and sat near the entrance to the café was this hard looking man with his beret on the back of his head stubbing out a cigarette and calling "Hey mate you two look like you could do with a beer or three, come and sit down and I'll tell you how I won the war single-handed." Well Wally didn't tell us that but, true to his word, he bought us beers and told us how, along with the other men there, they captured the bridge intact.

We stayed all afternoon soaking up the wonderful atmosphere of the 6th of the 6th watching Wally and the rest of the gang humbly telling their story to whoever asked – from ten-year-old boys to British and American veterans alike.

Wally and those men became firm friends of not only myself but French families in Bénouville and one such couple were Claude and Renée Potier who actually purchased a house yards from Pegasus Bridge solely to invite veterans to stay whenever they wished. This house became a second base for the men and over the years I have been privileged to be at many five-course dinners and impromptu parties where Wally entertained us with stories of not only the war – but his life in general.

I remember one such night when the Calvados had been flowing freely and Wally decided to retire to his "billet" upstairs.

"Bon soir mon amis et keep the effing noise down coz Wally wants his precious bye byes", was his departing statement.

Well the noise didn't abate – how could it with such company – when 30 minutes later the door burst open and there, completely naked save red beret in his right hand covering his private parts, was Wally. He took two steps into the room which was full with ex-this and ex-that and French and English ladies. He immediately apologised to females present and shouted in typical barrack room style:

"I requested bloody quiet now pleez I am going to bed – SHAD UP!"

With that he smartly threw his right hand up, placed his beret on his head, saluted, about turned and disappeared out of the room. Such a fine figure of a man when stood to attention! It's no wonder the Hun were a little worried in June 1944.

Wally was to me a truthful, hard working, sincere, no-nonsense man. He didn't suffer fools lightly - but once a friend – it was for life. When Wally talked and I mean seriously – you listened in awe what he imparted to you and how he delivered it was from the heart and the impact was such, that you were there with him in that Horsa glider – you could hear the whoosh as he opened the door – you could hear his heart beating as he scrambled out and ran with the rest into what could have been instant death. When he went to New Orleans on that sell-out tour I can hazard a fair guess as to who got the longest standing ovation!

The mind boggles! I now have this picture emblazoned in my mind of Dad –'stark bollock naked', giving that salute - I hope for everyone's sake that the only thing raised was his right arm!

'Mad-Dog' Robbie Jones après dinner

Those times for Dad were filled with not only joy but also sadness. Shortly after the birth of my first grandson, Jack, Dad and Louise along with Claude and Renée had to make a two day trip to my home to attend the funeral of Jack Bailey.

Jack's health had been deteriorating steadily – his lungs had finally lost their lifelong battle with a 40 fags a day habit. He had long since left Sydenham and died peacefully in an old soldier's home near regimental H.Q. in Winchester.

We all travelled to Winchester and attended, probably the highest profile military service ever given to a non-Commissioned Officer. At the end of the service we all walked out of the chapel to the sound of his beloved Edif Piaf singing 'Je ne regret rien' – 'I Regret Nothing.'

And that just about summed up my 'Uncle' Jack's life.

With Dad safe and happy in Vernon I thought it was about time that I attended one of the big ceremonies on D-Day itself. I was now going to see Pegasus Bridge in all its glory on June 5/6th for the first time and it was to the biggest event to date as the world looked on as it celebrated the 50th anniversary - and that turned out to be a week that was to change Dad's life situation for ever.

'Field Marshall Montgomery', Kirt Garcia and
a Wally Parr 'look-alike' !

The 50th Anniversary - The Triumph

As this was to be the first time I had been to Normandy on D-Day and I decided, for some unknown reason, to take a decent jacket, tie and trousers. I travelled with my brother, Bob, and we took the classic 'boozers route' to Bénouville: which is to walk to Lower Sydenham station, train to Waterloo East, main line train to Portsmouth, (picking up four pack of beers on concourse, swigging football hooligan style out of bag on train), short walk to ferry terminal at Pompey, (stopping in pub by car park for a quick one because we don't have to waste time in long queues with our car to get on ferry) check in at terminal half an hour before we are allowed to board (meaning we are forced to buy another beer in the rather grim bar, because what else can you do in the Portsmouth/Caen ferry terminal?) and then rather wearingly climb the long winding ramp up to the entrance of The Duc de Normandie ferry, bound for Caen. It actually docks in the port of Ouisterham, but maybe Caen fits easier on the tickets.

Before hitting the bar - where else? We nip into the book shop and browse through the many rows of D-Day memorabilia. I notice the official programme of events and flick through it quickly; the forward is by the Queen Mum followed by various articles written by Field Marshals and the Prime Minister. I make a note to myself to pick it up some time but something else grabs my attention and I leave it to one side.

Eventually we make our way up to main bar, which is roughly the size of a football pitch. These cross-channel ferries are, in effect, floating hotels. You could easily have a week long cruise on one, the only facility missing would be the out-door swimming pool. The atmosphere in the bar was quite unique. On other trips I had met the occasional veteran but on this trip the place was swarming with them! It resembled a Colonial Officer's Club. There were distinct pockets of men in regimental jackets and ties. A dozen or so with one regimental tie here, half a dozen green with something different there - nowhere could you see a merging of colours. Each group was surrounded by relatives and friends who protected their heroes from unwanted intruders. Occasionally a rival veteran, on his way to the bar and slightly worse for wear, would push pass and shout out a friendly insult, the reply would be just as sarcastic and laughter would fill the area - the atmosphere was good.

This was the night ferry, leaving just after midnight, it travelled at a slower pace than the day-time ferries allowing passengers more time to sleep and arrive in France around 6 a.m. The bar stayed opened most of the night allowing professional drinkers the pleasure of non-stop boozing. We reckoned to give it an hour or so and then to retire to our reserved reclining seats in the lounge on the lower deck. Sleeping in one of these is like sleeping in a dentist's chair with at least a dozen snorers within earshot. To lose consciousness, we reckoned we needed to hit the spirits.

Bob and I use these times alone together well. We have a unique brotherly relationship; I am eight years older and have over the years done my best to do the wise big-brother thing. I'm sure in his early teens I had the required effect, but obviously now, in our thirties and forties we are on equal standing and have a mutual respect for each other, learning and taking from each other as and when the need arises. Although we live less than a mile from each other we can go a couple of months without communicating. This is normal for us. When we do meet it is often with our wives and the conversations are on a different level than when it is just the two of us. Times like this on the boat take us into a realm that is true brothers, going back into a history that forms our very being, alcohol cements the union.

Before we became too sentimental we pick up our bags and find our way to the sleeping lounge and collapse into three hours of much needed sleep. Loudspeakers wake us with the announcement that breakfast will

Claude & René's house in Bénouville – note the extension
– built to entertain the many veterans who became their friends.

served shortly and that we will be docking in half an hour.

In no time, coffee filled, we are met by Claude Potier in the car park, in Ouisterham who drives us the 15 minute journey to Bénouville.

This is first time I have been here on June 5th/6th and I am amazed at the effort the locals put in to jazz the place up - the flags displayed everywhere reminded me of the Queen's Jubilee in London back in 1977.

Normally we would have stayed in Claude and Renée's house but the demand for accommodation is overwhelming and we are lucky to be offered a double bed for the night in their next door neighbour's house. We are greeted by Renée who leads us into their conservatory which was specially built to house a table that seats at least ten.

I had sat at this table a number of times before, experiencing their wonderful French dinners that lasted hours. That evening at the town hall there will be a special presentation given to Claude and Renée in recognition for the work they have done in making so many veterans welcome in their home.

Within the next hour people drifted into the dining room from various bedrooms scattered around the huge house. We meet up with Ted Tappenham and Wagger Thornton, somewhere still tucked up in bed is a certain Wally Parr no doubt snuggled into his beloved Louise.

Dad spins yet another yarn !
Ted, Charlie, Claude, Wagger and I try to ignore him.

Eventually we all gather for breakfast and Dad gives Bob and I the itinerary for the next 24 hours; The rest of the day is more or less free - that means drinking in the café opposite the Café Gondrée - then there is a special dinner given by John Howard at the Town Hall - followed by a Son et Lumiere presentation on the banks of the river at around 11 p.m. - the day ends at a quarter past midnight with the traditional ceremony of cracking open bottles of Champagne to commemorate the landing of the first glider 50 years ago. This certainly will be the longest day!

After breakfast we are taken next door to meet our hosts for the night. I have forgotten their names but their son Cedrick stayed with us in London a few months later as a thank-you present for their hospitality.

Our old friend Ted Barwick

By midday most of us were gathering on the west bank of Pegasus Bridge warming up for the days celebrations. The Café Gondrée was bustling with tourists and veterans from various regiments, reporters and TV crews were everywhere.

Dad and Co. made their base in the Café Les 3 Planeurs (The Three Gliders) on the opposite side of the road. Tension between Arlette Gondrée and D Company had been growing steadily worse over the years, as a relative outsider my observation seemed to be that somehow the message given to John Howard back on that historic night in June 1944: 'Capture the bridge over the Caen canal intact so that troops coming up from the beaches will be able to advance inland, has been changed to; 'Capture the Café Gondrée at all costs so that the advancing troops can advance inland after popping in for a cup of tea and a bacon sandwich'

Undoubtedly the *Café Gondrée* has a unique place in history as the first building to be liberated on D-Day but the danger was, and still is that it will take on a personality of its own and try to eclipse all other events.

In retrospect, I'm sure other veterans feel much the same with regards to the glider landings compared to equally important and dangerous operations carried out at the same time.

A couple of months before the 50th anniversary I had felt led to write Dad a personal poem regarding the forthcoming celebrations. All my life I have enjoyed writing, particularly poetry. It began with teenage angst-ridden ramblings and over the years progressed to thirty/forty something angst-ridden ramblings. Occasionally, more by luck than design, I would come up with something half-decent; the effort I had presented to Dad regarding the 50th anniversary was one of my better efforts.

Towards the end of the poem I cry out to all our fathers to put 'anger and hatred and bitterness aside.' The initial reaction would be to presume that I meant the 'enemy', the Germans and Japanese for example, while it is appropriate to vent feelings in that direction and for many it is necessary to release those emotions, I was more concerned with feelings much closer to home.

As I stood in the *Café Les 3 Planeurs* that day, I could look across at the *Café Gondrée* and sense the divide that existed, it was as if the road had formed a no-mans land. Slowly the more modern building that was the *Café Les 3 Planeurs* began to accumulate D Company memorabilia; the unwritten rule was that the café opposite was out of bounds, a hidden tension began to manifest itself between various groups of veterans, un-noticed by your run of the mill tourist.

My desire then and still today, is for differences to be put aside and when the day comes, the next generation, sons and daughters of proud soldiers, will be able to stand shoulder to shoulder, with not only relatives of any regiment but dare I say it even relatives of certain café owners. If this sounds naive, so be it.

The thoughts of division are soon put behind me as we get into the party spirit and start mixing with the guys. As we sit at the table French school children begin to arrive and thrust photographs and books in front of the veterans politely asking for their autographs in perfect English.

Signing autographs

It is strange watching your own father sign a photograph for a total stranger. It reminds me of a film star at a premiere or footballer outside a ground, the respect these kids gave was just as impressive, if not more, maybe the French education system had got it right when it came to giving priority to whom the real heroes were.

In no time it is mid-afternoon, the booze is kicking in and there is still another nine hours to go. I decided to go walkabout and sober up a little.

I left the café and walked across the bridge, which was now heaving with people. There was an air of chaos as traffic weaved amongst pedestrians who are basically ignoring the pavements. Every now and then a 1940's jeep passed filled with young men dressed in World War Two uniforms. Every detail, even down to badges and laces was correct, as was the history embedded in their brains. It varied between American and British regalia, the emblems on the jeeps matched the army. Most of the men were French, occasionally you would see some British guys playing the part.

As I approached the end of the bridge I glanced to my right and saw a small crowd of people gathered around my Dad's gun - a veteran, red bereted and blazer, was giving a brief lecture, arms pointing in various directions sharing his moment of glory.

I smiled to myself and suddenly realised that only two structures being admired by the tourists are original: My Dad's gun and the Café Gondrée.

The bridge everybody was making such a fuss about was a replica, the local authorities had replaced the original Pegasus Bridge a few years earlier to accommodate increasing heavy traffic and to allow larger ships to pass through into the port of Caen a couple of miles upstream.

I left the bridge and turned north and began walking along the east bank of the Caen in the direction of the sea. I quickly passed the floating La Peniche Restaurant permanently moored to the bank. For a number of years John Howard had hosted a private meal for the veterans here before conducting the ceremony at a quarter past midnight each June 6th. This year, due to the ever increasing number of veterans and hangers-on, he had hired the Town Hall for the commemorative meal.

Within a few minutes the crowds were left behind me, the only

The original Pegasus Bridge rusts away

sounds were helicopters bringing in dignitaries.

After half a mile I was in the middle of storage park, a moment later I turned a corner and in front of me, nestling between abandoned lorries and oil barrels, was Pegasus Bridge.

There was a stillness about the place.

I felt as if I had stumbled upon a lost village in the middle of the Amazon Forest, although of course I knew it was there all the time, the sight of it excited me yet quickly filled me with an overwhelming sadness.

As I approached I noticed the rust, eating away at its very history and the weeds creeping up its side, trying to strangle the memories of those that had walked upon it.

I was about to step up on to it when I noticed a wreath of poppies tied to the front beam. It looked clean and fresh against the grime of the metal - I reckoned somebody had performed a quiet private ceremony that very morning.

Alone I stepped on the bridge and began to walk. I was tempted to become a school kid again and run across, rat-a-tat-tatting my pretend machine gun and lobbing hand grenades everywhere in some vain attempt to capture what it must have been like, but I changed my mind and tried to act my age.

In the distance a veteran was walking towards the bridge. Small in stature his jacket which was heavy with medals seemed to slow his ageing steps. I stepped off the bridge just as he arrived. I didn't recognise the badge on his beret or the crest on his blazer. I politely nodded and left him alone to his memories.

Rob Curling, TV journalist gets an interview.

As I began to walk away an old jeep arrived with four young lads aboard, dressed as G.I.s. In no time they were out of the jeep and rushing over to the old guy who was now standing on the bridge. I hoped he managed to grab a few moments of quiet reflection before the gang arrived and bombarded him with a thousand questions.

By now I had sobered up. The hot Normandy sun beat on my face and reflected on the canal as I walked back in the direction of the café. Soon I was amongst familiar faces; the crowd was now thicker than ever.

A woman who was supposed to be the model that inspired the cartoon 'Jane', a pin-up for all the armed forces 50 years ago, had arrived and was having her photograph taken with any veteran that wanted to embrace her - the queue was quite long! To my right the TV presenter Rob Curling was interviewing Charlie Gardner. I read later that Rob considered this day to be one of the most rewarding day's work he did in his entire career. I got to know him throughout the day; indeed he got me out of trouble a few hours later when he gave me an extra roll of film.

Dad, as usual, was knee deep in people, as was all of D Company. The queue to the bar was huge; I was gasping so I picked up a half full glass of beer from our table and pretended it was mine.

As I guiltily finished the beer, to my surprise I heard a young man say: 'Hello granddad, it's me!' as he tapped Dad on the shoulder.

For a moment I thought it was some joker trying to muscle in on the action and then I realised it was my nephew Gary, the son of my older brother Chris.

Dad stared at him trying to get his bearings and think how many grandkids he had - he has six - and then the penny dropped.

'It's Gary, Gary Parr!'

Dad had not seen Gary since shortly after his son's, Chris, death over twenty years ago, my sister-in-law Val had moved to Ashford, Kent to begin a new life and we had more or less lost contact.

Somehow Gary had heard about his granddad's exploits and out of the blue had turned up on the off chance of meeting him. Now a young man in his early thirties, he had obviously inherited his mother's looks, but his father's free spirit.

His hair was long, his clothes reminded me of an old sixties hippie, the backpack on his shoulder made it obvious that tonight he would be sleeping under the stars. He had a friend with him whom he introduced and I bought us all a cold beer.

It was a weird feeling talking to a total stranger who I had known and loved as a small child. He had come to rediscover his grandfather, my father and it was the same blood lines that cemented our relationship in those first few minutes.

We filled in each others histories of the past two decades and then delved into the story that was Pegasus Bridge.

Dad, still in shock with the fact he had met his long lost grandson, gave Gary as much attention as he could, but the pull of various interviews and instant reunions kept dragging him away – brother, Bob,

Bob with Dad and his eldest grandson, Gary – the first time Gary and Dad had seen each other in over 20 years.

and I did our best to fill in the spaces.

Afternoon drifted into dusk. Many of the veterans had already wandered back to their rooms to grab an hour's kip before the next onslaught at John Howard's banquet. Eventually, Dad, Bob, Claude and I made a move back to Claude's place to grab a shower and a change into something half decent for the dinner. We said goodbye to Gary in the knowledge that we would keep bumping into each other over the next twenty four hours.

By eight thirty we were respectfully filing in to the huge town hall at the T Junction at the end of the road that leads away from Pegasus Bridge in Bénouville. The local community, the Mayor especially, had spared no expense in making the venue a place fit for a banquet. At the end of the hall two huge flags, one French and one British stood proudly together framing a massive picture of John Howard.

It was the classic head and shoulders shot that appear in all the books and articles.

We found our place and tucked into the French cuisine and fine wine. For an hour it was the usual banter that we had experienced all day at the café, for sandwiches and beer read decent grub and red wine. After

Claude receives a special award for his
services to the veterans

a while the ceremonies began to kick into place. The Mayor as expected
was running the show. The guest of honour was of course John Howard.
Various people came forward and sang their praises - Major Howard
accepted them with grace and dignity. After a while he was asked to
come to the front and make some
presentations himself. Although he
had suffered physically since the
war he could still manage to
shuffle along with the aid of
walking sticks. The highlight of the
evening from a personal point of
view was when Claude and Renée
were asked to go forward to
receive a special award on behalf
of the NVA (Normandy Veteran's
Association) in recognition of all
the work and hospitality they had
given to numerous veterans over
the previous years. The look on
their faces made us feel especially
proud to have them as our close
friends.

I took several pictures that

John Howard, in reflective mood, listens
to another tribute

evening; I have included one of John Howard sitting alone in a reflective mood. A man behind him is reading aloud yet another message, yet Howard seems somehow miles away. Perhaps he was thinking of the old times, when D-Day was remembered in a quieter more poignant way, far from the madding crowd. I got the impression that this night was the culmination of a life-times work, yet now as he sat there, goal accomplished, I detected an inner sadness, perhaps this was due to conflicts between certain individuals - I will never know. He had now taken on the position of an emperor or even a royal which left him almost apart from the rest, this was not of his doing or intention, no doubt he wanted to be in the thick of it amongst his boys, but it wasn't happening. Occasionally somebody would pluck up courage and come over and speak to him and then drift away quickly. I was tempted to go over and say something to him that hadn't already been said, but I couldn't think of anything original, so pride left me rooted to my chair.

The evening in the hall was coming to an end; people were looking at their watches in anticipation of the Son et Lumiere light show down at the canal and the midnight ceremony.

I had drunk several glasses of fine wine, life was good and I was full of confidence. 'Dad, I want to go out the front and recite me poem!'

He looked at me for a brief moment.

'Have you got it in yer son?' he asked.

Reciting my poem at the 50th Celebration

I nodded, and without hesitation he walked over to the Mayor and began talking. The mayor looked at his watch and drew in a long breath. Dad haggled and before I knew it I was out the front with a microphone in my hand. The noise coming from the audience was a loud babble as dozens of conversations competed with each other. I spoke as loud as I could explaining that I had written this personal poem for my father to commemorate the 50th anniversary but I would like to share it with everybody tonight in the hope that it might bless them also

As I began the first line less than half were listening.

By halfway through most were giving me their full attention, more by politeness than anything else. As I was about to enter the most powerful part of the poem, I quoted the lines;

'Even today old mates still meet,
Talking until the small hours, drinking whisky neat.'

At this point most of them burst out laughing, it had obviously touched home. The trouble was it wasn't meant to be funny.

The next lines were missed by many of them but, hopefully, some were touched:

'A shoulder to cry on, still battles to fight,
And they heal each others wounds, deep in the night.'

When I finally finished there was silence. The Mayor came over and

Midnight ceremony with Son et Luminere

thanked me and I returned to my seat. Dad slapped me on the back and handed me a glass of wine, which I gulped and then I began to shake from head to foot - don't ask me why. Weeks later I discovered that my poem was on page 47 of the official D-Day 50th Anniversary Commemoration Souvenir Programme of Events - a publication that sold over 30,000 copies. To this day I have no idea how it got there.

A few minutes later we all began to leave the hall and make our way down the road, across the bridge and into the special grandstand that had been erected beside the memorial. A firework and light show began. This lasted just long enough to take us into the quarter past midnight ceremony that marks the exact time when No. 1 glider landed on June 6th.

The evening was nicely finished with a glass of vintage Calvados handed to me by a grateful local. By 1 a.m. Bob and I were safely tucked up in the spare bed of Claude's neighbour.

Opening Champagne bottles just after midnight. An act to remember George Gondré sharing his Champagne on June 6th 1944

Forget June 6th 1944 - THAT had been the Longest Day!

The 50th Anniversary - The Tragedy

Next morning I woke with a medium to large hangover. I rose at 9 a.m. - my tongue followed shortly afterwards. Bob and I grabbed a quick coffee from our hosts and wandered next door to Claude's, only to be met by the sight of half a dozen dishevelled Normandy veterans dressed in vests and braces - not a pretty sight!

For a couple of hours we wallowed in the friendly banter that only these guys can muster. At one point I produced some photocopies of my poem and gave them a copy each. Barry Tappenden read his father's copy out loud to the rest of us - we all listened politely.

By lunch time all the guys were spick and span ready for parade. Dressed in smart trousers and with their regimental jackets weighed down by a chest full of immaculate medals, in the correct order of course, and the icing on the cake - their red berets.

The walk from Claude's house to the bridge takes about ten minutes, for old soldiers, twenty. The best route is down to the canal and walk the towpath. Claude's place is more or less in direct line between Dad's gun and the château. If Dad would have been off target back in 1944 Claude's house would have been built in a crater.

As we walked along the canal bank people began to notice the advancing party. We could see ahead of us the heaving crowds around the cafés and the bridge. To get up onto the road we had to pass between the Café Gondrée and the famous claret and blue sign that announces Pegasus Bridge. As we passed between the two the command was definitely not 'eyes left'.

No time for a drink as Barry Tappenden began to get D Company into some kind of order. I must say at this point, that no other person, with the possible exception of John Howard's daughter Penny, has done more to preserve and forward the memories of the veterans of Pegasus Bridge. He has also managed to involve his own family in the proceedings - his daughter Chantelle was to lay a wreath for her grandfather Ted 'Ham and Jam' Tappenham and this dedication would be an ongoing commitment that saw her ten years later, after her grandfathers death still attending the ceremonies to push Arthur Roberts across the bridge in his wheelchair.

At that time Barry was a Warrant Officer in the Royal Air Force based at Biggin Hill, Kent and marched in his own uniform.

Within a short space of time the band struck up a tune and the flag waving and cheering began. The road had been cut off from traffic for some time as the crowd on the pavements grew in size. Across the bridge

Three helicopters land to depict the original
landing of the three gliders.

three helicopters came into land in the area of the plinths depicting the site of the three glider landings. In the distance a huge plane deposited dozens of paratroopers -jumping from a couple of thousand feet.

Over the years, as I look at my ever growing collection of photographs acquired from a variety of sources you can notice the slow and tragic decline in the physical appearance of the veterans – for many it follows a sad pattern: crutches – wheelchair – death.

This is nature at its harshest.

Whether in war or peace nature has no way of telling who the heroes were and who the villains were. The 'good guys' found out that, as old age approached, they were dealt the same hand as the 'bad guys'.

At the 50th anniversary I noticed that Wagger Thornton could still keep up with his mates on crutches – this was a man in his seventies, a man that had dealt with his wounds for decades. I was tempted to compare him against today's generation. I am sure the 'Nanny State' would soon not allow him to march on 'health and safety' issues but I dismiss the thoughts as negative and counter productive. Grey hair and grey moustaches contrast against red berets as proud men protrude their chests and march in defiance of their years.

Howard, Wood, Sweeney and Edwards are in this brigade – they look the part, they are the 'Officers Club'.

Beside them, just as proud, just as important, are the 'lads' –

Tappenden, Gray, Thornton, Parr, Gardener, etc. no better and no worse.

As this motley crew march across the bridge the cheering of the crowd rises to a crescendo as they reach the east side and begin to veer right passing my Dad's gun and into the compound that houses the memorial.

David Wood & Todd Sweeney lead the boys across the bridge.
Arthur Roberts on a stick ...

... while Wagger Thornton stays the pace – on crutches

As the veterans marched across, Bob and I had walked parallel to them on the pavement of the bridge – somehow we felt that we did not qualify to march behind them as some of the relatives did. As we hustled through the watching crowd at least I could get some side-on photographs, something I would not have got if we were behind them.

When we reached the far side we pushed our way through the gathering crowd and took our position up, standing either side of our father.

To this day I have no idea who makes the decisions as to who is allowed to lay wreaths at these ceremonies – all I know is that today Dad was laying one and we were to be involved.

The first wreath was laid, of course, by John Howard – a he bent over the Mayor and his deputy were either side of him, holding each arm.

The cameras click as Major John Howard lays, probably, his last
wreath before being confined to a wheel chair

It is a symbolic gesture; they are saying 'All those years ago, in your prime, you supported us – now we support you.

'Other wreaths were laid.

I was particularly blessed by Chantelle. Barry Tappenden's daughter laying a wreath, this was symbolising the next generation, the grandchildren, and them realising the power and the importance of what took place all those years ago.

A photograph sent to Dad in 1994 by Penny Howard/Bates.
On the back it simply says 'Daddy & Tod Sweeney'

Lastly it was time for the Parr trio to do their bit – unsure of what to do we stepped forward, a pace behind Dad and waited.

Bob and I stand either side of Dad while Ted gives us encouragement

After a second or two he made a gesture to us to stand level with him. I felt the presence of the crowd around me as I reached out my right hand and touched the wreath, while Bob, on the other side touched it with his left. In unison we proceeded forward, bent down and laid the wreath at the foot of the memorial – then we stepped back a pace.

Dad then stood to attention.

One step behind as Dad salutes

As he did, Bob and I took one step backwards and as Dad saluted we kept our arms to our side and bowed our heads.

A short silence followed, the hustle and bustle of the crowd had long since ceased, and then, less than a yard from my ears, a lone bugler sounded the 'Last Post'.

I have heard this tune many times, before and since, but this rendition touched more deeply than any other – its power enveloped me and touched my very soul – tears unashamedly rolled down my cheeks. For a brief moment I was allowed to experience the real grief that only true comrades can feel over the loss of their loved ones. Perhaps for the only time, I was allowed to enter a special place – sacred ground. I felt honoured and privileged.

Shortly afterwards, it was all over and we walked back to the Café Les 3 Planeurs and drank alcohol.

This is D-Day plus two – you try to talk to people perhaps you had neglected the day before. It's not easy when both days have in fact been parties – booze has its good points and its bad.

Slowly we drifted back to Claude and Renée's to continue the day away from the 'tourists'.

Bob and I needed to gather our things from next door and finish off the weekend with a farewell drink with Dad and whoever else managed to make it back.

Renée as always had prepared a feast for the boys.

We spent a pleasant hour saying our goodbyes – it takes at least that in France. Not only have you got to shake hands and share a few words with each individual but you also have to kiss them on each cheek at least twice.

The last person I kissed was Renée – she got extra kisses and hugs in appreciation for all the hard work she had done in making the boys so welcome over the past few days.

Claude along with Dad drove us the short distance to the ferry – more hugs, less kisses and we were on our way.

On board the party continued – veterans, surrounded by family and friends were holding court. By now regimental jackets were off, ties undone, and berets resting now at not quite the correct angle. Nobody cared – the parade was over – let the fun begin. This was the night ferry – our hotel for the night – we drank in the atmosphere for a couple of hours and then retired to our 'room', a row of reclining seats and tried to grab a couple of hours sleep amongst a chorus of snoring.

By 10 a.m. the next morning Bob and I were safely back in London, risking our lives cleaning windows - trying to get back to some sort of reality.

It was at dawn the following day when I received a phone call.

It was Dad sobbing uncontrollably: 'It's Renée, she's dead!' He kept repeating.

Eventually I managed to calm him and get the facts.

René – a few days later she had sadly died

Apparently in the middle of the night Renée had got up to get some water from the bottles in the basement. Half asleep and in the gloom she tripped on the steep stone steps and fell down several feet receiving fatal head injuries.

Forty-eight hours later Bob and I were on the night ferry to Caen travelling to Renée's funeral the following morning.

The atmosphere on the boat was quite and sombre, so different from the carnival of a few days previous. Half empty with mainly English tourists there wasn't a red beret to be seen. In a corner we saw Ted and Barry Tappenden and the rest of their family. We joined them for a beer. We shared our shock; we talked of the future and remembered the past.

The boat drifted into Ouisterham on a morning mist – there were no welcoming hugs and kisses.

The funeral was due to be held in three hours time at the church in Le Port - from the graveyard you can look downhill to the bridge and café. We spent an hour in the terminal drinking strong coffee and eating croissants before taking the hour long walk to the church.

Normally we would walk along the canal path, but today we took the main road. A little way along we caught up with a grey haired old man, the solitary figure was Charlie 'Gus' Gardner.

The three of us continued our journey reminiscing over the good times we had shared at Claude and Renée's house.

We had slowed the pace for Charlie, there was no rush.

For years Charlie had missed out on the action while he nursed his wife through a long illness. It was only after her death that he made his first visit to Pegasus in June 1993.

In Stephen Ambrose's book Charlie is depicted as one of the four 'likely lads', those in the thick of the action and trouble. Parr, Bailey and Gray all had long interviews with Ambrose but Charlie was unable to find the time. All his exploits were given 'second hand' - such was his reputation. The fire had long since left Charlie's personality – he was now a deeply melancholic man.

We arrived at the church with an hour to spare. We sat in a café opposite and watched all the old familiar faces begin to arrive. Finally two large cars arrived. The first contained Claude, Louise, Dad and Irene, Louise's daughter.

The second car contained the coffin.

Bob and I barely had time to contact them before everybody entered the chapel.

A long beautiful service commenced. The church was packed, everybody that was involved in the Pegasus Bridge project was present; such was the respect bestowed upon Claude and Renée.

Afterwards a few of us were invited back to the house. John Howard was there - on hearing of the tragedy he had delayed his return to England in order to attend. It was more or less the same crowd as the week before, plus a few relatives.

The Major sat quietly in a corner, he looked confused and concerned. He was aware of the men that had died in the decade since the fortieth anniversary, he ran through their names in his head: Glider Pilot Bowland, Colonel Taylor, Sergeant Ollis, Corporals Godbolt, Porter and Stacey, Privates Jackson, O'Donnell and Bleach, General Sir Nigel Poett, Sergeant-Major Jack Bailey, Majors Fox and Smith and now to that list he could add Renée Portier a woman who had given so much to his beloved veterans.

Bob and I stayed a while. We ate at the huge table where we had spent so many happy hours.

Before we left I managed to share a few words of condolence, firstly to Claude and then to Dad and Louise. In my Dad's eyes I saw fear and uncertainty – he was unsure of his future, only time would tell. After an hour we gave a tearful kiss goodbye and began the long walk back to the ferry.

As I left, I placed my empty glass on the table, as I looked at it I remembered all the good times we had around it, the wonderful meals Renée had prepared for us that took until midnight to finish and the laughter that filled the air – joy turned to sadness as I wondered what the future held for Dad and Louise and whether the good times could ever be captured again.

It was the last time I ever ate at the huge table.

Healing each other's wounds

In many ways this chapter is perhaps the most difficult and probably the most controversial in the whole book.

It begins with a reunion.

Diane and I had driven to Portsmouth and picked up Dad and Louise from the overnight ferry from Caen. It was the mid-nineties and they were still fit enough to make the journey from Vernon, sadly those days have long gone.

Usually we would drive them straight back to London and spend the week at our place catching up with family and friends, but today we drove along the South Coast to the town of Brighton

Dad had made contact with an old friend and had arranged to meet him at the entrance to the main pier.

We mingled with day-trippers for a while and then, from out of the crowd, a grey haired, grey bearded man introduced himself to Dad.

It was Charlie 'Gus' Gardner.

Charlie had spent the last few years nursing his terminally ill wife and now, after her passing away he felt it was time to move on and build some kind of future for his remaining years.

After brief introductions we walked back to the car and drove a few miles further along the coast to Charlie's bungalow, which nestled in the shadows of the South Downs just outside Lewes in Sussex

We had arranged to stay overnight yet we wasted no time in unpacking but chose instead to take the short walk through leafy country lanes to his local pub which overlooked the cricket green.

Slowly the real ale and the wine relaxed inhibitions and we all drifted into a world of nostalgia and anecdotes. Diane, Louise and I took backstage as we observed old comrades reliving old memories as only they can.

I tried to put myself in their position and imagined me meeting old friends 50 years on. What would we talk about?

Football games we had played in or watched - walking trips in the Lake District - getting drunk at parties in the Swinging Sixties? Perhaps the feeling would be the same, but compared to the experiences of these two, I doubt it.

After a while Charlie informed us that he had got a few things in and would knock up a meal back at his place, but I insisted in buying everybody a meal in the pub. A night in these surroundings and free bed and breakfast more than compensated the price of five pub dinners!

Eventually we drifted back to Charlie's bungalow and fatigue began to set in.

Louise retired to her bedroom followed shortly by Diane to ours.

Then the Scotch came out. I stayed with the boys for a swift double and then respectfully retreated to give them space.

It was the rest of the evening that inspired the following lines in my poem:

'Even today old mates still meet,
Talking 'till the small hours, drinking whisky neat.
A shoulder to cry on, still battles to fight.
And they heal each others wounds - deep in the night.'

Here we are entering the 'Holiest of Holies', sacred ground where special work is done. Every war has a million stories and a million ways 'that the healing has begun'.

When I wrote the poem for my father just before the 50th anniversary it was untitled and still is, yet Dad instantly referred to it as 'Healing' - I now know why.

I'm not sure what time Dad and Charlie stopped crying on each others shoulders - only they know.

At this point I must return you to the first page of this book. I dedicated it to Peace which sadly can only be achieved through War. This original thought contains two opposites, War and Peace. The cement that bonds the two is Sadness.

In my introduction I stated that my purpose of this book was to preserve and honour the achievements of our fathers (and mothers) and to learn from their experiences so that it may never happen again. In my small humble way I also hope that the remaining survivors will somehow through reading these words find a way to be healed of their remaining wounds.

Over the past couple of decades I have observed and tried to understand how and why so many people have returned to the shores of Normandy to commemorated and celebrate that momentous event that is known as D-Day. I have tried to put it into context with battles before and after that date.

Obviously pre-1st World War events have sunk into the pages of history books. 1914 to 1918 veterans can be counted on one hand. Yet it is a sobering thought that within the next twenty years the same fate will befall the veterans that proudly march or are pushed across Pegasus Bridge and countless other World War Two sites.

What have we learned since 1945? The world has been at war more

Healing takes on many forms ....
'Setting history in stone'

Above - John Howard stands proudly in the street named after him

Below – John Tillet at the opening of a road named after the regiment

or less ever since.

The politicians of course have become crafty and no longer use the

'W' word. Instead they use words like 'crisis', 'conflict', 'invasion' and even

Healing takes on many forms ....
'Retelling the stories'

Wally Parr's gun – affectionately known as
'Me Gun' !

'policing'.

You can spin all you like my grey-suited friends but in Suez, Korea. Vietnam, The Falklands and more recently The Gulf, Iraq and Afghanistan, men and woman are still risking their lives in the name of

War.

'Is there a difference between then and now?' I ask myself.

In my naivety I thought there was. On the face of it the driving force behind World War Two was one of survival, indeed preservation. Hitler presented himself as a force that would crush Europe and perhaps the whole world.

Yet when I observe from a distance with a different mind set, I see something sticking out like a sore thumb slap-bang in the middle of all this turmoil and it troubles me.

It's 'neutral' Switzerland.

'Big deal' you may say, why worry about a country that yodels and makes cheese.

Yet when I see a picture of Roosevelt and Churchill sitting either side of Stalin - I question the concept of 'good guys and bad guys'.

In war, the whole concept of right and wrong blurs into a grey mess.

For good guy Joe Stalin, read good guy Osama Bin Laden - providing they are bringing down the bad guys, be it fascist Hitler or commie Soviets.

Healing takes on many forms ......
'Re-enactment

Re-enactment preserves the memory. The 'future' connects with the 'past' - by living in the 'present'.

I look at the conflicts of the last century and see a simple pattern emerging - it is not preservation that prevails but power. Deep in the heart of all world conflict is money

Perhaps the dirtiest, most evil expression one can use when it comes to describing war is not genocide or blanket bombing but a 'Swiss Bank Account', as it bankrolls both sides.

The one question that haunts me, mainly because I will never find the answer is this: 'Who rules the rulers?'

Maybe at this point I should ease up on the heavy stuff and leave it to my good friends Michael Moore in the US and the likes of John Pilger in the UK.

Who will listen to an uneducated window-cleaner?

If I cannot heal the nations perhaps I should attempt to touch individuals. After all, it is these people that combine together to create nations.

Obviously there is the story of Wally Parr - just as close to home is

Healing takes on many forms ....
'Comradeship'

Army meets Navy – Dad and father-in-law, Bill Davies

my father-in-law Bill Davies. He spent the war in the Royal Navy.

My wife, Diane, and I were childhood sweethearts; we grew up together in the same block of council flats. Bill and Dad were neighbours for many years, there was occasional friendly banter about the war, Bill's Navy vs. Wally's Army - it never got deep.

Towards the end of Bill's life we spent a holiday with him in Spain. One night over a meal, for the first time ever, Bill opened up to me and shared his war experiences.

He described being on a ship that was torpedoed while in the Pacific. His mates at the back of the boat were killed, he survived. For a while he shared other experiences. In the end I paid more attention to the tears beginning to well up in his eyes and the trembling in his voice. Within ten minutes he excused himself and went to the toilet.

When he returned we discussed the paella.

A few years later, for Christmas, I gave Bill a framed copy of my poem. He thanked me, shook my hand and it remained on his living room wall until he died.

I've even learnt lessons from my own generation.

We have life-long friends who live in Gosport Hampshire, Iris and Pete Jenkins. On one visit recently I decided to make a trip to the D-Day museum a couple of miles along the coast at Southsea. The girls went shopping while Pete and I decided to do a gentle pub crawl to the museum.

After about our third beer it suddenly occurred to me to ask Pete about his Dad's wartime experiences. As he spoke I saw a tension release in his face.

For many months he had heard me rattling on about Wally Parr this and D-Day that and now it was his turn. He quietly and calmly informed me that his father was a Bevin Boy. I had a vague inclination what this meant but he continued to educate me.

Apparently the Ministry of War implemented a policy that dictated that a certain number of able bodied men should not be called up for action but instead would be conscripted to work in the nations coal mines.

The lottery result was decided by the last digit of your National Health number.

Pete's Dad spent five years sweating his bollocks off for the war effort. He probably worked harder than the average squaddie but never heard a shot fired in anger.

In retrospect, no coal meant no industry, along with countless other men and women he was digging for victory.

Pete was proud of his Dad and rightly so.

We ended the conversation with Pete commenting that is was many years before the Government recognised the value of the Bevin Boys and allowed them to march with the rest of the war veterans on

Remembrance Sunday.

Healing takes on many forms ....
'Remembrance'

Sister, Pat, her husband, Jim, and Dad
visiting Den Brotheridge's grave.

As we go deeper the healing gets closer and more personal.

At the ripe old age of 41 I was accepted to run in the London Marathon. Ever since attending the first race ten years before I was determined to complete it before I was 40 - I was a year out.

The night of my acceptance I rang my Dad, he was delighted. Within an hour he was back on the phone to me. He couldn't believe the coincidence, Barry Tappenden, son of 'Ham and Jam' Ted, was also running in the same race. Dad had already been on the phone to John Howard and told him that two of D Company's sons were running to probably raise money for the NVA.

That night I slept uneasily.

The following morning I drove the short distance to Dad's place. As I entered the room, he could see that I was troubled.

'I don't want to run the marathon for D Company Dad - I want to run it for me!'

He stared at me not knowing how to react.

'For once forget the bloody war and be proud of me!' I cried.

Dad stood up and walked halfway across the room inviting me to meet him halfway.

I reciprocated and we met in the middle of the room and embraced. Before he spoke we wept simultaneously. 'Of course I'm proud of yer, you silly bastard, you know that!' I knew he was genuine, he spoke Cockney not posh, 'Get out there and do yer best, that all you can do', he continued.

Healing takes on many forms ....
'Commemoration'

Every picture ....

.... tells a story

We both learnt a valuable lesson that day.

As a teenager growing up in the Swinging Sixties I had been told by a number of people that what my generation needed was a 'damn good war'.

I was beginning to learn that perhaps the people that told me these things were transferring their guilt and hurt onto me, this was the only way they could ease their pain.

I transferred my own hurts and energies into getting fit for the marathon.

In the spring of 1991 I stood in Greenwich Park ready to give it my best. As the sounds of 'Chariots of Fire' rang out through the loudspeakers 20,000 runners braced themselves for the off. My family and friends were yards from me, I could feel their presence.

As the cannon blasted away from the Greenwich Observatory, heralding the start of the race, there was only one voice I heard above all the mayhem;

'Oi son,' it began, 'by the way I'm proud of yer!'

I ran the marathon in 4 hours 26 minutes - crap time by most standards - but I did it.

I raised eighteen hundred quid for a local hospice. It was similar to the one that cared for my brother Chris until his death from Multiple Sclerosis.

I ran the marathon for my brother – I wrote this book for my Dad.

So where do we go from here?

I have examined the terminology of war and delved deep to ascertain my own interpretation.

My generation, the baby boomers, look back on recent conflicts like The Falklands and are shocked to realise that more soldiers have committed suicide since returning from that war, than the number of deaths while fighting. Somehow in 50 years time I can not see veterans commemorating events that were orchestrated by a Prime Minister who thought she was Winston Churchill!

Likewise the napalm bombing of Vietnamese villages and the 'shock and awe' bombing of Moslem cities will eventually rot the pages of history books that rarely tell the truth. I have the utmost respect for men and women that fought in these conflicts and I do not doubt their bravery for one second – but I am not sure we will be marching and holding ceremonies for these events in the distant future.

Meanwhile old men in their eighties struggle to come to terms with their war memories.

I knew a man who refused to buy anything Japanese right up to his death. Such was the pain inflicted by the barbarism of his war

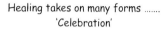

Healing takes on many forms ....
'Celebration'

For Ted Barwick (above 4th right) and his brothers it was getting involved (Honiton 1984).
Below Ted meets Arthur Roberts, Wagger Thornton and Ted Tappenden while Brother, Bob, videos.

treatment.

Many men cannot forgive others because they cannot forgive themselves. They tell themselves that perhaps they could have done more to save a stricken comrade - again there must have been countless incidents of so called 'friendly fire', brothers shot by brothers.

A million stories - a million ways to be hurt.

They must look back on the world and ask 'was it worth it?' My prayer is that each person may find a way to be healed. It may entail getting drunk with an old comrade through the night - or it could be the simple act of laying a single poppy in a foreign field far from the maddening crowd.

For others it will be the public display of marching, chest full of medals, to the sound of a brass band and cheering on-lookers.

Whatever it is my friend, please do it.

Soon all the veterans will be gone.

Personally their experiences have taught me this:

A Pacifist sees a tank, stands firm, and it runs him down.

A Peace Lover sees a tank, stands firm, and if the tank continues, picks up a PIAT gun and takes the bastard out.

There is a big difference.

A War-Monger sees a tank 2,000 miles away, invades the country and takes it out – 'just in case.'

The singer Joni Mitchell wrote in her masterpiece 'Woodstock' that she saw 'bomber planes turn into butterflies'.

One day I believe this will happen, but only by the actions of peace lovers not pacifists.

Even one of the greatest peace lovers of all time, Jesus Christ, knew that on certain occasions he had to take violent action - smashing up the tables of the money lenders in the temple for example - to achieve his ultimate aim of Peace on Earth.

You will often hear the expression 'Hawks and Doves'.

Perhaps there is a middle way.

Could it be that we were all meant to be 'Doves' - but with a sting in our tails?

PEACE BE WITH YOU.

Healing takes on many forms ....
'Memorial'

Penny Howard/Bates looks on at the
unveiling of her father's bust in June 1995

Bridge over Troubled Water

It is always difficult to actually pin-point an event or indeed a time when you can say: 'that is where it all went pear-shaped.'

Up to the 40th anniversary everything was 'hunky-dory'. I asked Penny, John Howard's daughter what the atmosphere was like in the old days, the post-war years when it was all quiet in the 'Eastern Front'. I have reproduced an email she sent to me, it sums up perfectly those early carefree days: *'David Wood actually went back with my father to Bénouville in 1946 – I've got a couple of nice photographs of them, Also Jim Wallwork went with my parents – our two families were very friendly when Jim lived in Manchester before moving to British Colombia.*

Jim went quite often in the fifties with my Dad – nice photograph of he and Dad in the Café with dear Georges Gondrée having champers in 1954 (10th anniversary). In the 1950's the Sandhurst Staff College took a group of cadets every June, in theory to study the battle tactics (in fact to have a beano). So Dad was very involved with that doing lectures etc. he adored it because he was back in the army, officer status restored.

This continued well into the 60's and so the D-Day Anniversaries were very much officers only, because the ordinary folk just couldn't afford to travel abroad in those days. I went over in 1947 with my family for the first time and then went again in 1954 when I was ten (we flew with the car, Barry! This amazing aircraft that opened up at the front for about 4 or 5 cars – those were the days!) There are photographs of us by the pond on the LZ looking at what was a sizeable chunk of glider left.

I went again when I was 15 on my own for 6 weeks to learn French – that's when I stayed with the Gondrées and really got to know them….. I can recall it being so quite there, and so primitive in the living arrangements. I recall Jack Bailey calling in for a few days. A chap called Gordon Ramsey used to go then too for the D-Day anniversary. Todd or David would show occasionally but they were posted abroad so much of the time then.

The Staff college jollies suffered from the 'cuts' of the early seventies and ended much to my fathers chagrin, but then the Swedish Navy took over the lecture tours because it was the Cold War and apparently the Normandy coastline was very similar to the Swedish coast opposite the Russian one! The Swedes continue going to this day – I can't recall when Daddy met Peter Wetterberg but it was early on. My Father would stay at the Café Gondrée in those days of course, when Madame Gondrée was alive – she adored us all and I loved her dearly .The Staff

College chaps would keep going there on their own accord after that – always a good crowd of old friends would turn up each year – it kind of gets you like that.

Those were the glory days sitting in the sun outside the Café Gondrée. I went again when I was 18 with Dad that would have been 1962. Then they made the film 'The Longest Day' and that really was what started the ball rolling. My parents went over in 1962 for the filming and bless her; I think it was the highlight of my Mum's life, living it up with all those stars. She came home and told me she'd met 'ever such a handsome young man named Sean Connery, he's going to be James Bond in a film soon and if it's a success they may make another one....'

Stephen Ambrose, then a history lecturer specialising in military matters, brought a group of his friends over and visited Pegasus Bridge in 1982 and met my Father – it changed Steve's life and that's when he decided to write the book. It came out for the 40th anniversary in 1984 – the rest is history!

I went over again in 1984 with my youngest daughter Kerry and Dad rented a small place in Ouistreham because the Wallwork clan were coming over from Canada. Not saying it wasn't exactly the Ritz, but Jim got out of their car and said "Bloody hell John, I didn't realise we were staying in a garden shed!!" That stretched the old man's bonhomie a bit.

1984 was when the men turned up in force for the first time – it was a wonderful re-union. I can remember being really moved because these guys who hadn't seen my Father for 40 years would snap to attention at the sight of him and salute, saying "Sah!" Amazing!

I think that was the first time I met your Father. Arlette and Georgette Gondrée would bring Champagne over the LZ at midnight on the 5th for the toast, but their mother started the tradition. My Father would book the floating restaurant 'La Peniche' and pay for the dinner for all the men and their wives and the Gondrée girls, and later the Mayor of Bénouville too. That's when the meal on the evening of the 5th began. Happy Days!'

Happy days indeed. Undoubtedly the combination of the 40th celebrations and the Ambrose book changed the atmosphere at Bénouville forever. When ascertaining whether it was a good thing or a bad thing depends on which way you view it. For the quiet dignified group that attended on and off for the previous 40 years, the crowds that attended in 1984, it must have been quite a shock.

But for others it was a revelation – as Penny recalled men were reuniting for the first time in decades and the public at large were beginning to recognise the importance of the events that took place in 1944.

When I made my first trip way back in 1986 the atmosphere at the Café Gondrée couldn't have been more convivial. I was welcomed in the café by Arlette, even being taken into the 'inner sanctuary' out the back – any friend or relative of the boys from Pegasus was a friend of hers - but not for long.

I suppose in the end it all boils down to egos and personalities. It is not so much what came first, the chicken or the egg – but what came first, the bridge or the café.

The obvious answer of course is the bridge. To all intents and purposes, if at the Western end of the bridge, back in 1944 there was a haystack, it would have gone down in history as the first haystack to be liberated. The objective was to stop the enemy advancing over a strategic bridge – not stopping them popping into a certain café for a strategic cup of coffee!

The beauty of the bridge and to a certain extent the café, is that they both give a focal point to concentrate on – unlike many other battle scenes, which often consist of non-descript fields or forest, with at best a nearby cemetery that enables loved ones, comrades and visitors a place to concentrate their grief.

With Pegasus Bridge and the café you have the potential to have a setting that is both historical and interesting – sling in the odd museum and you have a darn good day out.

As the crowds increased throughout the 1980s so did the business profits at the café. Maybe, in my opinion, Arlette began to think that perhaps she and her café were becoming more of an attraction than the bridge itself.

The life of the café was now entering a period of its history that was to prove more turbulent than its occupation in World War Two.

The café was original bought by George and *Thérèsa* Gondrée in the 1930s. George Gondrée died in the 1960s but not before he enjoyed a long rewarding life entertaining the small band of veterans that made the annual pilgrimage. The Gondrées also owned the land alongside the café. In 1972 they leased the land, under a 25 year contract, to the D-Day Commemoration Committee for a museum to house the many artefacts that were being provided by the veterans and their families.

The original museum was opened on June 6th 1974 – the 30th anniversary. The driving force behind the scheme was Raymond Triboulet who presided over the D-Day Commemoration Committee, which had paid for the construction of the new building. Triboulet was a former minister and the first Sub Prefect after the liberation. The museum was inaugurated by General Sir Richard Gale; General Omar Bradley 1st American Army Commander was also present along with John Howard and a few others.

On that day Bill Millen's bagpipes where among the many extra articles donated,

The Gondrées had three daughters, Arlette and Georgette, both alive on the night of the invasion, and Françoise, born in November 1944. Their mother died a short while after the 40th celebration leaving the three daughters in charge. Not surprisingly Françoise didn't hold the same vision as her elder sisters and by 1988 wanted out. This sparked a legal battle began between the sisters – the elder girls wanted to preserve it as it was, while Françoise allegedly was not so keen.

The summer of 1988 saw the café boarded up as the girls locked horns – the atmosphere on June 5th/6th was subdued.

In early December the lawyers had decided the outcome of ownership would be decided by auction. Ancient French law decided that the auction should be conducted under 'burning candle conditions' – this simply meant that the last bid placed before the candle expired was the winner.

It took place in a solicitors office in nearby Caen – Arlette's original bid of £28,500 was soon bettered by Françoise's £31,500 and she feared the price would end up much higher – in the end the price at the end reached a massive £160,000, fortunately Françoise's last gasp bid of an extra £5,000 was made a fraction of a second after the candle went out and the solicitor deemed Arlette the successful bidder!

I have newspaper cuttings of the time showing Dad and Ted Tappenden celebrating outside the boarded-up café arm in arm with Arlette and Georgette, the headline reads:

'Saved – French 'shrine' for our liberating Tommies.'

In the article Arlette expresses her relief and refers to her 'Uncle' John Howard and how pleased he will be – reminding people he was not present due to an impeding operation.

The balance of £160,000 plus costs would be needed to be raised by the new-year – readers were invited to send donations to the Normandy Veterans Association (Café Gondrée) Fund, no doubt the target was reached and the NVA still continues to do good work to this day.

Relationships between the veterans and the Gondrée family were presumably at an all-time high – everybody should have been looking forward to the next big event in 1994 – the 50th anniversary.

Unfortunately the French authorities put a spanner in the works when, in 1993 they decided to replace the original Pegasus Bridge with a brand new replica – quite simply the old bridge was worn out and could not handle the increasing heavy traffic passing over it and the ever widening shipping passing underneath it.

April 1994 – The new bridge is lowered into position ready for
the 50th anniversary celebrations

Naturally the veterans didn't want the old boy melted down for scrap – they would have liked it to be preserved and kept in the immediate area. In contrast Arlette Gondrée had a much better idea – ship it over to England and place it in a military museum. This is only my own personal speculation, but I feel her thinking may have been that if it was placed on the opposite bank it may have drawn the crowds away from her beloved café.

She was not only fighting the British boys on this issue but also many of her French counterparts

When I arrived for the 50th anniversary to see a brand new bridge spanning the canal and the boys drinking in the Café Les 3 Planeurs opposite, I knew the writing was on the wall. The Ox and Bucks boys had won a partial victory at that point – the original bridge was still in Normandy but lay rusting in an storage park half a mile away on the east bank.

The 50th anniversary came and went and by 1997 relationships had reached the point where the boys spent all their time seated at the café opposite, Les 3 Planeurs. As new photographs and newspaper cuttings became available they were placed on the walls of their new 'home'.

Around this time things began to really hot up. The original museum was built on land, now owned by Arlette, and leased to the D-Day Commemoration Committee for 25 years in 1972. Under French law a landowner can take ownership of any building at the end of a land lease so another bitter battle was about to erupt, not only over the future of the original museum but also as to who owned the artefacts housed within.

In the original brochure of the new Pegasus Memorial Museum there is a short succinct paragraph depicting the period between the closing down of the old museum and the opening of the new, it reads; 'Certain differences with the owner of the land on which the old museum was built forced the museum to close its doors in 1997, leaving a vacuum for the veterans, their families and friends.'

The rift between Arlette and D Company was not the only apparent division. In the two cafés facing each other sat men on opposite side of the fence – in Café Gondrée were the 7th Battalion Paras, on the other side sat Howard's men. I have in my possession an article that appeared in one of the national dailies, the headline reads;

'Yes, we'll bun-fight them on the beaches.'

Perhaps the journalist wrote the headline with tongue in cheek – all I know is, in my opinion the rest of the article is confusing, to say the least.

There is one picture of Arlette in front of the café, the caption below says: 'FORCES DARLING: Arlette Gondrée helps tend Paras after the Battle of Pegasus Bridge.'

When you read the article, and if you didn't know the history, you could easily get the impression that it was the Paras that liberated the bridge.

'I know my boys will not let me down,' she says.

'We are prepared to mount a show of strength – a second Normandy landing – if needs be.' Claims one of the proud and strong Paras supporting her.

The article gives the impression that her 'wicked landlords' (my words), the Normandy Landing Committee who own the museum next to her, want to throw her out of the café which of course was nonsense.

The opposite side of the story is given only five lines:

Newspaper clippings from the day

'Raymond Triboulet, the committee's 91-year-old president said: "With the collaboration of the English we are going to do everything so that the landlord, Madame Gondrée, is relieved of control".'

In the confusing article there appears to be two landlords – thankfully the 91-year-old landlord won the day and didn't evict her from her home as the article suggested would happen – but did manage to build a museum elsewhere.

Around 1996 to 1997 the boys of D Company were fighting battles on two fronts – always dodgy, ask Adolf – their beloved bridge was lying rusting a mile or so away and if they were not careful there would be nowhere to keep the artefacts and preserve their memory.

If the bridge was to be preserved and the new museum was to be built, money and organisation would be needed.

Many charitable bodies already existed. The Trust to Preserve the History of the 6th Airborne Division into Normandy, being one of them. The Patron was none other than His Royal Highness the Prince of Wales KG. KT. PC. GC. GCB. AK. QSO. ADC(P). The Vice-Patrons were Excellency's, Major-Generals and our old friend Raymond Triboulet OBE. The Chairman was Lieutenant-General Sir Michael Gray (no relation to

Billy!) KCB. OBE. FBIM. F Inst D. My Dad was involved in all of this and being resident in France had his ear very much to the ground. I have kept numerous letters sent to him over the years from some very high ranking officials, including Brigadier J.F. Ricketts CBE. ADC. Sir Michael Gray and Viscount Montgomery – I am honoured that they were all sent and received on first-named terms.

Another body formed around that time was the 'Association de Defense pour la sauvegarde du pont Pegasus et de son site Bénouville (Calvados)' – roughly translated it says: 'Keep the Bridge in France!'

The English president was chosen to be none other than Corporal Wally Parr AC/DC OBE (Old Big 'Ed)!

Lieutenant-Colonel Neville Jackson, Vice-Chairman Airborne Assault Normandy Trust, wrote to me giving me an example of the role my Father played: *'Barry, When Mrs. Arlette Gondrée-Pritchett was appealing against the French State's ownership of the Café Gondrée, and using the name of British veterans in support your father wrote (with assistance/backing) the letter below to the Prefect of Lower Normandy. Her appeal either failed or was abandoned!'*

ASSOCIATION DE DEFENSE POUR LE LA SAUVEGARDE
DU PONT PEGASUS ET DE SON SITE BÉNOUVILLE (CALVADOS)

From the English President
Wally Parr,
27 Rue de Bizy
27200 VERNON
13th October 1999

Monsieur le Prefet de la Region Basse Normandie Prefet du Calvados

Dear Monsieur le Prefet.

CAFÉ GONDRÉE

I was in the first glider to land at Pegasus Bridge on D-Day, and for many years I have been a member of veterans' associations as well as the English President of the French Bridge Association. I am also a resident in France ....

The letter then explains to the Prefet that contrary to some reports there was much discord among various bodies regarding state ownership of the Café Gondrée. It then goes to some length to explain the breakdown of certain relationships during the previous few years, especially over the positioning of Pegasus Bridge. The letter ends by saying that various newspaper cuttings were included to verify the situation.

If you read the letter you don't have to be a genius to work out that the only part of the letter that Dad was actually responsible for, was his signature – but at least it produced the desired result, as all action taken by Mrs. Gondrée-Pritchett was either abandoned or fell on stony ground.

That was in 1999 when the issue was over who owned the café – but the most fierce battle took place back in 1997.

On the 31st March both The Times and The Independent carried stories relating to the impending confrontation that would occur on June 6th that year when the lease on the old museum would expire. I quote: 'But Arlette Gondrée is unsentimental, "My lawyers and a locksmith will be there at 8 a.m. on 6th June and they will have to leave" she warned, "the building is in desperate need of repair and I am fed up with 25 years of bad behaviour." Mrs. Gondrée vehemently opposes a proposal to develop the museum into a memorial park –"some kind of Disneyland" as she refers to it.'

'I do not want to see commercialism,' she says, 'it is the café that is the living memorial and the real museum'.

All very interesting – Dad, at this time, was keeping me informed with telephone calls and sending me newspaper cuttings – the reference to Disney Land made him think that the whole story was becoming a bit of a 'Mickey Mouse' saga.

Indeed, Arlette, a bailiff and a locksmith were there on 16th September for what the press were to describe as a 'dawn raid'. Marc Jacquinot and the Mayor of Bénouville – tipped off by the press – were there to meet them and to stop the seizure of the museum. The pictures in the British National Press the next day were not of her waving from a first floor window at the café, as they were the previous March, but instead it showed her stumbling over a low wall in the resulting scuffle.

Yet despite all the conflicts, the bridge stayed in France and eventually ended up in the grounds of a brand new museum along with many of the original exhibits, housed on the opposite bank to the café.

Sadly Major John Howard never saw the culmination of all his campaigning. He died on May 5th 1999 aged 86.

He was given half page obituaries in both the Times and the Telegraph. The latter quoted his daughter Penny as saying: 'He was one of the few men that changed history – yet he would reply to her and say modestly that he was simply in the right place at the right time and there were many just us brave.

Both articles contained many tributes – The Times carried a picture of him beside the Bridge, with the café on the opposite bank in the far distance.

John Howard obituary (The Times May 7th 1999)

The Telegraph showed him alongside Richard Todd the actor that played him in the film 'The Longest Day.'

He died thirteen months before the new museum was opened – he missed out on the memorial that would preserve his epic feat for decades to come.

John Howard DSO and the Croix de Guerre avec Plume – rest in peace.

It was in February 2000 that Dad found himself taking one of the slowest walks of his life – The Daily Express carried a full page article showing him walking in front of the old bridge as it was

Major John Howard

being towed from it place beside the storage park to its new position a mile or so up the canal in the grounds of the soon to be opened museum. The headline read: 'Pegasus Bridge takes wing to new place of honour.' The main picture shows Dad, wearing jacket, beret and medals walking in front of the bridge - a smaller picture is of Arlette, the article gives the impression they are on the same side - don't believe everything you read in the papers!

Dad with a picture taken on the day the bridge was moved to the new museum

Not only were there several newspaper reporters present but also a couple of TV and satellite companies.

'I worked at giving interviews all afternoon,' recalls Dad, 'I sweated me nuts off - a talk here, a photograph there and all I got out of 'em was a couple of cold beers.'

It's ironic, millionaire 'celebrities' charge a small fortune for appearance money - yet a guy who could have done with a few bob gets bugger all. Having said that, in all honesty, the only thing Dad wanted was publicity for the bridge and the museum - the beers were a very much appreciated bonus.

Thankfully by the time June arrived the museum was built and the bridge was safely housed in its gardens. Prince Charles having flown down

The crowds await the arrival of Prince Charles at the opening of 'Pegasus Memorial' in June 2000

by helicopter from attending the 60th anniversary of the evacuation at Dunkirk formally opened the museum on June 4th 2000.

Myself, Bob, son-in-law, Gary, and my nephew, John, decided to make a 24 hour trip to witness the opening. It was the usual overnight ferry and a march up the canal in the early hours and meet Dad at the café. The walk along the canal is usually a pleasant stroll but this time it was slightly more hard going due to the fact that Gary had won £250 on the one armed bandit on the boat and it was in pound coins! He kept them in a carrier bag and we had to take turns in carrying the bloody things. The day was good; more so for Gary and John as this was their first trip. The crowd was huge and we had no chance of getting anywhere near the museum although we did get to the front of the crowd to see Prince Charles march past and perform the official opening.

After the ceremony we all met again at the café and did the usual. Around late afternoon I noticed many of the veterans beginning to wander off in the general direction of the châteaux. Eventually the only veteran left was Dad – I asked him what was happening and he told me that they were all invited to a reception at the Châteaux de Bénouville with Prince Charles that evening and it was then that I saw his gold embossed invitation sticking out of his top pocket. I asked him why he was not going and he told me it was more important to stay and have a beer with his boys as he hadn't seen us for a while. This deeply touched us all and led me to getting in another round! It was on this day that I met an amazing guy called Geoff Baulk – here is yet another example of the next generation picking up the vision of Pegasus Bridge. Geoff

MEM○RIAL PEGASUS

RANVILLE-BENOUVILLE

lived near Bletchley Park, the home of the famous Enigma code breaking story, and had been fascinated by the Second World War story from an early age. When, at the age of 16, he was asked at school to read a history book of his choice for a school project, he chose 'Pegasus Bridge' by Stephen Ambrose. His parents David and Linda had told him stories about his relatives in the Second World War and this book only added to his enthusiasm. At this point he became a volunteer at Bletchley and started collecting memorabilia. Somehow he managed to make contact with my Dad and in April 1997 he made his first trip to the bridge and met all the boys for the first time. According to Geoff's dad, David, the young lad was moved to tears when he stood upon a piece of living history and actually met his heroes, including Major Howard, he later described it as 'one of the greatest days of his life'.

Bletchley Park - the home of the museum run by Geoff Baulk and his parents

Geoff, with the support and encouragement

Dad 'squares up' to his old sparing partner 'Tich' Rayner at the opening of the new museum in June 2000

of his parents, then set about putting together a unique exhibition dedicated to D Company, in the grounds of Bletchley Park. I visited this labour of love last year and was amazed at the quality and diversity of the exhibits – one of my favourites is a life-sized model of Wagger Thornton firing a PIAT gun. On the day I visited Tich Rayner was there in his full gear ready to give any visitor a personalised tour of the museum. Tich also makes regular visits to local schools and gives the youngsters talks on his exploits.

David and Linda give much of their time to the project and Geoff is now so involved that he has joined the TA and has also done a sponsored parachute jump to raise funds for the building of the new museum in Bénouville.

In 1998 he bought a genuine 1942 Ford jeep and was in Bénouville with it on the day we met him at the opening of the museum. He was dressed in full World War Two uniform with every detail perfect. I spent some time chatting to him about how he got involved. As the evening drew to an end we said our farewells to Dad and Geoff, but when Geoff realised we were walking back to the ferry and carrying all that money he offered to give us a lift back to the terminal in his open topped jeep – it is an experience I would recommend to anybody!

It was around this period that Dad met up with a couple that were to become close friends with him and Louise and provide a lifeline between Vernon and Bénouville. Their names were Terry and Hilary Bond. Terry had become captivated with the whole Pegasus Story when he saw the Charles Wheeler interview for the 50th anniversary. Terry and Hilary

Hilary and Terry Bond share a drink with Louise and Dad

then decided to visit Normandy and for a number of years attended the D-Day celebrations while watching the veterans from a distance. It was in 1999 that Terry finally plucked up the courage to approach Dad and say hello. They hit it off immediately and in no time Terry and Hilary were visiting Dad and Louise in Vernon and their circle of Pegasus friends spread far and wide. On a number of occasions after this Terry thought nothing of arriving on the ferry at dawn, checking into his hotel and then making the two hour drive to Vernon to pick up Dad and Louise and take them straight back to the bridge. At the end of his stay he quite happily did the same return trip. Bob, Pat and I are eternally grateful for the love and help that Terry and Hilary gave to Dad and Louise.

Along with John Howard, another man never to experience the new museum was his old friend Stephen Ambrose who sadly passed away in the autumn of 2002 without ever being able to make a visit.

His international reputation had grown considerably after he wrote his epic work 'Band of Brothers' - post publication he found himself rubbing shoulders with the likes of Stephen Spielberg and Tom Hanks. Their film 'Saving Private Ryan' adding to the world-wide interest in D-Day.

At a memorial service held outside the D-Day museum in New Orleans, former president George Bush Senior was one of the many mourners who paid tribute. Ambrose was primarily a war historian, but above all he loved to tell stories - including one about a bridge in Normandy.

His son Hugh Ambrose summed up his father perfectly when he said: 'he earned every dollar that ever crossed his palm, but I'm not sure he ever worked a day in his life.' That's the kind of job I would like!

Personally I would like to give thanks to a man who gave a bunch of ageing veterans a new lease of life and also for taking my Father to New Orleans and allowing him to spin a yarn or two.

As I end this chapter I feel deeply troubled – I have called it 'Bridge Over Troubled Water' and I have tried to the best of my ability to share the conflicts between various parties.

My wife, quite rightly, has reminded me of the words in my poem that say: 'Put anger, and hatred and bitterness aside.' When I wrote those words I wasn't only referring to the Germans or the Japanese – but I was also talking about the in-fighting between, not only French café owners, but also various groups of English veterans. I am very much aware that the generation that fought so hard to give us the freedom that we have, and all too so often take for granted, will one day be gone - and when that day does arrive, I want to be able to stand shoulder to shoulder with fellow sons and daughters of these brave men and be united in joint respect. Therefore perhaps we should all let bygones be bygones and start afresh – what happened on Pegasus Bridge back in 1944 is far, far bigger than any of our petty squabbles.

The Lull before the Storm

I suppose one of the motivations for writing this book came from my great-niece, Gemma. In her late teens, like most kids of her generation, she surfs the Internet constantly - even this reference would be alien to most men of D Company! One day in a moment that bordered between boredom and curiosity, she typed the words; 'Wally Parr Pegasus Bridge' into a search engine and was astonished at the number of hits she recorded. On several hundred sites there were recorded references, not only to my father but numerous other connections, all relating to D-Day and events surrounding Pegasus Bridge. She immediately rang me and it was then that I realised that the next generation was ready to hear and listen to the story I wanted to tell.

While on the phone to Gemma she told me to go to a site called Wild Bill Guarnere - it is a military-based site that refers to a character from 'Band of Brothers' and deals with many aspects of the military especially World War Two. As she watched over a particular chat room she notice that two guys were comparing 'Wild Bill' to Wally Parr in Pegasus Bridge – she immediately logged in and introduced herself as the great-grand daughter of the very man they were discussing. The guys were Yanks and in true American style went totally over the top typing in expressions like 'O my God!' 'Get out of here!' etc. The next day I logged in and informed the forum that I was thinking of writing about my father's exploits and when I received over a hundred replies from people all encouraging me to go for it and where could they buy a copy when it was finished, it was then that I knew that the time was right.

Over the past few years I have gathered a growing circle of friends through my involvement with D Company and this is largely due to the power and influence of the Internet. I asked two such friends, Danny Greeno and his dad Chris to email me telling me how they first got involved and what was their vision for the future – the response is both typical and exciting: *'Since childhood my father, Chris, had been interested in both world wars (his grandfather Albert, was killed on the first day of the battle of the Somme in 1916) and as a consequence we spent many family holidays in Northern France. We knew that Pegasus Bridge existed but we didn't know where and to what extent. During our family holiday in 1990 my Dad drove over the bridge by accident and vowed to return one June. He visited Normandy on the 50th anniversary but chose to go to Arromanches. Whilst watching the celebrations on TV he saw a lot said about Pegasus Bridge and decided to go there in 1996. On the ferry over he met a certain Ted Tappenden who seemed very welcoming and forthcoming with information and invited Dad to join in* most of the celebrations. Through Ted, Dad met Arthur Roberts and Tom Packwood. In 1999 after hearing so much about this wonderful place, I went with Dad. Sadly Ted had died earlier that year but I was lucky enough to meet Tom, Arthur, Dougie Allen, David Wood and a certain Wally Parr. I felt so welcomed by these men who had such great stories to tell. Dad and I have returned almost every year since and will so for as long as we can. We have a real love of Bénouville, not just the history but the place itself. A beautiful and tranquil place. Very much in contrast I imagine to 1944.

We have met many people there over the years and consider many to be friends. I decided two or three years ago to build a website dedicated to the men of D Company. I have been very lucky to have met many of these incredible individuals and although the museum is a great dedication to them, I worry that the memory of the men themselves will gradually fade over the years. My site (when eventually finished!) will be a pictorial dedication to the 180 men who fought and suffered to make Bénouville, Herouvillette, Escoville and many other places safe for future generations. I wanted to share my experiences, stories and many photographs of this place and the men associated with it to ensure that it is never forgotten.

The Internet has and is making the bridge more and more famous. The visitor numbers each year continue to increase. This in many ways is a good thing and need to continue for future preservation but............many of the tourists have not been fortunate enough to meet the men who made it famous and therefore are 'perhaps' missing the point a bit.

Personal accounts like Denis Edwards', Penny Howard/Bates' and Barry Parr's will help to educate what these men were really like. Funny, courageous, full of character and an absolute joy to know!

Tich Rayner spends much of his time touring schools to share his wealth of knowledge and experience which is FANTASTIC. I would like one day for my website (www.mypegasus.co.uk) to be used for educational purposes and enjoyment. I will be forever be searching for more information and hope that new books and websites will help to keep alive the memories and stories of such gems as Ted, Tom, Arthur, and Wally.'

It is embracing such enthusiasm as Danny Greeno's and his generation that inspired me to go for it!

Having found the motivation, I decided, along with my wife, Diane, to make a short visit to Dad in Vernon. My youngest daughter Sandra works for a local travel company that specialises in short breaks to Paris on Eurostar – we have used them many times, it is a good way to have a romantic break and also pop down to Vernon from Paris and take in a few hours with Dad and Louise.

I bought myself a smart brief case, some new shiny pens and pads and finally a Dictaphone tape recorder to interview Dad at his place – I looked like a 'proper writer' - all I had to do now was write!

After a good night in Paris we got the train out of Saint-Lazare and made the 50 minute journey to Vernon. We were knocking on the door in time for lunch – in my new bag I had bought the usual 'goodies' that you bring ex-pats, in Dad's case it is strong hard Cheddar cheese, he hates the Normandy soft stuff, best back bacon, (according to Dad the French pigs ain't the same) and lastly Steradent false-teeth cleaner, because the taste reminds him of England. For Louise we always bring her a couple of large bags of pear drops sweets – she tasted them in England and loved them and according to her, you can't buy them in Vernon, so she hands them out to her envious neighbours.

When we knocked on the door of their tiny apartment there was a look of utter surprise on both of their faces - true to form Dad had got the dates mixed up and thought we were coming for lunch on the following day. Diane and I breathed a sigh of relief as Louise is one of the worse cooks on earth, so we happily settled for eating the bacon we had brought followed by the pear drops for desert

Meanwhile Louise went into a panic because she hasn't done her hair or dressed up so she headed for the cupboard and proceeds to take large swigs of wine out of a huge plastic container – we had only been there five minutes and it was already shaping up into a rather interesting afternoon!

I began by informing Dad that he has been 'Googled' on the Internet, he immediately grabbed himself by the balls and says that it must be painful – I continued to tell him that if you hit a search engine his name comes up hundreds of times, at this point he went crossed-eyed and sarcastically said 'Wow!' I quickly realised that he was not into all this Internet stuff and resigned myself to simply telling him that he was more famous than he thought – this he grasped.

To the smell of bacon, I switched on my tape and Dad began to talk and talk and talk – for nearly two hours he shared his war story. I thought I knew it backwards – but from deep within came new stuff, and even the old familiar stories took on a new freshness as his yarn telling skills kicked into action. The real hero of the day was Diane as she struggled to keep Louise occupied a few feet away from us – in the background on the tape you can hear the girls occasionally singing Edif Piaff songs as the wine begins to flow.

Diane knows little French and there are only so many ways of showing Louise the dozen or so pictures of our grandkids. Now and then Louise would swoon over to us and tell me 'her beloved Wally is ze D-Day cockney ero!' – Dad replied with; 'Oui, mon cherie, mon poppet' and sent her on her way.

In the run up to the 60th anniversary Wally Parr, being resident in France, is in more demand than ever – not only is he local but he's also cheap. Mind you, a TV company paid him a visit a few weeks before we arrived and they came from China! They turned up six strong with several large cameras and yards of back-cloth so they could transform Dad's tiny flat into a studio – there is hardly room to swing a cat around so God knows how they managed it. It would have been interesting to see the finished product – I wonder if they used dubbing or subtitles, either way the editor would have had a right old task translating his rich language.

During the weekend of the 60th anniversary in June Dad also made the front page of the local paper in Vernon – for a long time they had made a big thing of the fact that a British veteran had set up home with a local girl – the picture on the front page showed Dad clenched - fisted baring his teeth, it was taken in his flat with Dad dressed in his vest, his hair uncombed, it was supposed to depict him as a fierce warrior still scaring the hell out of the enemy – it scared me and the horses weren't too happy!

Soon it was time for us to leave and return to the relative calm and sanity of Paris. As we said our farewells Dad mentioned that he was being driven up to the bridge with Louise on the following Wednesday by a national French magazine who wanted to give some interviews and take some photographs of him and Louise *in situ*. I immediately decided to travel over from England for the day and do some more research.

So it was that I found myself on the Tuesday midnight ferry at Portsmouth bound for Caen – this trip was a far cry from the usual madhouse journeys I encountered in the summer, I discovered that I was the only foot passenger and there are only a couple of dozen cars queuing at the quayside – the bar is so empty I felt like I was on board the Marie Celeste! After a few drinks and an hour or so of writing I drifted of to sleep and woke to a cold Normandy dawn.

The coach took me from the huge ship to the customs hall, I was the only person on board, as I approached the check-in a solitary customs officer appeared from behind a screen and slowly checked my passport. He gave me a strange look and then welcomed me to France. I gave him an equally strange look and was tempted to say sorry for disturbing him but changed my mind.

As I ate a long breakfast in the terminal I watched the sun rise over Trouville and Deauville to my left - the stiff brandy in my second coffee started to warm my bones. It was nearly eight o'clock. Dad would not be arriving until midday I had plenty of time to kill. I had to use it wisely – getting tipsy before 9 a.m. is not a good idea!

As I began the walk along the canal to Bénouville I glanced over my shoulder to the ferry - smoke was bellowing from its funnel, it would wait patiently for me until mid-afternoon and then return me home in time for the last train to London – no profit made today, but wait until June!

As I walked inland the cold wind hit me full in the face. There was a tourist sign-post that amongst other pieces of information informs me

Pegasus Bridge – deserted on a cold March day

that this path eventually leads to the Pyrenees many hundreds of kilometres away – I got the impression that was where the wind was coming from. I passed through early morning fish-markets, business is quiet – tourists and the summer sun are a long way off. Soon I left civilisation behind and shared the morning with the odd swan and the occasional super-fit French cyclist racing along the tow-path. As I continued my walk along the canal, history, almost in slow motion, began to lay its cloak before me. In the distance the spires and towers of Caen town appeared out of the morning mist, many of the buildings are relatively new, having been rebuilt after the carnage of 1944 - from where I was walking the town could be any new town anywhere in Europe, it gave me a sense of lacking soul. Around a bend and the bridge appeared – the Café Gondrée rests beside it, shutters closed, it was dwarfed against the size of the bridge and the Château de Bénouville a few hundred yards behind it. A quarter of a mile from the bridge I photographed La Peniche floating restaurant with the outline of the original Pegasus Bridge behind it – to the right of it was the impressive glider wing shape of the new museum. I looked at the rather run-down Peniche and tried to imagine the meals provided by John Howard for the veterans on the evening of the 5th June each year – those must have been quite intimate times, a far cry from the banquets of the 50th anniversary, yet this must be the price paid by the ever increasing army that wishes to share in the exploits of D Company.

As I walked towards the bridge there were little signs of life. The wind was cold, I needed a wee, a drink and a sit down – Dad has assured

The Café Gondrée (left) faces The Café Les 3 Planeurs
- both on the opposite side of the fence

me that the café opposite the Café Gondrée, the Café Les 3 Planeurs, would be open. Dad had a good relationship with the owner Chris, so much so that he would provide accommodation for him and Louise during the 60th anniversary. The 'overt' sign on the door calmed my soul.

I walked inside and was reminded of how much this relatively modern building had become a shrine to the Ox and Bucks. Everywhere there were photographs and memorabilia - John Howard and Co. filled every available piece of wall space. I was particularly impressed by a piece written by Barry Tappenden, son of Ted, it depicts the return of the old bridge back to its resting place in the grounds of the new museum and he had the good sense to produce it in both French and English.

For a while I browsed and took photographs, unlike the café opposite, photography is allowed. I got the impression that neither café owner sent the other a Christmas card!

A lady was standing behind the counter; I confidently walked up to her and announced that I was Barry Parr, son of a certain Wally and that I would be meeting him in this very café at midday. She smiled and informed me that he would be arriving at 1 p.m. As we shook hands I ordered a large beer and I was charged the full tourist rate - so much

Marc Jacquinot in the museum foyer
- my poem is bottom middle

for connections.

After a couple of beers I decided to walk across the bridge to the museum - it had been opened since the end of February; preparations were already underway to make this its biggest year ever. Dad had rung the curator Marc Jacquinot and told him that I would like to interview him and get his life story. I hoped Marc would not be too busy with the season's first influx of tourists.

I stepped into the foyer closing out the cold March wind behind me and instinctively looked to my right and saw four regal documents, expertly framed in brass. The largest of the four was a plaque commemorating the opening of the museum by Prince Charles in 2000. To the left and the right and slightly smaller, were plaques recognising the main driving forces in bringing the museum into existence.

Directly beneath the Prince Charles plaque was another document, just as regal – I began to read it and it was a split second before it registered that it was my poem!

The museum foyer

When Dad said they had 'stuck it in the new museum' I presumed they had placed it in some cabinet somewhere near the toilets!

Like a winning Lottery ticket holder I read through the poem twice just to check that it had actually happened. 'Barry Parr, son of Wally Parr No. 1 glider' at the bottom silenced my doubts. A wave of emotion sent tingles through my head – I walked back out through the door into the car park and sobbed like an idiot.

A few minutes later I returned to the foyer and studied my poem yet again. They had used the original poppy and photograph of Den Brotheridge's headstone in the mounting process that I had used when I originally gave it to Dad. For some stupid reason I checked for grammar and spelling mistakes – there were none.

After composing myself I walked to the desk and introduced myself to the person stood behind, adding that I was hoping to see Marc Jacquinot. The person I spoke to was Mark Worthington, a lovely guy, who is responsible for the day to day running of the museum. He informed me that Marc would be along in half an hour. We spoke briefly about the placing of the poem and I thanked him for the excellent job they had done.

He then suggested I had a good look at the exhibits until Marc arrived. Taking me by the arm we walked past the people queuing for tickets and he ushered me through the turnstile.

I felt accepted, he made me feel special, and I got in for free!

The quality and variety of the exhibits was breathtaking – it was a far cry from the amateurish, if well intentioned, effort of the original museum beside the Café Gondrée.

It would have taken at least two hours to absorb all the information on offer – as usual I concentrated on any D Company exhibits but was becoming more aware that I should broaden my horizons.

When the museum was opened in 2000 none of us could get anywhere inside because of the high security and our lack of time, this was my first real visit. I wandered around for a while and then drifted back into the foyer looking for Marc.

He was still amongst the missing, so I browsed through the bookshop. The relative serenity of the place was soon broken when a coach load of people arrived and swarmed into the foyer.

Soon a dozen or so were standing in front of the four plaques – I strolled towards them and noticed that three or four of them were reading my poem.

My emotions were touching both ends of the spectrum – part of me felt like Leonardo da Vinci standing amongst the crowd as they viewed the Mona Lisa – while another part of me felt like a complete plonker.

The plonker in me decided to speak.

'See that name at the bottom: Barry Parr? That's me. I wrote that.'

I felt uneasy the second I said it and I'm sure that if I had been with anybody I knew I would have kept quiet with embarrassment, but what the hell.

Immediately people called over their friends and they began having conversations with me. I explained my Dad would be arriving soon and I also shared the story of the poem. They were genuinely interested and for the first time I was receiving feed-back on a personal level as to how people were influenced by the magnitude and importance of the events on D-Day.

I had just walked the tightrope of humility and hopefully I hadn't fallen off.

Shortly afterwards the people drifted towards the ticket desk and Marc arrived.

The first thing that strikes you about Marc Jacquinot is his appearance. The eternal bachelor, he feels he has little need to impress. His clothes are not so much worn as lived in; his flyaway hair knows not the French or English for 'comb'.

With his spectacular moustache and sexy French accent he treads the fine dividing line between either being taken for a tramp or a film star – with Marc what you see is what you get

The place was now fairly quiet; I had time to get Marc's life story and some of the facts regarding the moving of the museum.

Originally from Lille, born in the late 40s his first job was as a teacher – which explains his excellent skill as a curator and lecturer.

After ten years of teaching he decided to drop out and cycle round the world – as you do!

He spent the next decade travelling throughout the world including Africa and Australia. In 1988 he returned to Normandy and decided to settle down.

A job as curator to a museum at the Café Gondrée was advertised and although he had never heard of Pegasus Bridge he applied for the job and got it – being multi-lingual probably clinching the deal.

He learnt fast, the story fascinated him and an added bonus was the wonderful relationships he built up with the veterans.

At this time he lived in a rather derelict 'mobile 'ome' a mile or so north of the bridge on the bank of the canal in the middle of an storage park. I have already shared the story of his famous barbecue and why his dog, Ranville, is the fattest dog in Normandy.

Marc shared his favourite story about his dog: He is called Ranville because he found him; you've guessed it, in Ranville. For a number of years he was Marc's constant companion, never on a lead, he followed behind him wherever he went. Every day he would follow him to the museum and sit outside all day scrounging scraps from the customers eating at the café next door.

Once, during the 50th celebrations, Marc came outside and Ranville was missing. In desperation he looked up and down the road and then shouted at the top of his voice; 'Ranville! Where's Ranville!?'

Immediately a veteran, slightly worse for wear, rose from a nearby table, pointed eastwards with an outstretched arm and proclaimed:

'Ranville? It's about a mile that-a-way!'

We got onto the subject of how the museum was transformed into its present situation. We discussed the erratic behaviour of the owner of a certain café. Inevitably I brought up the famous incident of the early morning visit from Marc and others to retrieve memorabilia from the old museum. Arlette, of course, was having none of it and stood her ground. There was a picture in the English national press of Arlette falling over a small wall in the resulting scuffle – Marc is pictured alongside. I ask him the obvious question: 'Was she pushed or did she fall?'

For a few seconds he remained silent, contemplating his answer – then a broad smile appeared on his face and the twinkle in his eyes said it all, 'I can't remember my friend, it happened so quickly!'

After the exhausting summer of 1994, the 50th anniversary, Marc decided he needed to unwind. Most of us would probably choose a warm beach and put our feet up, not so with Marc – he decided to fly to North America, buy a bike and cycle down to Florida, a journey that took him three months! And that just about sums up the man that is Marc Jacquinot.

In due course another coach arrived and Marc had to leave me and continue his duties.

I strolled out into the car-park, the sun was higher, the breeze felt warmer. I walked down to the canal and stood beside the Peniche floating restaurant. It looked pretty run-down. In the silence I strained my ears to see if I could hear long forgotten distant echoes of men raising glasses and crying 'Up the Ox and Bucks!' All I heard was the wind lapping waves against the hull.

From the boat I could see the sun sparkling on the water beneath Pegasus Bridge a hundred yards in the distance.

Leaving the canal I walked up the incline to my Dad's gun. When I arrived, half a dozen British squaddies were leaning on the railings looking into the gun pit. One of the guys was pointing up to the château – he had obviously read 'Pegasus Bridge'. I chatted with them for a while and shared my Dad's story. It emerged that they just returned from a tour of duty in Kosovo. No one needed to say it, but we all knew that they would never return in the future to commemorate their battle in the Balkans – the reasons and methods of present day wars are different.

Walking back across the near-deserted bridge gives me a real sense of history. I was going in the same direction that the boys took just after midnight all those years ago. There was little traffic on the road, once again I was tempted to break into a run and go rat-a-tat-tat with a pretend machine-gun and throw hand-grenades like I used to do in the playground as an eight-year-old. I declined and continued to walk.

I walked past the café and stopped at the spot where Dad found Den Brotheridge. I moved on to place where Wagger Thornton fired his PIAT at the tank and tried to imagine what would have happened if he had missed. I continued to the T junction, now a roundabout, and stopped where the tanks once stood. I turned right and walked the few hundred yards to the church where Renée was buried. I found her grave, beneath her name was Claude's, it showed his date of birth, a blank space awaited the attention of the stone-mason somewhere in the distant future. From the graveyard I could see the turret of the bridge and I was reminded that Dad would soon be arriving.

Walking back down from the T junction it occurred to me what a non-descript scene lay before me. After all it was only a couple of ordinary buildings beside a fairly ugly bridge – yet it held so much public attention. In the surrounding countryside between here and Caen much bloodier battles took place during the eight week period leading up to the liberation of the city. There are rarely visited fields that saw hundreds of men fall, these veterans often get much less attention than the boys from the Ox and Bucks – I could easily understand the resentment between some of these guys.

There were a few cars parked outside the Café Les 3 Planeurs so I presumed that Dad had arrived. I went inside but Chris informed me that they were running late and would be at least another half an hour. I ordered the inevitable grande bière and I was introduced to a friend of Dad's called Marc Lomo. In pigeon English we chatted about Dad and he shared with me the many good times they had had together. He brought out a few photographs from his wallet; there was a good one of him and Dad meeting Prince Charles. I used my digital camera, set on macro to photograph it – this was a big mistake as I failed to alter the switch and the rest of the day's photographs were hopelessly blurred.

In the next moment the door opened and Dad entered with Louise and a couple of journalists. Dad filled the room with his presence – his maroon blazer, medals and beret dominated the small café. After hugs and kisses and drinks the journalists took Dad and Louise outside to get the usual photographs beside, the café, bridge, gun and landing plinths.

Interior of Café Les 3 Planeurs

We finally landed up in the museum, after a quick tour we were taken out the side entrance into the grounds. The original bridge stood proud surrounded by guns and jeeps. Mark was flooding us with information about the 60th anniversary. The highlight would be the unveiling by Prince Charles of a full scale replica of a Horsa glider. He took us to a huge area with a concrete shaped cross set in the grass – this was to be the site for the glider, he informed us that there was still much work to do to get it in position in time for the unveiling.

Soon we were back at the café where the journalists bought us all lunch and drinks. I tried to get Dad to one side to get more information for my book, but the journalists took all his time and attention – it was right, there is no such thing as a 'free lunch'.

Time was now running short. I said my goodbyes to Dad and Louise and Marc Lomo kindly gave me a lift back to my ferry which had been patiently waiting for me since dawn.

As the huge ship pulled out I look backed up to the canal. In three months time this place would hold its biggest celebration ever. The British Government has announced that after the 60th anniversary there will be no more official celebrations – it will be up to the local Mayors and veterans to keep the memories alive.

In 2005 it will be the 61st anniversary but all eyes will be on the 60th celebrations of VE and VJ day in England.

On June 5/6th 2004 it will be Pegasus Bridge's greatest moment – it is of vital importance that they do it well and get it right!

The 60th Anniversary - Saturday Night

Thanks to the Internet my circle of friends interested in the events at Pegasus had grown steadily. The most notable was a guy named Dean Croucher. He could have lived anywhere in the country but fortunately he was only round the corner in Bromley. I have met many people whose knowledge of D Company puts mine to shame – as I mentioned in the introduction, my only qualification is that I am my father's son – so when I listen to people like Dean I am in awe.

The first time Dean visited he arrived with stacks of information and loads of questions. I was particularly impressed with a document he had produced that not only had the seating plan of all three gliders but he was also in the process of compiling a named list of each occupant and a brief personal history of each individual. He was going over to Normandy for the 60th anniversary and was hoping that I could arrange a meeting with some of the D Company boys. Dean is an elite firearms officer, protecting the occupants of No. 10 Downing Street and he had persuaded some of his fellow officers to come with him and do a series of sponsored marches for the British Legion and the Normandy Veterans Association.

Dean Croucher (far right) and his mates

The good news was that Dean and his mates were travelling on the same midnight ferry as my son-in-law Gary and I – the party was about to start early!

We travelled over on Friday June 4th, the ferry was packed but I sensed quite a few of the veterans were already in Normandy perhaps attending the services at Arromanches that day.

We soon congregated in the bar and the beers started to flow. We talked until 3 a.m. I met Dean's mates, most were too young to have a dad in the war, but all had uncles and granddads whose histories they were uncovering. I met a family from Yorkshire, the daughter surrounding her 87-year-old father like a protective mother hen. He landed on D-Day plus 20 and got a real pasting liberating Caen. Every story was unique – us relatives showed no rivalry as we drank in a common bond. The only place Dean and I could find to sleep was the soft mats in the children's play area – I haven't a clue where Gary ended up.

At 7 a.m. we parted company with Dean and his crowd – they headed off in a mini bound for a meeting with their French counterparts while Gary and I began our now familiar trek along the Caen canal. I am pleased to know that this time Gary was unsuccessful on the one-armed bandits. I didn't fancy just the two of us carrying all those coins.

Since 9/11 the world has become a jittery place – especially when many of the world's leaders are congregating in a small corner of France. For a few months I had been receiving letters informing me that I would need special passes to get into various events. As we walked along the canal path we noticed heavily armed police spaced out at regular intervals – none seemed particularly bothered with our presence until we rounded the final bend and the bridge and café came into view and then it was only a quick glance at our passes and not even a peep into our overnight bags - so much for security.

From a distance the bridge and the Café Gondrée looked splendid. Flags abounded, even from here there was a carnival atmosphere – it was a far cry from my last windswept visit back in March.

To my right the campsite was heaving with people. American and British flags stand proud beside each camouflaged tent. Every other vehicle was a genuine 1940's jeep or ambulance – whole families were sitting around tables eating breakfast in full World War Two uniforms, everything was correct down the finest detail. They were living out a lifestyle for whatever reason. Maybe some did it for the fellowship and comradeship; they were fulfilling a basic need to be part of something, to share a Blitz or Dunkirk experience. Perhaps for others, they were disillusioned with the present, fear the future so chose to escape to the past, the 'good old days.'

It's more than likely they were just plain fascinated in this period of our history – whatever the reason they all seemed to be having a bloody good time.

A minute later and we were outside the Café Les 3 Planeurs, although it was only 9 a.m. both cafés were heaving. Chris the owner had put up an additional outside bar to cater for the masses. Stalls were selling memorabilia in the forecourt – the whole area took on the atmosphere of a foreign bazaar.

In the road outside temporary scaffold had been erected to accommodate TV cameras, crews and presenters, fifty yards up the road towards the T Junction I could see a huge crane with another camera mounted on top no doubt to show the world aerial pictures of events over the next two days.

Gary and I found a table outside and ordered our first beers of the day, he doesn't drink tea or coffee - so don't blame me!

I introduced myself to Chris, he remembered me from the March trip, I enquired about Dad and Louise, they were staying in a room above the café, they did it every year, which was just as well because most accommodation had been sold out for months. We left it an hour and then I weaved my way through the crowds and went upstairs to find Dad. This day was going to be busy to say the least – at 1 p.m. Dad, along with the rest of the lads, would be going to the museum and meeting Prince Charles for an unveiling of a full-size replica Horsa glider. In the evening there would be a civic reception at the Town Hall in which the veterans would be presented with a special 60th anniversary medal and after the dinner and speeches they would be expected to walk over the bridge to attend the midnight ceremony followed by speeches, fireworks and vintage Calvados and Champagne. In between all of this the boys would be expected to give interviews, sign autographs and answer any questions that were thrown at them as well as drink the odd drink that was going.

As I climbed the stairs I thought to myself that I doubt if he would be able to stay the pace.

I entered the room and one look at Dad confirmed my worst fears – he was sat on the bed half-dressed, his grey hair long and dishevelled. He had made a half-hearted attempt at shaving and as I looked at this sorry state his hands were trembling as he attempted to pin his medals on his jacket. Beside him in the bed lay Louise and although it was warm, she was fully immersed under the covers, a pair of eyes gave me a feeble welcome - it was obvious she was going to take no part in the day's proceedings.

I helped Dad to get ready and find his walking stick. Within fifteen minutes we were descending the steep steps into the bright June sunshine. The forecourt was busier than ever, fortunately Gary had had the good sense to find us a table in the shade. I left Dad with Gary and joined the queue for three cold beers.

For the next hour or so a conveyor belt of people approached our table – some chatted to Dad for a couple of minutes others stayed longer, occasionally somebody simply shook his hand and said nothing.

As the time approached for the unveiling of the glider more familiar faces appeared. Penny Howard/Bates and her husband George were standing by the roadside giving an interview – I seized the opportunity and from my rucksack got my original hardback copy of 'Pegasus Bridge' and managed to speak to her and got her to sign the book – she found a space above her father's name near to his familiar trademark 'Ham and Jam'. I shared my intentions of writing my Dad's war story and in turn Penny told me she is hoping to have a book about her father published soon, there was no rivalry; instead we encouraged each other.

Amid the gathering chaos a strangely familiar face appeared from the crowd. 'You know who this is?' remarked Dad.

I looked at this guy in full Ox and Bucks gear, medals sparkling but looking ten years younger than the rest. Slightly drunk I racked my brains and stared blankly.

'It's Billy Gray you stupid sod!' continued Dad.

Billy Gray gives an interview

Slightly embarrassed I embraced him – it had been ten years since I last saw him and he hadn't aged in the slightest. We chatted for a while and then he signed my book having failed to do so at the 50th anniversary.

Dad and Billy were the last two survivors of the original four who were called 'scallywags' in Ambrose's' book - Parr, Gray, Bailey and Gardner.

I always missed Jack Bailey at these times – to me he will always be 'Uncle Jack' from my childhood – it is ironic that the man that was most loyal during the wilderness years of the fifties, sixties and seventies should have passed away before this finest hour.

The fourth, Charlie Gardner, had lost a long battle with illness a few years previous – no longer would he and Dad 'talk until the small hours, drinking whisky neat.'

I was reminded of how Stephen Ambrose treated Dad in his book – in all he is mentioned on 48 separate occasions, as much as the other three put together, of all the regular soldiers only Wagger Thornton comes close with 20 mentions. No wonder some veterans have shown animosity towards Dad – one even suggested perhaps it should be renamed 'Parr Bridge' instead of Pegasus. I think I can see where Ambrose was coming from – he was attempting to write a personal oral history and to achieve that you needed characters and Dad was certainly that.

It was soon time for us to cross the bridge and head for the unveiling. Before we left Dad asked me to check on Louise, I found her fast asleep in her bedroom, curtains closed – this proved to be a bonus because I could now use her VIP pass to see the unveiling close-up.

I reassured Dad that she was okay and we set off to walk the couple of hundred yards to the museum. Once over the bridge we hit a brick wall of people all lining the aptly named Rue de John Howard. We found a gap in the barriers and by showing our passes to the guarding policemen we were shown through. For the last couple of hours the museum had been closed to the public in preparation for the royal visit. As we approached the main entrance guards blocked our way. There was no need to show passes at this point, Dad's beret, uniform and medals are our passport - Gary and I grabbed an arm each of Dad and hoped nobody was counting numbers.

We walked through the foyer and bookshop of the museum and into the gardens. The relative calm of the museum was quickly broken by the hustle and bustle of friends and relatives gathering in anticipation of the eminent unveiling. The garden, as always, was dominated by the original

Pegasus Bridge, it stood silent and proud, allowing people to walk up and down it and tread on the footsteps of history. I looked up at the huge dent caused by the impact of the unexploded bomb and once again reflected on what might have happened if it had gone off. All around the gardens were armoured vehicles and guns of varying sizes – amongst it all

The boys await the arrival of Prince Charles

Mark Jacquinot spotted us and beckoned Dad towards him, as always he was in complete control.

We passed through one more guarded barrier into the VIP section – the guy ignored Dad but checked my pass carefully, he looked at me strangely, trying to work out why a nice English boy should be called: Louise Claret. Needless to say I got through and escorted Dad into a row of seats underneath the wing of the replica Horsa and made a hasty retreat into the VIP seating area to await the arrival of Prince Charles. Somehow Gary had managed to creep behind me and was in an excellent position to take photographs and use the video camera.

For events like these you usually have to be seated at least thirty minutes before the dignitary arrives, which always seemed a waste of time because inevitably they have unexpected conversations with somebody interesting and the schedule is thrown out the window.

By now all the boys were seated under the wing of the glider awaiting the arrival of HRH – this was the first time the boys had all been together since last year, the usual banter and handshakes ensued. Colonel Tillett stood nervously, he was the most senior surviving officer and he looked uncomfortable resting on his crutches in the intense heat. Colonel David Wood was wandering around doing most of the organising. Jim Wallwork was sat inside the glider, beret off, mopping his brow as he waited to be introduced to Prince Charles. The rest of the crowd that didn't have seating passes were pressing up against the barrier that separated them from the veterans – Mary Ann Nightingale, the TV

Five minutes later Dad was shaking hands
with our future king !

presenter was standing in front of a camera crew, powdering her nose, waiting for a live link-up at any moment.

As the tension mounted I took my seat and awaited the arrival of Prince Charles. Fifteen minutes later and nothing had happened.

As I looked across at Dad seated in line I noticed that he is tossing and turning in his seat in obvious discomfort. After a few more moments he beckoned me over and I strolled across in the full glare of the worlds press. As I bent over he whispered in my ear. 'It's no good mate; I've got to have a slash!'

The three beers from the previous hour had caught up with him. Without hesitation I grabbed him by the arm and we meandered over to a quiet corner behind the VIP seats and found a spot behind the shed that houses the remains of an old Horsa. Officials looked on in slight panic. Out of the sight of the immediate crowd I joined Dad in relieving myself against the shed. Half-way through I looked to my right and realised we were in full view of dozens of people congregating outside on the Rue de John Howard – some were cheering and waving at us, I declined to wave back bearing in mind what I had in my hand!

A few minutes later I escorted Dad back to his seat and returned to mine, pretending nothing had happened.

With no time to spare the crowd began to react, cameras zoomed into action as Prince Charles and his entourage emerged from the museum. Polite applause greeted him as he was shown to his seat. I was seated directly behind him, two rows back, he was slightly blocking my view of Dad and the boys and I was tempted to lean forward, tap him on the shoulder and ask him to move slightly to the left but my better judgment told me to keep quite and be thankful for being so close.

From his viewpoint Prince Charles could see the glider, the veterans and Jim Wallwork – by now the boys had sat upright, almost to attention, while Jim had put his beret on, despite the heat in the fuselage.

A rather dignified gentleman then greeted Prince Charles in French. After a few paragraphs he stopped and Marc Jacquinot repeated the message in English. The Frenchman then continued his message stopping once again for Marc to translate. This time when Marc began to speak the microphone packed up – he gave it the customary few flicks but it failed to respond – Marc continued to speak without the mike but unfortunately I couldn't hear him even in the second row. After a brief stoppage the mike was replaced and the speeches continued without a hitch.

After the speeches Prince Charles walked over to the glider and began the unveiling. To do this literally would have taken a cloth the size of a tennis court – a symbolic cutting of a ribbon at the foot of the steps did the trick instead. As the crowd cheered and clapped, His Royal Highness gave a royal wave and climbed the few steps up to the fuselage shaking Jim Wallwork by the hand as he entered the glider. The pair spent several minutes inside – a picture of Jim and Prince Charles sitting at the controls was to be beamed around the world by the next day.

Charles gets tips from veteran Jim Wallwork, the first glider pilot to land
Picture by Steve Prenergast

His Royal Highness was genuinely interested, aware that Jim had probably performed the finest feat of flying in the entire Second World War. He asked him how he managed it.

'Practise, simply practise', was the modest reply.

They chatted for a while longer and the pair shook hands as the Prince stepped outside into the June sunshine.

As he walked down the steps all the boys seated under the wing rose up and stood in line for the inevitable handshake.

The first to be greeted was Major Tillet; he did his best to give a dignified handshake while balancing on crutches. The Prince moved down the line – Nobby Clark, Billy Gray, Tom Packwood and then Wally Parr. As the Prince chatted to Dad I got over-excited and left my seat to get some close-up pictures – I got to within a few feet before security guards blocked my way. I managed to take a few pictures before they stopped me, but they turned out useless as I was pointing directly into the sunshine. Prince Charles spent a couple of minutes giving each veteran his full attention – I got the impression the short conversations were non-repetitive such was his knowledge.

One of my most endearing memories was to see a young lad called

Robbie standing out the front in a red beret accompanying his granddad Corporal Bob Ham – a timely reminder that future generations are taking up the vision of preserving the memory of D Company and Pegasus Bridge.

In no time the Prince and his hangers-on moved on to the next engagement acknowledging the waves and the cheers as they left.

Immediately the barriers were let down and the area around the glider was flooded with well-wishers and the media. The veterans were

Dad with HRH Prince Charles

soon giving interviews and posing arm in arm with total strangers. As I was trying vainly to protect Dad from too much hustle the huge frame of Ted Barwick pushed through the crowd and I realised I have no chance. Ted is the brother of Pete Barwick, after much back slapping we enjoy a few minutes banter catching up on old times – we have had many a beer with the Barwick family, even travelling down to their hometown of Honiton in Devon and experiencing his wife Rose's hospitality.

After saying our goodbyes to Ted we slowly edged our way out of the museum grounds and fought the oncoming tide of people as we headed back to the café and a cold beer.

As the day drew on I began to think about the rest of the days arrangements – my brother, Bob, was due to arrive any moment having travelled over on the morning ferry. For a long while we were having problems finding overnight accommodation but thankfully this had been solved by a friend of a relative who had agreed to put us up in a mobile home along the coast providing we didn't mind being transported there either on the back of a motorbike or in a sidecar!

Having solved our sleeping problems we then had to decide who would accompany Dad to the Mayor's banquet now that Louise had dropped out.

As I pondered these problems the conveyer belt of people began to arrive at our table at regular intervals.

'Hello Wally - remember me from last year?' a stranger asked.

'Yes mate, how are yer?' he would occasionally lie.

At one point I felt a tap on my shoulder and looking round noticed it was my nephew, Gary. The last time I had spoken to Wally's eldest grandson was at the 50th anniversary - in the ensuing decade Gary had aged little, his long flowing hair still reflecting his free hippy spirit - I doubt he felt the same about me!

In between outsiders, Gary managed to grab a few moments with his granddad. As they spoke brother, Bob, arrived, all of a sudden we were in the middle of a family reunion oblivious to the outside world.

As Bob, the two Gary's and I caught up on a decade of family gossip

Dad gives his last interview to the BBC

Dean Croucher arrived with a few of his mates and a couple of bottles of Dakota special edition beer for Gary and me - what a friend!

I introduced Dean to Dad - in the hustle and bustle of the café forecourt Dean went down on one knee and showed Dad various artefacts from his backpack. In the few precious moments he had, he tried to get as much information from Dad as he could – the irony is that Dean probably had more information about D Company and Wally Parr than Wally Parr himself! Out of respect for one of his heroes Dean kept calling Dad 'Mr. Parr', I interrupted, rather stupidly, and insisted he called him Wally – I think it broke the ice, After this Dean rang Dad on a regular basis and even paid him a visit in Vernon.

A group of London Policemen dressed in kilts started to play the bagpipes – don't ask! Surrounding people, including ourselves, started to clap and sing along to the tune of 'Scots Porridge Oats', it was all getting a bit manic as the beers and wine started to flow and it was only four in the afternoon. Dad decided that if he is going to stay the pace he would need a couple of hour's kip. I took him by the arm and led him upstairs to his bedroom – Louise was still in bed but awake, Dad hung his jacket and tie on a chair and snuggled in beside her despite the heat. I closed the window to muffle the awful sound of the bagpipes – Bill Millin eat your heart out!

Downstairs brother, Bob, and I had a decision to make – Dad had an invitation to the Mayor's banquet which stated 'Wally Parr and guest', it was obvious that Louise was not up for it and as I worked my way into the Glider unveiling I suggested it was only fair that Bob accompanied Dad to the dinner. Bob insisted I go because he was wearing scruffy Green Flash trainers but I offered to lend him my half-decent shoes but he was having none of it. I suggested we toss a coin but got no response – I then offered one potato, two potato and then in desperation playing a game of paper, stone, scissors to decide the outcome, but all this drunken rubbish was getting us nowhere.

Two hours later Dad appeared at the bottom of the stairs – minus beret, medals and tie and we still hadn't decided who would be joining him.

By now nephew, Gary, and his mate had gone walkabout, we would see them again tomorrow – tonight they would have the same sleeping arrangements as they had had for the 50th celebrations – under the stars.

The four of us began the slow stroll up to the Town Hall. After five minutes we were outside the imposing building. A hundred or so invited guests were milling around sipping fine wine provide by waiters. We stood amongst familiar faces and soon a tray of wine was thrust in our faces – we gratefully accepted and did our best to mingle, hoping nobody would spot Bob's trainers!

Penny Howard/Bates at the medal ceremony

I managed to grab a few words with Jim Wallwork; I told him of my intention to write my book and would welcome any comments of his flying experiences and his trips to New Orleans with Dad. He gave me his card and suggested I write to him. I also caught up with Geoff Baulk, the young lad who was doing so much work at Bletchley, again I asked him to write to me and give me information for my book. After catching up with a few others a French voice made an announcement from near the entrance and it was all eyes forward.

This was the time of the evening when the surviving Veterans were to be given a special 60th anniversary medal – in essence it was a longevity award, thanking each individual for still being alive.

We all knew there would be very few takers at the 70th celebrations.

As each veteran came forward Penny Howard/Bates stood beside the mayor and gave each member an encouraging smile – she was trying in her own special way to take the place of her much missed father.

Most of the guys were still in regimental jackets and ties – for some the was barely room to pin on yet another gong, but in Dad's case there was plenty of room as his jacket was bare – he looked like he had just dragged himself out of bed, which wasn't far from the truth.

Dad receives his medal

Ceremony over, people started to drift into the main hall. Inside a couple of dozen large tables were laid out, ready for a banquet. Panic and confusion set in as Bob, Gary and I stared at each other wondering what to do.

'Don't panic lads –follow me!' was Dad's response.

Sheepishly we followed him inside; he found a table near the front and instructed us to sit beside him. For the next ten minutes I stared at the entrance watching people file into the hall – places were being filled rapidly, eventually people stopped coming and there was still half a dozen empty seats. I breathed a sigh of relief and poured myself a glass of fine French red wine.

A pleasant hour followed as we ate a four course meal provided by God knows who – whoever you were, you did the Ox and Bucks and their relatives proud.

Towards the end of the meal people began to get up and wander over to other tables and chat with other buddies. At one point I noticed Billy Gray being ushered out of the door and being seated in front of a TV camera and crew. Marc Jacquinot had accompanied him and was helping with the translation. Billy was a relatively quiet sort of chap and it was good to see him getting the limelight as compared to the likes of Dad.

In due course David 'Lackery' Wood stood up and began the proceedings. He started by naming the veterans present – first on the list was Arthur Roberts, described by Colonel Wood as probably 'the finest soldier ever to fight in the second world war.' We all suspect that this is said with slight tongue in cheek and may be something to do with the fact that 'Robbo' was in Wood's platoon.

Somewhere in the middle he introduced 'Tich' Rayner as the only man in the war to be shot by a dead German – the mind boggles.

Finally, almost as an afterthought, he finished with 'a man that needs no introduction' – Wally Parr.

The evening then entered a more sombre mood as relatives of departed veterans were welcomed. The longest standing relative present was Margaret Brotheridge – a widow of sixty years, this was followed by Ted Barwick, the brother of Pete, another war time casualty. To me the most poignant moment was when Barry Tappenden was introduced – if any man deserved to still have his father with us it was Barry. His dedication was such that, even after his father's passing, he was still heavily involved in events surrounding D Company. On an even deeper personal note I thought of Jack Bailey, my old 'Uncle Jack', the eternal bachelor, there never was to be a wife or children to stand and honour him. Other names drifted through my head Charlie Gardner, and Wagger Thornton to name but a few. Then Colonel Wood finished the roll call by acknowledging last but certainly not least Penny Howard/Bates.

The evening drifted on with the odd presentation here and there and then before we knew it we were all being ushered out and sent back in the direction of the bridge in preparation for the fireworks and the traditional midnight ceremony.

The four of us, much worse for wear, linked arms and followed the crowd heading for the café. I'm not sure if Dad's feet were actually touching the ground by the time we arrived back, all I knew was that he had had enough, the day's events had finally caught up with him and it was time for his bed.

With Dad safely tucked up Bob and I joined Gary at a nearby table for yet another beer. The whole area was now heaving with people. Although darkness had fallen the light from the cafés and the TV camera-lights kept the visibility good. As we drank our beers four huge figures approached us staring at us from underneath visors and helmets

- the leather suits and boots added to their menace.

The next moment they took off their helmets and underneath were the smiling faces of Tom Friar, his mate, 'Tank', and a couple of other guys who were to be our transport to our over-night accommodation.

After buying them a beer they agreed to stay a while to see the fireworks – I also suggested that perhaps I could get them into the museum. I haven't a clue why I suggested this, bearing in mind that it was nearly midnight and the place was closed to the public, perhaps I was more intoxicated than I thought.

Needless to say, after a few minutes, Gary, our leather chauffeurs and I made our way across the bridge and headed for the museum. As we approached the entrance I could see two heavily armed gendarmes blocking the way – I felt vulnerable when I realised I was without my Dad, my passport to anywhere. Full of Dutch courage, I faced the guards, produced every pass I had on me, mumbled something about No. 1 glider, Major Howard and garçon of Wally Parr and much to my surprise they let us in – tonight I could blag for England!

Inside I quickly showed them around, it was obviously closed to the public, but on the main counter was a couple of bottles of 50-year-old vintage Calvados – beside it was a dozen or so glasses, no doubt in preparation for a small reception after the midnight ceremony. I poured myself a large glass and offered the others a taste – they wisely declined my kind offer. I downed the drink in one large swig it had the effect of drinking rocket fuel with attitude! Feeling rather guilty I suggested we left.

Outside the fireworks had finished – the quarter past midnight ceremony was about to begin. The crowd gathered was huge it overflowed past the landing zone and engulfed Major Howard's bust and my Dad's gun. There was no way we could get anywhere near it so we decided to let the actor Richard Todd and the rest of the crowd get on with it.

Fighting our way back to the café we found the rest of Tom's mates guarding their huge Triumph motorbikes. They took one look at me and decided that for my own safety it would be best if I did the trip in a sidecar. Bob had gone missing and when I phoned him he told me he decided to do his own thing – perhaps he wasn't in the mood for hairy rockers!

Soon Gary and I were speeding along the coast road to our mobile caravan site at Saint-Aubin-sur-Mer. The cool night air and the breakneck speed soon sobered me up and within the hour we were safely bedded down on a makeshift double bed in someone's kitchen.

I am about to have a sobering experience in a side car

As I drifted off I was reminded of the 50th celebrations – at the time I considered it to be my 'Longest Day', looking back at the previous 24 hours I came to the conclusion that June 5th 2004 had become my 'Longest, Longest Day!'

The 60th Anniversary - Sunday Morning

There is a brief moment in time – somewhere between deep sleep and awakening where reality doesn't exist. Before the truth kicks in you begin to panic. Where am I? What did I do last night? Did I hit a policeman or insult the Mayor? Worse still did I stand out the front and make a complete arse of myself or perhaps I seduced a Colonel's daughter or fulfilled some other deep-rooted sexual fantasy? As I slowly opened my eyes I came face to face with Gary's smelly feet. 'Reality' kicked in and I breathed a sigh of relief when I realised that I had done none of the above. Within a few minutes a total stranger handed me a cup of strong coffee and I got to work on the hangover.

Tom and the rest of his crowd were gathering outside and were busy going through the day's itinerary. These middle-age rockers go by some amazing names: Richard 'Tank' Turner was the man that would eventually write the report of the week that would appear on the web site of the Bexley Triumph Motor Cycle Club. Then there was 'Stainless' Bob and 'BMW' Ray to name a few, another girl, Aussie Liz had flown halfway across the world just to do the D-Day week. The main organiser was Tom Friar, the caretaker at my sister-in-law's school and like my policeman friend Dean his knowledge of the events surrounding D-Day put me to shame.

They had a couple of veterans with them; one named Tony was an 80-year-old who landed at Gold Beach with the Sherwood Foresters. Still a keen biker he had travelled over to France in a sidecar, no namby-pamby cars for these guys! The other was Tom Burnett who served with the Devonshires.

For many of the huge crowds in Normandy, today is 'Beach day.'

World leader's, most having never heard a shot fired in anger, will stand in solemn lines and extol the evil and tragedy of war, before the likes of the 'two B's', retreat behind closed doors and plan the next conflict.

Security was at its highest. Tom's campsite was a mile or so inland and for them to get us back to Pegasus Bridge without the proper passes would have been a nightmare, so we decided to get a taxi to take us back using the inland road hoping it would be much clearer.

Quietly panicking we go to camp reception and find an English speaking person who arranges us a cab. In true cabbie tradition he takes us 'round the houses' but we decide to simply relax and enjoy the early morning Normandy sunshine. Before we knew it we were at the roundabout in Bénouville – here the journey ended as a roadblock prevented the car entering the village.

We paid off the taxi and thought we could now stroll down the road to the bridge as large as life and twice as handsome. But the gendarmes manning the road block had other ideas. We both spent a frantic couple of minutes rummaging through our rucksacks looking for the relevant passes, secretly worrying that we hadn't dropped them the previous night in a drunken stupor. Thankfully we found them and both agreed that today we would act more sensibly.

Five minutes later we were outside the Café Les 3 Planeurs and I ordered the first two beers of the day – it was only 10 a.m. but the sun was already hot and it was still the best cure for a hangover.

Soon nephew, Gary, and his mate appeared, it was obvious they had spent the night under the stars – normally they got little hassle, but this year they were moved on constantly, each time having their rucksacks thoroughly searched.

June 2004 was sandwiched between the terrorist attacks of 9/11 in America and the 7/7 attack in London which was to occur the following summer – at this point in time we were living in the nervous 'If' before the inevitable 'When'.

As we drank our beers Bob appeared through the crowd emerging from the direction of Caen. I stared at him for a brief moment he too looks dishevelled from a night under the stars and I wondered what he had been up to all night – brotherly instinct satisfied me that it was 'none of the above'.

Apparently he had spent the entire night walking to Caen and back – in my spirit I suspected he has gone through some sort of 'spiritual experience' – almost a 'dark night of the soul'. At times Bob can be a very intense and private person – I have and always will respect him for that, I decided not to delve too deep – instead I convinced him that it was his turn to buy the next round.

Our café table was soon filled with glasses of lager; the only thing missing was the great man himself. Half an hour later Dad came out of the door accompanied by Louise – this was the first time his good lady had breathed fresh air in over 36 hours. Dad found her a seat in the shade and came over and joined us. Bob gave up his seat at the table and after a quick embrace with Dad went and sat with Louise and engaged in an O level French conversation.

Dad's attire was back to full military parade neatness – always an individualist, he still chose his maroon military jacket in contrast to every other veteran's blue blazer. The heat prevented him from doing up his top button and the beret would only be worn at the last moment. On one of the few remaining areas of his jacket that didn't display a medal he had managed to pin his latest gong, presented to him on the previous night. For a brief moment I admired the array of medals before me – I recognised his basic three from my childhood, affectionately know as 'Pip, Squeak and Wilfred' you got those for simply turning up. They weren't the originals of course, as kids we were allowed to play with his medals and I remember the star shaped one made a brilliant Kung Fu weapon if you threw it at the door – it also doubled up as a sheriff's badge if you played the goody. We were also allowed to play with his beret with the hole in it and for a while I had his silk map of France pinned to my bedroom wall. Today his beret is on display in the D-Day museum in New Orleans – but I haven't a clue as to the whereabouts of his original medals and silk map.

Dad makes the front page !

Back to reality – it was time for the parade. Dad had to hastily gulp his first beer of the day and it didn't satisfy his thirst. We were into our third and the cold gassy French beer was having trouble going down – as we got up Dad noticed that Bob had left half his beer in the glass, after putting his beret he reached down and finished of the remains, 'Waste not – want not.' He whispered.

Across the road near the Café Gondrée the usual Ox and Bucks suspects were gathering. The contrast between the 50th and 60th anniversary was staggering. The words 'more' and 'less' came to mind - more outsiders, less veterans. As the numbers dwindled and the mode of transport used by some of the veterans attempting to cross the bridge changed from year to year one thing remains constant – and that was Barry Tappenden.

Ever present year after year, yet again he was organising the boys into some sort of marching order. He had also managed to install the same enthusiasm into the rest of his family. His daughters had been laying wreaths for years and after the death of their grandfather, Ted, one of the daughters, Chantelle, was at the front pushing Arthur Roberts across in his wheelchair.

I am very much aware that I am less qualified or knowledgeable than many others to write a book such as this but again I repeat my message at the beginning: 'I am simply my father's son.'

Without warning the band struck up and we were off.

A massed band with brass and drums blazing has an energy of its own which immediately transfers to the crowd who respond by clapping, cheering and waving. Behind the band marched the veterans followed by the local Mayor and officials, then local school children, then the relatives and finally a multitude of hangers-on.

As the veterans broke into step I began to worry that Dad would not stay the pace. His stick dug into the ground allowing him to get a boost every other step – I saw Arthur in his wheelchair and wished there was room for Dad. For the first time ever I tagged onto the relatives marching behind the veterans. I walked on the road instead of joining the crowds on the pavement – rightly or wrongly I somehow felt qualified.

It probably took less than five minutes to march across the bridge – roughly the same time it took to clear the bridge of the enemy back in 1944!

Under a blazing sun we soon reached the other side and filed off to the right and entered a cordoned-off area by the memorial. The crowd was huge, people were standing on the rails protecting Dad's gun in an effort to get a better view.

That day we had the 'Pomp and the Circumstance' sitting side by side. The 'Pomp' was the marching bands and the crowd's adoration. The 'Circumstance' was the laying of a wreath in a few minutes time when the people would fall silent. The 'Pomp' was corporate and welcomes recognition. The 'Circumstance' was private and is sometimes even a lone figure laying a single poppy in a quite field as he remembers a fallen comrade. The 'Pomp' feeds the ego. The 'Circumstance' feeds the soul. Both feed off each other. For true healing they must go hand in hand.

As I embraced these thoughts I settled down in a chair in the second row – the first row was taken up by the boys and the Mayor. In

The final march for Dad & Tom Packwood (right)

front of me was Arthur Roberts in his wheelchair.

The ceremony was much the same as the one conducted ten years previous. It pleased me to see Geoff Baulk, the young lad that was doing so much work for D Company at Bletchley, laying a wreath in his TA uniform. After a few speeches and some more wreath laying, a lone bugler struck up the last post. He was part of the local youth band – it was a long way off from the perfection I had heard at the 50th anniversary but in its inexperienced naivety I sensed an innocence that in many ways made it more poignant. It gained an extra dimension when a young girl played a drum roll afterwards – as she played, Arthur Roberts and the rest of the boys stood to attention and saluted.

While I stood behind Arthur I took a photograph of the memorial looking through Arthur's saluting arm. It turned out to be a very moving photograph – it was to be Arthur 'Robbo' Roberts' final salute – a few months later he died.

Arthur Roberts gives his final salute

When the ceremony was over local school children filed past the veterans seated in the front row and gave each of them a carnation, it was red, white or blue – colours that united two flags and two nations.

I filmed the boys receiving their flowers, the camera captured strange reactions at first, but in the end the overwhelming picture was one of humility and childlike innocence – for some strange reason I was reminded of the 60's protest song: 'Where have all the flowers gone.'

By now the June heat was overbearing. Slowly we made our way back to our table at the café and much to our surprise our seats had not been taken and there was still some lukewarm beer left in our glasses – gasping as he was, even Dad couldn't be tempted to take a swig this time.

As we refilled with a cold beer somebody on a nearby table announced that Ronald Reagan had died. I recalled the time somebody shot him in an assassination attempt and he told his wife. 'Honey I forgot to duck!' – Dad piped up and said he should have used the same quote when Mum first visited him in the hospital in Scotland back in 1944.

With grandson, Gary, me & Bob – ten years on

Meanwhile my new found biker friends were continuing their full week's program. It was a classic well balanced tour, taking in beaches, cemeteries, the town of Saint-Mere-Eglise with its famous model of the stranded paratrooper hanging from the church tower and, of course, Pegasus Bridge and Ranville.

I envied these guys. My visits to Normandy over the years had given too much emphasis to the Bridge and D Company – my only experience of Normandy beaches had been sunbathing and watching the topless birds at Cabourg in the early days when Claude had his apartment overlooking the beach.

One of the highlights for the Bexley Triumph Motor Cycle Club was on Friday 4th June when Tom Friar managed to organise the bunch and get them in one piece to a place called Abbaye-aux-Dames just outside Caen. Here Tom 'the elder' and Tony were presented with their special medals to commemorate the 60th anniversary – each medal had the veteran's name and war-time serial number engraved on it and was presented by a local school child.

As the crowds dispersed locals and visitors alike were amazed as

Tom and Tony, both over 80 meticulously pulled on their riding leathers over their regimental blazers and roared off on their motorbikes with the rest of their 'Easy Rider' mates.

Richard 'Tank' Turner, one of the bikers, wrote an excellent report of the week for their website – with his permission I am delighted to reproduce some of it here: *'Our friends from last year, the ex-paratroopers John Hunter and Jimmy were at the Gondrée Café and we sank a few more beers and baguettes. Tom and Tony were in their element and were pressed by many of the serving British paratroopers at the bridge for tales of D-Day. After a while most of us drifted off to the Pegasus museum and then to Ranville Cemetery, where one of Tom's old wartime comrades is buried. It was a hot day and as we walked up the hill towards Ranville Church and cemetery, Ray noticed a piper in army uniform at the top of the hill. Ray spoke to him and advised him that Tom was following us up the hill and as Tom was a veteran of D-Day and was in a Scottish Regiment, it would be nice if he could play for Tom and Gwen.*

The French piper drew himself up to his full height and said, "It is my obligation, my duty to play for the veterans." With that he cranked up the bagpipes and slowly marched down the hill towards Tom and Gwen playing 'Flower of Scotland.' Tom and Gwen were slowly climbing the hill but when they got within ten feet of the piper, they stopped and waited for him to finish. We all stopped, the traffic stopped, transfixed at the scene and then the piper finished playing, Tom shook his hand and the spell was broken. We continued to Ranville cemetery

There was loads of security at Ranville, loads of gendarmes, snipers on the church tower and lots of well built men in dark glasses wandering about, a bit excessive to deal with a few bikers I thought, but you can't be too careful...

We were wandering around the cemetery, Tom had found his friend Bobby Greenslade's grave and was paying his respects when this very well dressed woman in a big hat comes up to me and says "your friend at the grave, was he at D-Day?" I say yes, he was in the Devonshire Regiment. Next thing, along comes this well dressed bloke in a slightly smaller hat, he introduces himself to Tom as General Wellesley, the commander of the Devon and Dorset Regiment, and as the regiment had amalgamated with the Devonshire Regiment some years previously, was in charge of all the Devonshire graves. His aide-de-camp and secretary, both in full dress uniform, accompanied General Wellesley. When chatting to Tom, he mentioned he was at the cemetery as one of various important people who were there to meet the German Chancellor but he had a bit of spare time and, if Tom wanted, he would show us other Devonshire Regiment graves in the cemetery, Tom agreed!

So it came to pass that, under the watchful eyes of gendarmes, police, snipers and men in dark glasses we were shown around Ranville Cemetery by a General and his entourage. We left the cemetery just as the German Chancellor arrived; one of the motorcycle outriders was holding a pistol as he passed! We were also told, at the cemetery, that each soldier's grave was the responsibility of a child in one of the local primary schools and the children helped to maintain the graves in their pristine state. We made our way back to Pegasus Bridge where we found Tony still telling tales to the young Paras and still knocking back the beers. We joined Tony for a few more beers and then it was time to go back to the caravans.'

Sadly, as with Arthur Roberts, this was to be Tom Burnett's last visit to Normandy. He died in April 2006, the funeral service began at the Pied Bull pub in Farningham, Kent, a place were all the bikers used to meet every Tuesday and Tom collected the subs. From there he was given a full 'bikers escort' to the cemetery – the service was well attended, the praises many, from not only his many biker friends but also by his many army contacts. The service ended with a prayer read by a member of the Normandy Veterans Association: 'They shall not grow old as we who are left grow old. Age shall not weary them nor years condemn. At the going down of the sun and in the morning, we will remember them.

Unlike his fallen comrades in 1944, Tom did grow old, but he never grew weary or was condemned – Tom Burnett rest in peace.

Meanwhile back in Normandy for bikers read 'Old Bill in uniform'. Dean Croucher and his mates had planned for months a week long sponsored walk through the lanes of Normandy at the 60th anniversary to raise funds for the NVA and British Legion.

Although I knew the two groups, bikers and coppers, through different channels I knew they had a common bond and by a strange coincidence they began their journeys in France at the same place – Saint-Aubin-sur-Mer. Who knows, that first night they may have been drinking in the same bar – one mention of Wally Parr or D Company and the bond would have been made.

For bikes read feet. The boys began the week by cementing relationships with the mayor and local gendarmes. Dean and his crew all worked as elite firearms officers standing guard outside 10 Downing

Street and the Houses of Parliament, so it seemed appropriate to present the mayor with a bottle of whisky from the House of Commons and a Metropolitan police helmet. I hope for the Mayor's sake he didn't think he had to drink the booze out of the helmet!

The plan was to do a variety of walks each day dressed as London Bobbies and then return back to base and take a rest. These guys were

Arthur Roberts shows the letter that announced his passing back in 1944 !

all as tough as old boots – but in Dean's case it was new boots that let him down, as after a couple of days he had to give up walking and drive the support van because he was in agony with blisters.

In all they raised over £1700 for the two charities, I enclose a section of the diary they produced afterwards – Sunday June 6th seemed a typical day!

We all got up at 06:30 hrs to get uniforms on. At 08:00 we left for the Bayeux Cemetery. We noticed lots of Gendarmes at nearly every road junction. As we arrived we sneaked in behind a black Range Rover (VC 15) that appeared to be carrying someone important. Lots of veterans were coming up to us to comment on how nice it was to see British Bobbies, and how safe they felt. We met the military security at the cemetery and were given a perimeter hedge to stand in front of. Brian and his Special Branch knowledge got us introduced to Geoff Hoon the Defence Minister. As we approached him many of the veterans began to clap and cheer us. There was delay in the arrival of President Chirac. A lot of the veterans needed seats in the heat and were constantly given water. As the two helicopters arrived with HM Queen and President Chirac the down draft caused dust to engulf us and nearly blew off our helmets. We witnessed the ceremony and sang hymns. As the Queen spoke with the crowds at the end, Paul and Peter were seen in the BBC coverage. We shook hands with Tony Blair and the Duke of Gloucester. Then refreshments at the NAAFI where we met Conservative leader Michael Howard who donated some cash to our charity walk. We heard that Ronald Reagan had died. After the ceremonies at Bayeux we went to Jerusalem Cemetery where a 16-year-old soldier was buried. In the cemetery we met with a coach party from the Nottingham NVA (5 Branch). They collected donations for our fund raising. We then drove to the Tilly-sur-Seulles cemetery. We saw French children waving to us as we drove along the road. Peter whilst giving directions in the mini-bus during the day said. "Right o'clock". Peter met Air Chief Marshall Hodges. On the way back to the apartments we saw a fly past with a Lancaster, Dakota and two Spitfires. Later during the evening some of us went to the beach in Saint Aubin. Dean was dared to run in the sea naked, which he did much to the amusement of the locals. By the end of the day we had collected a total of £210.'

This is just a thumbnail sketch of what the boys did – a day that was an exercise in not only 'name dropping' but also 'trouser dropping'! The following November Dean invited Gary, Diane and I to a presentation evening where he put together an excellent video show and presented two good sized donations to representatives of both the NVA and the British Legion. Well done boys – it is guys like you that make the future secure.

As the bikers and Bobbies got on with their business we sank yet another beer. Louise was sat against the wall in the shade – the look on her face told us she wanted to go home. Terry and Hilary our friends from Bristol joined us for lunch – in his wisdom Terry had booked a table in the restaurant out the back of the café for all of us. Afterwards he would drive Bob, Gary and I to the ferry and then return and take Dad and Louise back to Vernon – a four hour round trip. I am eternally grateful for all the time and effort Terry and Hilary has put into Dad and Louise over the past few years.

As we made our way into the restaurant, the owner Chris handed Dad a handwritten note. Once seated at the table Dad found his glasses and spent a couple of minutes reading it. Looking over his shoulder I could see it was full of neatly written writing. When he was finished I asked him who it was from.

'It is from David,' he replied quietly, 'he's very sorry he never got to chat to me yesterday and he hopes we can meet up again sometime.'

'Who the hell is David?' I asked confusingly.

'David Montgomery – Monty's Son.'

'Oh that David,' I replied naively.

It then struck me that this carefully written note summed up the true meaning of D-Day – from the top to the bottom they were in it together. I was reminded of one of Dad's favourite quotations: 'No man is an island.'

We had an enjoyable lunch with a pleasant surprise at the end, brother, Bob, paid for the lot – that's one I owe you bruv!

Then we said our usual goodbyes and ten minutes later Terry was dropping us off at the ferry. Little did I know at the time but in effect that meal was to be our 'last supper'.

The Caen/Portsmouth daytime ferry reminded me of your typical provincial tennis club. Four by fours towing two-year-old caravans litter the car decks. Well-spoken families share with total strangers the details of their epic journey up from Provence or the Dordogne. Their young children are still pale skinned - thanks to sensible factor-twenty sun block. The bar is strangely quiet while the duty free shop does a roaring trade in yuppie style bargains.

Once on board the three of us decided to go our separate ways. Bob headed to the reclining seat lounge and some much needed sleep. Gary went walkabout in the direction of the amusements and shops. I grabbed a large beer and climb numerous steps to the uppermost deck. In the sun and out of the breeze I grabbed a comfortable chair and began to reflect on the previous forty eight hours.

The highlight of the weekend wasn't what I expected it to be. The obvious choices, meeting royalty as they unveiled gliders, medal presentations or last post wreath laying ceremonies were all good, but sunk into insignificance compared to one personal moment.

It was on the Saturday afternoon around three o'clock. Prince Charles and his entourage had left the glider area at the museum and moved on. For a while we all mingled around wondering what to do next.

Dad with my son-in-law, Gary

The heat was intense; the crowd was swarming over the bridge from the café side eager to get a look at the glider. I looked at Dad, he was tired and thirsty.

Along with Gary we decided to try and cross back from the museum to the shade of the Café Les 3 Planeurs. It seemed like thousands of people were walking in one direction while we try to go in the other. As we left the museum the first obstacle we hit was a metal barrier preventing us from crossing the Rue de John Howard. We eventually found a moveable gate policed by a heavily armed French soldier - he was letting nobody through.

I took Dad by the arm and approached the soldier; 'Monsieur, mon papa il et un D-Day 'ero, numero une glider. Il et tres fatigue. Ouverat le porte silvuplat.'

My failed O level French didn't make any impression. 'Open the gate son - I'm bloody gasping' shouted Dad. He took one look at Dad, saluted and let us through. So much for an education.

As we approached Pegasus Bridge the crowd grew bigger. We felt like three tired salmon swimming upstream and then all of a sudden we had the 'parting of the Red Sea' experience. People were actually stepping aside and letting us through, even though there was little room for them to manoeuvre.

Occasionally somebody would tap Dad on the shoulder and whisper 'Merci Monsieur'.

Again another would murmur 'Thanks mate'. A couple of times polite applause would break out as we passed. I continued to lead Dad through, touching his arm. I wanted people to know that I was part of this man. On Pegasus Bridge, the pavement is very narrow and a continuous iron barrier prevents people from spilling onto the road, yet somehow we continued through against the tide of people. Near the end of the bridge we encountered a group of English squaddies in Para uniforms.

'Out of the way lads,' cried the guy in front, 'genuine 'vet' coming through'.

Obviously the young man had become a little tired of hearing stories from middle aged pretenders. I thanked them and a few yards later we were in the shade of the café.

Dad was close to exhaustion, the hand that was holding his stick was shaking. A large Scotch and a cold beer would soon cure that. His first concern was for Louise. I went upstairs to their room above the café and found her asleep with the curtains closed. The weekend had become too much for her, I left her sleeping. By the time I returned to our table Gary had got the drinks in.

As we sipped on our beer we spoke little, resting in the atmosphere. I looked over to Dad, his tie, jacket and beret were off and laid on the chair next to him. The old man that sat opposite me, the person that I knew as my father looked tired.

This weekend his audience wanted yet another performance.

For just one more time they wanted to see the young tear-away that raided the cookhouse – the nutter that couldn't spit sixpence – the exhibitionist who had had so much fun with a big gun – the man that knelt down and touched the blood of a dying comrade.

But even if the world was a stage - this actor had had enough.

This day was the finale. Today the curtain was coming down for the last time – no final bows no more encores.

It was then that I thought of his life long expression that he used to live by: 'Bite on the bullet, shoulder your pack and soldier on'.

Bite on the bullet? That can't be easy when your false teeth are over twenty years old and they nearly fall out when you smile. Shoulder your pack? You're kidding; it's all he can do to carry a jacket around with a chest full of medals.

Soldiering on? Have you tried it on a stick, aged eighty-two, with shrapnel in your leg and your favourite footwear is carpet slippers?

Perhaps by next year, Dad will be like Arthur Roberts on parade and be pushed across the bridge in a wheelchair. Can you imagine Wally's reaction to that?

'Call this a march-past; it's more like the bloody chariot race in Ben Hur!'

Very few people get close enough to Wally Parr to look him in the eyes. If they did they would be surprised. They are basically hazel, but round the edges they have a distinct blue ring. It's as if God couldn't quite make up His mind. Like the majority of us Dad occasionally talks out of the back of his head. Fortunately, most of the time he puts his brain in gear and talks through his mouth. Lately, with increasing regularity he had spoken through his eyes, which are the windows of the soul.

As these thoughts enveloped me a small crowd began to form around our table. A camera would click; a video camera would start up as people moved around the back of us to get into the picture. In the corner a French school-boy stood patiently with a pen and a photograph picking his moment to ask for Dad's autograph. Beside him a huge Canadian clutched the paperback version of Pegasus Bridge. Inevitably there was the usual television crew waiting to pounce and get a free interview.

In due course Dad managed to oblige everybody. Lastly he dealt with the camera crew. They asked the usual questions and he gave the usual answers, sprinkled with the Wally Parr cheeky cockney humour.

Then he finished with his own personal message that he has been using increasingly over the last few months. His eyes shone intensely: 'Irrespective of your class, colour, creed, religion or nationality, may I suggest that you ask the prophet of your choice to surround you with his love and may that love, not only surround you, but be within your heart, not only now, but through each of all your eternities and above all may your God go with you'.

It was then I realised that after sixty years, the anger, the hatred and the bitterness had finally been put aside, and I thought to myself - How much longer will it be before it's me that stands there and remembers him with pride?

The National Press Remembers

Coming Home

In England, the summer of 2005 was long and hot – the climate was perfect for a nation to celebrate the 60th anniversaries of both VE and VJ days. The government, in its wisdom had decided that it would not officially celebrate any World War Two events after that event's 60th anniversary – for the previous five years the unfolded history from 1939 onwards had had its day and then rested back into the private memories of those that took part.

True to form the 61st anniversary of the raid on Pegasus Bridge was a very low-key event. In contrast to the blazing sunshine of mainland England, the Normandy coast was drenched in depressing rain – it started at the midnight ceremony and continued throughout the next day and didn't stop until the rather meagre crowd had dispersed. Penny Howard/Bates summed it up perfectly in her Christmas newsletter when she described at as a 'bit of a damp squid'. Dad had tried to make the effort to travel up from Vernon but increasing pain in his bones meant that the 61st was the first anniversary he had missed since the 40th.

Meanwhile back in Britain the party began.
Prince Charles began the proceedings by laying a wreath at the Cenotaph on the 8th May to commemorate VE day. In between the final wreath laying on the 21st August to honour VJ Day the government had planned on Sunday the 10th July to hold a National Commemoration Day – a huge gathering that combined the two events.
Despite months of planning and preparation to get the day perfect nobody could have foreseen that London would be attacked by terrorists in the week preceding. The Queen in her speech referred to the atrocities that fell upon the people of London on July 7th 2005 and called upon this generation to dig deep and see as an example, the 'Blitz Spirit' that prevailed amongst the nation 60 years previous.
While watching the events un-fold that Sunday I decided to ring Dad. He had missed the 61st celebrations through poor health and I thought he may have needed cheering up, I knew he could not see the televised events as his only life line was Radio 4. When I rang through it was obvious that he was in pain and his mood was subdued. I described the scene in Trafalgar Square and when I mentioned that Richard Todd had been interviewed and broadcasted across the nation he cheered up no end.
Personally I found the day slightly bizarre – the date was July 10th yet we were supposed to be celebrating a 'victory' in Japan while in actual

fact 60 years before our brave soldiers were still dying and being tortured by a barbaric regime. The official reason given for this date was that it did not interfere with our beloved MPs long summer sojourn – no doubt on the proper VJ Day, 21st August most of our parliamentarian representatives were laying on their fat arses getting a sun-tan.

In contrast Prince Charles on that date was again at the Cenotaph laying a wreath. Beside him Viscount Slim laid a wreath at the foot of his father, the 1st Viscount Slim, and afterwards he made a short speech: 'The Burma Star is most grateful that they and all who fought and suffered in the Far East have been recognised and remembered.'

That summer had been memorable – many events had been held, I had seen my oldest Grandson, Jack, aged 7, march with his Beaver group through the streets of Bromley waiving a Union Jack and trying to remember a great-grandfather he had never met, I had seen Vera Lynn stand on a stage - golden voice long since departed, but wearing a smile a big as The White Cliffs of Dover. Once again I was proud to be a Londoner as evil bastards tried to bomb us into submission – yet as the Lancaster Plane flew over and dropped a million poppies each one said: 'We shall not be moved – we shall not be defeated.'

Our grandson, Jack, at the VE Day celebrations in 2005

Yet at the beginning and at the end of these goings on – Prince Charles had laid a simple wreath and saluted – somehow he had managed to keep a sense of solemnity to the proceedings.

In a strange way I felt we had almost become mates – although of the same age and city, our worlds couldn't have been further apart- yet we nearly brushed shoulders - he walked a few feet past me when he came and opened the museum in 2000 - he sat two seats in front of me blocking the view of my Dad when he unveiled the glider in 2005 and my poem is placed beneath his plaque at the entrance to the museum – the fact that we both think Spike Milligan is a genius is but an aside.

Cleaning windows hardly taxes the brain so to alleviate the boredom I usually listen to talk radio on my headphones. Over the months I had become bit of an addict ringing in to a couple of the presenters on a wide range of topics. On the week leading up to the 60th anniversary of VE Day one of the topics up for discussion was: 'Have you got a real life TV character in your family?' Most people rang in and said they had an uncle that was just like 'Dell Boy' from 'Only fools and Horses' - but I managed to get through to James O'Brien on LBC and share with him that we had a real life Windsor Davies from 'It ain't half hot Mum.' I proceeded to amuse him and half of London with stories of my Dad screaming at his grandkids and telling them to 'get those shoulders back!' It passed a couple of minutes of boredom and then I was back to cleaning windows.

A couple of days later was general election day and I knew that on that day all radio stations were not permitted to discuss politics – I had read previously that a survey conducted had found that a vast majority of teenagers thought that VE day and VJ day was something to do with sexually transmitted diseases or AIDS and was probably highlighting the problem in Africa!

I thought this day would be a good opportunity to put London's youth in the picture, so I emailed James O'Brien at LBC and tried to set up a discussion as to the importance of the next generation being aware of what VE/VJ meant - for good measure I mentioned in the email that I was writing a book about my father and I also included my poem in the hope that it would inspire the editor before they went on air. To my utter surprise the programme opened up at 10 o'clock with the theme: 'What does VE Day mean to you?'! James O'Brien mentioned me calling in a couple of days previous and before I knew it I was calling in and having a long conversation with him – as we were coming to an end he asked about my book and to finish he asked me to quote my poem on air.

Before I had time to panic I found myself at the bottom of my ladder, mobile phone in hand, reciting it to the largest listening audience in London! I managed to get through it without mucking up – he thanked me and they went to an advertising break. Apparently after I put the phone down the station was flooded (probably two dozen!) with callers trying to get a copy of it – that evening it was put on the station's web site and hopefully it blessed a few folk.

At that time progress on this book had ground to a virtual halt – family life and full time working had eaten into any time I had put aside to writing.

Then on September 22nd 2005 events were to occur that changed my life forever.

I was at work, cleaning windows – my mind was elsewhere - in a couple of days my wife Diane and I were to take a well earned break in Combe Martin, North Devon, a place that Dad had recommended for our honeymoon back in 1969, a place that D Company had march through back in their training days. We had returned many times over the years and as I worked away I made mental plans for our walks in the coming days. Then in a second it happened – while at the top of my ladder I moved my scrim from my right hand to my left, the slight movement caused my ladder to shake and instantly it shot out backwards and I came crashing down and smashed my right leg on a hard patio floor.

I have fallen from my ladder a few times over the past twenty-eight years but this time I did it good and proper. I was rushed to the Princess Royal University Hospital in Farnborough, Kent and it emerged that I had broken several bones in my right leg and ankle and I would never be able to climb a ladder again and may have a permanent limp – my window cleaning days were over.

It was time to 'bite on the bullet'. I was determined to not make this the worst thing that had ever happened to me but the best. For months I had been struggling to finish this book but had always had problems finding the time – now with at least six months recovery ahead of me I had time a-plenty.

I was in hospital on traction for a few weeks – I wrote constantly. Eventually I was allowed home and all my handwritten notes were gradually transferred to my computer.

Then one day the phone rang – it was Dad.

Obviously distressed, he told me he was being taken to hospital in Vernon as the arthritic pain in his body was getting too much. Feeling totally useless I wished him well and told him to keep me informed.

A couple of days later we managed to contact the hospital and get some information as to his condition. It was rather vague but we did learn that Louise was staying on the floor above – we thought that this was the French national health being rather kind and allowing Louise easy access to visit.

Three days later Claude rang me and told me that Louise had died – he also informed me that Dad was on regular morphine injections and he was to receive radio therapy – we feared the worse.

At this point my brother, Bob, came into his own – I was incapacitated and my sister, Pat, was in Lincolnshire - Bob took control and did it well. He travelled to Vernon and assessed the situation – in no time he had organised a private ambulance and within a week my sister, our partners and I were at Lewisham University Hospital, London ready to receive Dad and to get him some treatment through the NHS – Bob drove back on the same day with 16 years of our Dad's life in the back of his car.

Within a few days the hospital told us they could do nothing

It is at times like this that you begin to understand the true meaning of the word 'Comradeship.'

Denis Edwards always was and still is the driving force that cements the very fabric that keeps these old comrades informed and together.

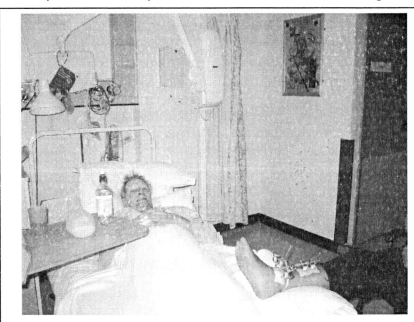

At the end Dad was more concerned about my physical condition than his own

Most of these old boys have even managed to embrace the complexities of the Internet and emails. In no time the word was out about Wally Parr's condition. The response to my family and I was overwhelming. My brother, Bob, had paid the £1200 cost of the private ambulance out of his own pocket – I couldn't help, I had just lost my business and would have to downsize my house just to survive - yet within a few days Colonel John Tillet had sent me a cheque for £500 from one of his own charities and had put me in touch with other agencies who covered the remaining £700. If you ever wondered what happened to your poppy donation, now you know.

I answered every email with as much detail as I could.

We visited Dad one day and there beside his bed sat Nobby Clark. I gave him the special 'left hand' handshake that only he receives! Dad was much brighter that day, they gave each other the usual banter and ribbing that only they really understand – yet after a while Dad went quiet. Nobby read the signs and left soon afterwards, allowing my wife, Diane, to use her home care skills to get him reasonably comfortable.

Another blessing was the day Penny and George Bates arrived. They came to our house for a coffee first and then afterwards Diane drove us to the hospital. Penny asked if she could take him in a small bottle of Scotch to buck him up – it seemed a good idea to me but when we saw the size of the ward-sister we all agreed perhaps not!

Dad did his best to entertain Penny and George but the light was fading – I felt a special affinity with Penny, we both had fathers that were a bit special – we both wanted to preserve their memories for anybody prepared to listen.

That evening I had a bad fall on my crutches and thought I had done even more damage to my leg – it was probably one of the lowest points of my entire life – it was then that I remember the half bottle of Scotch that Penny had left with us. I saw most of it off that evening- 'shrapnel medicine' as Dad would say - he would have smiled at that.

One of Dad's favourite sayings was: 'Whatever you lose – never lose your sense of humour'.

The week he stopped cracking jokes I knew the end was near. The day he died Hilary and Terry Bond had travelled up from Bristol to see him. That was a good thing – Hilary and Terry had done more than most to make his life enjoyable during his last few years in Normandy.

The moment he lost his final battle he was in the room on his own. That too was a good thing – that way nobody could claim the honour of being the last to say goodbye – anyway he hated farewells.

I have a problem with grief – my problem is that there is no 'normal way' – no person should be able to dictate how anybody else should react – when a loved one dies there is only one way to react and that is your own personal way – there are no rights or wrongs in the grief game.

When my Dad died my overwhelming emotion was one of relief.

Months before the man I knew and loved had left me - his lust for life had gone - so also had his lust for living. His final act was to see Louise on her way before he, himself, moved on.

God help the angels, the day he died – they better had been in 'ship - shape and Bristol fashion' the first time he inspected them!

The Union flag covers the coffin

In no time the machinery that is a funeral swung into place. Two days after his passing the Sun newspaper printed the first obituary. It was the size of a postage stamp tucked away in the bottom right hand corner of page 45, it read: 'SADDEST DAY - D-Day hero Wally Parr, whose bravery inspired 1962 film The Longest Day, has died aged 88 in London'.

Trust the 'Current Bun' - I think John Wayne may have a few words to say about the inspiration for the film – and as for his age, they were only five years out!

In contrast, a few days later, I received a phone call from Charles Owen of the Daily Telegraph with regards to publishing an obituary on the day of my father's funeral. His attention to detail was all you would expect from a quality journal – they even sent a motorbike courier to pick up the appropriate photograph. We had now gone from the sublime to the ridiculous

On the day of his cremation The Telegraph placed him in pride of place on its obituary page. It covered half the page - to the right and below him were Tory Peers, World famous philosophers and Hungarian international pianists. The title at the top of the page simply read: 'Wally Parr.' On a line below is stated: '*Soldier who landed in the leading glider during the assault on Pegasus Bridge in June 1944.*'

In the previous weeks they had given a similar treatment to a certain George Best and the actor Richard Prior – all three had one thing in common: they were all flawed characters that had for one reason or another captured the public's imagination – I'm not sure what it is, lets call it the X-factor.

The funeral was well attended – age had taken its toll on D Company,

A guard of honour led by David Wood (right)

A Tribute to Dad

Colonel David Wood, Tom Packwood, Tich Rayner and Nobby Clark were the only surviving members to attend. Billy Gray had been in constant touch with me since Dad's return to England but was unable to arrange transport from Northampton. Denis Edwards had hoped to attend but was unable to leave his sick wife. Sadly Colonel John Tillet couldn't leave his sick bed.

Penny and George Bates sent flowers but had to honour a previous long standing engagement.

Sixty years of history arrived at Hither Green Crematorium that day – in fact for 'history' read 'his story' as we shared in one man's life. We had hired a hall for everybody to drink his memory afterwards and at the back we had a display of items collected over the years. In pride of place was his famous maroon jacket with its array of badges and medals. A book of condolence was to be handed around so that people

Robbie Jones and I drink to Dad's memory for England – he would have liked that

attending could record their personal messages.

Barry Tappenden and his family had arrived early that day and gone to the funeral parlour and dressed the coffin with the union flag and then placed a black cushion on top with Dad's medals placed in the middle.

At the service friends and family, old and new sang hymns chosen by my sister, Pat, and heard my brother, Bob, recite Kipling's 'If', a favourite poem of Dad's that inspired them both. Brother-in-law, Jim, read the eulogy sharing the highlights of my father's life. After that I struggled to the front on my crutches and recited my poem to the congregation – my one fear was that I would break down half way through – fortunately I made it, only to go to pieces moments after when a bugler from the Coldstream Guards broke into the Last Post.

To the end Dad was a man of surprises – in his last months he had made two final wishes:

My wife, Diane, looks on proudly at our three grandsons, Joe, Harry & Jack

The first was that his ashes not be scattered off Pegasus Bridge or over his beloved gun as you would have expected – but instead to be laid around an old oak tree in our local park. It was a much loved place of his, where he used to walk barefooted in the morning dew - a place where he saw his children and grandchildren grow up. It is called Home Park and we as a family would feel at peace knowing that he has finally come home.

Secondly he had asked for a quiet funeral, all very low-key. The problem was, that if you knew Dad as we knew him, you would quickly realise that he didn't always say what he meant – Wally Parr doesn't do 'meek', in fact he is not too clever at 'humble' either.

'The meek may inherit the earth,' he once said 'but they don't bloody well win yer wars!'

With this in mind after giving him a full Monty funeral I decided to take him on one more trip to Normandy.

Technically the ending of my book was to be when I left Normandy after the 60th anniversary – in the time it took to write my story Dad's health was to deteriorate and the new ending was his passing and the funeral. Events then demanded another ending when I decided to take some of his ashes back to Normandy and scatter them over Pegasus Bridge and his No. 1 Gun during the 62nd commemorations on June 5/6th 2006.

So it was that my wife, Diane, and I along with our friends Dean Croucher and his wife Sue set off to Portsmouth to finally lay the old man to rest.

Penny and her husband George had been working flat out, during the weeks leading up to this time, ensuring events and political differences merged and hoped all went well between the local Mayor, the airborne boys, the 7th Paras and Arlette Gondrée. I am sure Penny is well aware of the saying: 'You can't keep all the people happy all of the time!'

Needless to say events over the next few two days were to go smoothly.

We travelled overnight to Normandy; the ferry was due to berth after 7 a.m. As I mentioned previously, the secret with these trips is to hit the bar and drink as much and as long as you can, because you are eventually going to retire to the reclining-chair sleeping lounge which means you are going to join around 100 other passenger who are fidgeting and snoring in what are basically dentist's chairs – if you get two hours kip you are doing well. What didn't help was that the four of us didn't settle down until about 3 a.m. after having half an hour of drunken school-kid giggles.

Dawn in Normandy was clear and sunny. We were met by our old friends Terry and Hilary Bond who escorted us to our hotel just outside Ouisterham. The place was pure 16th Century Norman full of character, the hostess Françoise couldn't have been more welcoming, first giving us a free continental breakfast and then giving up her own private bedroom because the place was fully booked.

This was Sunday the 4th and was to be a free day. Dean had brought his car and we all agreed today we would do the beaches. It's ironic; in all the years I've been coming over I had never really explored the full length of the actual invasion.

We made it as far west as Omaha Beach – 'Saving Private Ryan' country. Two things impressed me, the size of the beach and the height of the hill the fully equipped infantrymen had to climb. When we eventually visited the cemetery at the top of the hill, I was not surprised at the magnitude of the place bearing in mind the task they had to perform.

There is a marked contrast between the British War Cemetery and the American counterpart. At Omaha the size overwhelms you – it is at least three times the size of my more familiar cemetery at Ranville. The immaculate lines of white crosses remind me of all that is regimental with the United States Military – the perfection of the crosses stand in line like elite Marines on parade at West Point.

Diane and Sue at the bridge

Unlike Ranville there are no flowers planted around the bases – I like to feel that grieving relatives have sowed plants and even trees in their homeland America – that way they can pay their respects daily rather than on a once in a lifetime pilgrimage to far-off Europe. For those that do make the trip the communal gardens and monuments surpass anything I have seen before.

Unlike British War graves the exact ages are missing on the headstones – perhaps it is irrelevant, we all know that these brave men had one thing in common – they died young and they died in their prime.

Another difference I noticed was that where English graves give you the regiment of the deceased, the US graves simply gave the State in

America from where the soldier originated – this told me that irrespective of what unit or regiment they came from, they ultimately died for their Country and for the common good.

Despite the subtle differences between Omaha and Ranville I was acutely aware and proud to know that we were on the same side and above all we were victorious allies.

From Omaha we travelled eastwards and arrive at Arromanches in time for lunch. The Mulberry Harbours still lay a few hundred yards out to sea, an ongoing monument to the expertise of the Allied Forces. It was Napoleon that said 'An army marches on its stomach.' It was the harbours and Bailey Bridges that enabled arms and supplies to get through to the troops as they advanced inland and eventually to Berlin. Quite simply the last few months of the war was won by the nation that could provide the best solution to supply and demand.

The narrow streets of Arromanches were packed with people visiting the numerous shops and restaurants. Tourist-tat pretending to be second world war memorabilia fill the shelves – it reminded me of a mini-Blackpool or Brighton, to me the town was 'D-Day on Sea', I enjoyed what I could and then we headed back to an excellent late evening meal in Ouisterham.

Next day, Sunday the 5th, I woke to my own personal D-Day.

Ceremony at the replica glider

On this day I would be scattering my father's ashes over the old

Pegasus Bridge in an official ceremony and afterwards there would be a more private affair where I would be scattering the remainder over his gun.

Enjoying Champagne with one of Dad's old friends

Nobby, Tich, me and Barry Tappenham

The next generation – Geoff Baulk (left) and Chantelle Tappenden carry their wreaths

For weeks I have been wondering what to wear – there is a thin dividing line between going over the top and looking a plonker and under-dressing and showing lack of respect. Over the years most of us veteran's sons have managed to cock it up – one will be in a suit while the one next to him will be wearing shorts and trainers. I decide to go the middle way and wear one of my Dad's beige jackets with an Airborne Division badge sown on it. The tie I wear is an AANT (Airborne Assault Normandy Trust) one given to me by Norman McKay at my father's funeral – I trusted I was now qualified to wear it in public. It all seemed appropriate despite the intense heat.

We entered the museum an hour before the midday ceremony. For the first time Diane saw my poem on display in the foyer – she proudly photographed me sitting beneath it – I breathed a sigh of relief, thankful that nobody on the museum committee had decided to take it down and replace it with something better.

In the museum itself we bumped into Nobby Clark and a few minutes later met up with Tich Rayner who was brought over by the Baulk family. I was then told that David Wood would not be making the trip due to last minute health problems – the expected three members of D Company was now down to two and the evening meal at the Mayor's hall will not have Colonel Wood as the Master of Ceremonies.

I would have loved to have met Billy Gray one more time, but due to previous illnesses, the health insurance for the trip was astronomical. Billy was probably Dad's closest friend and he had helped me with loads of information after Dad had died - thus enabling me to fill in some gaps in my book. Denis Edwards couldn't make it as he had to look after his sick wife and Jim Wallwork lived too far away in British Columbia.

Claude and I ioin the march

Nobby and Tich were the only ones there from the old crowd – they looked lonely, it is obvious that they miss their mates.

I briefly chatted with Marc Worthington from the museum and then Marc Jacquinot arrived and informed me of the running order of the first ceremony. In no time I found myself pushing through the crowds on the old Pegasus Bridge, with my wife, and standing in line with Penny and George Bates on the middle of the bridge opposite a small plaque. After a while Penny and the Mayor laid a joint wreath and then Marc asked me to step forward and spread my father's ashes. They were in a small gold box – I am relieved that the surface of the bridge is in fact a grill and his remains slipped through as I gentle scattered them. I heard numerous camera shutters click - none of them would capture my thoughts. I stepped back a couple of paces and bowed my head for a few moments – for the rest of my days I would never feel qualified to salute - I turned and walked back in line and hold Diane's hand hoping that I had given him the dignity that he deserved.

I had completed the first part of my odyssey - next will be his gun and finally his tree.

Scattering Dad's ashes on Pegasus Bridge

As we left the bridge the heat intensifies, my tie made me feel hot under the collar but I was determined to keep it on until my second task was fulfilled. Next, we lined up beside the replica glider for another wreath laying – I had hoped to take Diane inside the glider and sit in the seat at the back where Dad had sat but there was a rather elegant rope blocking the entrance. After the glider ceremony we moved a few paces to the right and witnessed the unveiling of a chair and a blessing by the regimental padre.

After this, all official duties are over for the time being and I found myself joining an orderly queue as we lined up for a welcoming glass of ice-cold Champagne courtesy of the museum. I was continuing a great Parr tradition of scrounging free drinks from the French – it started way back in 1944 when Dad grabbed his first glass of Champagne from Monsieur Gondrée at the café.

It was time to relax and catch up with old friends, Barry Tappenden informed me that he was planning to run 65 miles to Bénouville in 2009 to remember the 65th anniversary – he wanted me to join him, we ran the marathon together way back, I informed him that after my accident I probably couldn't run 65 yards, but he was having none of it.

It's good that the next generation is making plans for the future, I am sure I will be involved in the 65th celebrations even if it is only waving them over the finishing line with my grandkids!

For the next half-hour I was introduced to total strangers as the son of Wally Parr – they then embark on stories and anecdotes about the time they met him and how he touched their lives, I felt like the son of a famous celebrity. Occasionally I looked over my shoulder and half expect to see the old man in some corner giving a group of admirers his usual banter.

Diane and I make our way back to the café

This is the first time I had been to Normandy without him – and it was the first time I got a deep feeling of loss. In London I was used to him being on the other side of the Channel – but it was there in France that it finally sunk in.

Before I found time to feel sorry for myself a rather distinguished gentleman introduced himself as the Mayor of some town or other and told us he knew my Dad well – upon seeing our empty glasses he invited the four of us to join him in the car park and take up the offer of more cold Champagne or vintage Calvados – any friend of Dad's is a friend of mine! I informed the people that would be joining us at Dad's gun that we would be meeting just after 1 p.m.

Two glasses of Champagne later I was standing beside Dad's gun pit and about to begin. Tich Rayner joined Diane and me at the front – we wait for Nobby but he failed to arrive. I began by sharing a few words – I told them about the numerous photographs I have of Dad leaning on his gun and sharing his stories with anybody prepared to listen – I mentioned him firing into the maternity hospital, filling the water-tower with holes and sending the gun-boat back in the direction of Caen. We all smiled as I recall Jack Bailey making his brew of tea and Dad letting off a round and filling his cup with dust.

Then I turned to Penny and reminded her of the time her father finally lost his patience with Dad and screamed at the top of his voice: 'Parr - stop firing that bloody gun!'

After I finished speaking Diane handed some ashes to Tich who gently dropped them into the gun pit – a few seconds later I recited a short poem I had written for the moment and then released the remainder. Shortly afterwards Nobby appeared and I asked him and Barry Tappenden to join us at the front. By the time we finished the crowd had grown somewhat although most of them was unaware of what had taken place.

John Howard's bust

Eventually we all made our way back to the Café Les 3 Planeurs, as I walked back with the two empty boxes I was a little disappointed that Claude and our old friend Robbie and Rose Marie had failed to show up for the ceremony. We all go back a long way – they live in France and I had emailed them especially and wanted them to attend more than anybody else. You can imagine my surprise when I approached the café and saw them knocking back the beers. They were even more surprised when they noticed the boxes that once contained their old mate Wally's ashes. The confusion was soon sorted when they informed me that my email stated I would be scattering the ashes on the 6th – although in fact I did it on the 5th, my mistake – us Parrs couldn't organise a piss-up in a brewery!

That evening we had the usual banquet at the Town Hall. David Wood was missed as the MC – the Mayor did his best to hold the fort and make us welcome.

In some ways it seemed like a strange wedding feast – Tich and Nobby were the Bride and Groom, yet the best-man, the ushers and all the close friends that had been on the stag night were missing.

An era had passed and it would be almost impossible to rekindle it.

At midnight we all met at John Howard's bust and joined in the celebrations with Penny and George. At 15 minutes past midnight the Champagne was opened by George and we continued another great tradition. As he opened the third bottle the cork flew up in the air and eventually landed right on the top of Major Howard's bust - Diane and Sue tried unsuccessfully to stifle their giggles, but I just smiled to myself and rested in the fact that this confirmed something I always knew – that John Howard was a real 'corker'.

Tich and Nobby at Den Botheridge's grave

- 264 -

The next day we all meet at Ranville Cemetery beside Den Brotheridge's headstone – he is buried against the wall in the grounds of the churchyard; the much larger national cemetery was added after the war.

Tich and Nobby laid a wreath and took the salute, they looked even more like lost souls at sea and I feared the weekend is catching up with them.

Opposite, a company of Royal Green Jackets stood on parade – a lone bugler sounded the last post after we had observed two minutes silence. It would be the first of many 'Last Posts' I would hear that day, the expertise of the playing would vary – yet the passion and emotion of each rendition would remain constant.

We met an American couple who knew John Howard and Dad, he gave me his card and asked me to email him some photographs of the weekend – I noted that he was a member of the 'Over the Hill Gang' it is nothing to do with a battle but something to do with being over 50, he invited me to join it if I was in his neck of the woods anytime.

We moved over to the main cemetery – the place was much too crowded, I preferred to wander around it out of season.

Eventually we made our way back to Bénouville and a much needed cold beer.

Barry Tappenden checks that all is in order

Shortly after midday Barry Tappenden gathered us into some sort of order ready to march across the bridge to attend the main ceremony at the memorial beside the landing zone. It was at this point that I was informed that I would be laying a joint wreath with Claude. It then dawned on me that everybody on parade was suited and booted and there was me in light trousers and an open-necked short sleeved pink shirt – I stuck out like a sore thumb!

Needless to say I performed the ceremony with Claude and if nothing else I provided light summer contrast to the dark blazers. At the end local school children came amongst us and gave each of us either a red, white or blue flower – my wife Diane has kept mine and preserved it as a permanent reminder.

After lunch we attended yet another service in nearby Escoville. We skipped the next one at Herouvillette as Dean wanted to talk us through the action in and around Escoville. This was a particular interest to me because this was where Dad did most of his sniping and where he was wounded. As usual Dean's knowledge put mine to shame and we passed an interesting hour.

Exhausted we finally sailed out on the midnight ferry – mission accomplished.

Scattering Dad's ashes under his favourite tree

Three weeks later I managed to get my brother and sister together and the three of us along with Diane and Pat's husband, Jim, decide to perform the last act and scatter the remainder of Dad's ashes around the old oak tree near to where we spent our childhood.

It was a perfect summer evening - the light was just beginning to fade.

I felt my story was just about to come full circle - in death, as in life, my father was once again about to become reunited with France and his beloved Homeland – the Mighty Oak symbolised all he stood for.

In turns we each spread some ashes and quietly rested in our own thoughts as we reflected upon how this one man had affected us in our individual lives.

Then as the last rays of sun dipped in the west I made one last symbolic gesture and scattered a circle of ashes around his favourite tree and quoted the poem that I had recited back in Normandy - when I had last leant against his beloved No. 1 Gun:

'YOU BIT ON THE BULLET
AND YOU SHOULDERED YOUR PACK
WE THOUGHT YOU HAD LEFT THIS PLACE
BUT NOW YOU ARE BACK

YOU AND YOUR COMRADES
DID WHAT YOU MUST
NOW IT'S ASHES TO ASHES
AND DUST TO DUST

+ +

'HAM AND JAM'

Wally Parr
1922 - 2005

Acknowledgements

I would like to thank the following people for making this book possible:

Hugh Ambrose for giving me permission to quote from his father's book.
Denis Edwards for not only allowing me to use his book material but also to have access to his archives.
Billy Gray and Nobby Clark for filling in the gaps left by Dad, particularly post Normandy.
Penny Bates for sharing her experiences in Bénouville pre-40th anniversary years.
The many friends who encouraged me to 'Go for it!': Colonel Wood, Colonel Tillet, Denis Edwards, Tich Raynor, Marc Jacquinot and the Pegasus Memorial crowd, Dean Croucher and his mates, Tom Friar and the biker boys, Robbie Jones, Claude Potier, the Baulk Family, Danny and Chris Greeno, Terry and Hilary Bond, Kirt Garcia and Barry Tappenden who also 'did the business' at my Dad's funeral.
Most importantly I would like to thank Colin Evans for doing all the technical-computer-thingy stuff that brought this book into physical fruition. Over the past two decades, through thick and thin, no man has been a more loyal friend - if I had to choose any man to be beside me in a slit-trench it would be him.

Last but by no means least I would like to thank my family, who over the past two years have constantly encouraged me and have never for one moment doubted me, particularly my daughters Jennie and Sandra.
And last but certainly not least I would like to thank 'long suffering' Diane, who has had to ride my roller-coaster mind as I lived and breathed this book. If I am to be known as ' son of Wally' then she is 'wife of Barry' - and for that I am eternally grateful.

November 2006.

ISBN 142511073-8